BOTH A SERVANT AND FREE

A PRIMER IN FUNDAMENTAL MORAL THEOLOGY

By Father Brian Thomas Becket Mullady, O.P.

New Hope Publications

Nihil Obstat
A.R.D. Hugh Barbour, O. Praem., S.T.D.
Censor Deputatus
Imprimi Potest
R.P. Emmericus Vogt, O.P., M.A.
Prior Provinicalis
Die 11 Octobris 2010

Copyright 2011 Brian T. Mullady, OP
All rights reserved.

With the exception of short excerpts for critical reviews, no part of this work may be reproduced or transmitted in any form or by any means whatsoever without prior written permission from the publisher.

New Hope Publications
P.O. Box 10
New Hope, KY
www.newhope-ky.org

ISBN 978-1-892875-53-2

Printed in the United States of America

For
MSGR. Richard Loomis, Joseph Fessio, S.J., and Hugh Barber, O. PRAEM.
with much respect and gratitude.

CONTENTS

PREFACE ix

INTRODUCTION xi

CHAPTER ONE
THE HUMAN SOUL 1
Introduction 1
Ancient Approach of the Platonists 2
Modern Philosophy and the Soul 3
The Church and Aristotle 3
Powers of the Soul 4
Sense Powers of Knowing 6
Sense Powers of Desiring 9
Spiritual Powers 14
Ethics and Human Nature 16

CHAPTER TWO
THE NATURE OF MORAL THEOLOGY 23
Towards a Definition 23
Scripture and Tradition 25
Role of the Magisterium 25
Intrinsic Evil 27
Infallible Teaching? 30

CHAPTER THREE
HUMAN HAPPINESS 33
Acting for an End 33
Perfection and the Will 36
What is Happiness? 38

MAN IS FREE: THE GENUS OF MORALS

CHAPTER FOUR
MORAL RESPONSIBILITY: THE VOLUNTARY 55
The Voluntary 55
A Human Action or Omission 57
The Will 60
Double Effect 61
Fear 63
Morally Responsible Passions 65
Ignorance 70
Emotional Problem vs. Moral Problem 74

Circumstance	77
Other Considerations	81
Summation	91

MAN IS A SERVANT: THE SPECIES OF MORALS

CHAPTER FIVE
FREEDOM AND TRUTH: GOODNESS AND EVIL — 95

The Intellect: Objective Norm for Human Freedom	95
Philosophical Difficulties With Morals	98
The Problematic Moral School of Karl Rahner	99
The School of Moderate Teleology	104
The School of Fundamental Option	107
The School of New Natural Law Theory	109
Summation	112

CHAPTER SIX
THE INTELLECT: OBJECT, INTENTION AND CIRCUMSTANCES — 113

The Object of The Act	113
Circumstances	124
Intention	128
Moral Wholeness	130
Answers to Modern Problems	131

CHAPTER SEVEN
THE PASSIONS — 137

The Place of the Passions in Morals	137
Stoicism	137
The Hedonist Idea of the Passions	138
The Correct Idea of the Passions	140
Formation of the Passions and Freedom	141

CHAPTER EIGHT
LAW — 147

Law and Morals	147
Law: An Ordinance of Reason	150
Law: The Common Good	152
Law: Authority	153
The Natural Law	154
Human Law	156
Divine Positive Law	160
The Old Law	161
The New Law of Christ	167

CHAPTER NINE
CONSCIENCE — 173
    The Problem of Conscience — 173
    Conscience is a Practical Judgement — 175
    Conscience and Certainty — 177
    The Mistaken Conscience — 178
    An Informed Conscience — 180
    Freedom of Conscience — 181

THE FREE SERVANT — SPONTANEITY AND HEAVEN

CHAPTER TEN
VIRTUE — 187
    Virtue and Freedom — 187
    The Nature of Virtue — 189
    How One Obtains Virtue — 189
    Kinds of Virtue — 191
    Prudence — 191
    Justice and Charity — 192
    Fortitude and Temperance — 193
    Growth in Virtue — 194
    The Theological Virtues — 195
    Heaven on Earth Begun — 199

CHAPTER ELEVEN
SIN — 201
    Recovering the Idea of Sin — 201
    Sin, Malice, and Vice — 202
    Sin of Omission — 204
    Physical and Moral Evil — 205
    Sin and Guilt — 206
    The Gravity of Sin — 207
    Sins of Weakness — 208
    Sins of Ignorance — 210
    Sins of Malice — 211
    External Causes of Sin: God, Material Things, The Devil — 212
    Original Sin — 213
    Actual Sin: Mortal and Venial — 214

CHAPTER TWELVE
GRACE — 219
    Grace and Moral Theology — 219
    God's Love and Man's Love — 220

What is Grace?	222
Definition of the Kinds of Grace	223
How One Gets Grace	224
The Effect of Grace: Justification	226
The Effect of Grace: Merit or Reward	229

CHAPTER THIRTEEN   233
    I Want to See God   233

ENDNOTES   241

PREFACE

When in the early 80s I arrived as a newly ordained priest to the Roman Angelicum to study spiritual theology, I knew that I had to make an effort to acquaint myself with the theology of Aquinas. It was my joy therefore to attend some courses that were based directly on the texts of Aquinas, which I read in Latin. Among these were those offered by Fr. Brian Mullady, O.P. on the *De Malo* and by Fr. Mullady's mentor, Fr. Quintin Turiel, O.P. on the relationship between nature and grace. The struggle with the mediaeval Latin and its terminology gave me access to the Dominican Order's greatest thinker and to the clarity of theological principles that allow for convictions within faith. I am therefore grateful to Fr. Mullady for his role in my early theological formation.

Among the theological themes that Fr. Mullady introduced me to, were: the importance of objectivity in morality, centered around the moral object, which can be rationally known, against the proportionalist attempt to tie morals uniquely with a subjective intention; the distinction between the rational direction of the emotions in virtuous living and the neurotic repression of the emotions as explained in an exemplary way on the basis of Thomistic principles by Anna A. Terruwe and her disciple Conrad Baars; the location of the natural desire to see God within the intellect, that is, as an extension of intellectual curiosity and not in the will that allows for a Chalcedonian, distinct and unmixed presentation of the orders of nature and grace, of philosophy and theology without the subordination of the life of faith to purely natural criteria and agendas and without the treating of the order of grace as an extraordinary, purely optional and basically unnecessary factor without which nature could supposedly attain its ultimate fulfillment; and finally, the distinction between the moral order and the political order with its penal system to the perspective of which the moral order is not to be reduced. These themes, learnt through Fr. Mullady, have been with me ever since and they have stimulated my further research, my teaching and my writings.

It is therefore a great pleasure for me to write these few words of introduction to Fr. Mullady's book on the principles of Christian moral action. The life of grace, freely imparted by God, in no way denies the natural capacities of the human mind to perceive the inner logic and truth of moral action. The Christian indeed is *Both a Servant* in that he responds in truth to the order grounded by His Maker and in humility towards His Redeemer, thereby becoming transparent to His grace, *and Free* in his personal maturity, undertaking through the cultivated personal virtues the moral challenges and responsibilities that face him, which enables him to untangle himself from the shackles of sin.

Wojciech Giertych, O.P.
Theologian of the Papal Household

INTRODUCTION

Man is at the same time "both a servant and free."[1] This text from St. Augustine is an excellent summary of the traditional Catholic teaching on moral theology. Since the sixties, there have been many theologians who believe that the traditional systematic approach of Catholic theology, which emphasizes man's service of the Natural Law coupled with his freedom as a Person, could not be sustained. Karl Rahner, for example, speaks about the possibility of writing a fundamental catechism which would be valid for the whole world in very disparaging terms.

> Can we reckon with the possibility that a single basic creed can be formulated at least for the whole of Catholic Christianity? . . . Or is something like this no longer conceivable to begin with? I think that we have to answer this question with the second and negative alternative. . . . In order to show the impossibility of a single, new, basic and universal creedal statement we may perhaps call attention first of all to the fact that attempts to create a common and universally valid world catechism and to introduce it officially have collapsed, and have met with the unambiguous resistance of both preachers and catechists.[2]

Nowhere has this malaise in systematics seemed more evident than in moral theology. The great many opinions on the foundation of morals have led to a dizzying skepticism on the part of many moralists as to whether there can be absolute moral norms. So great has this skepticism become, that Pope John Paul II felt called to write an encyclical, *Veritatis Splendor*, on the very subject of absolutes in morality. Such an encyclical would have been inconceivable in the times before Vatican II.

The outcry which greeted *Veritatis Splendor* on the part of moral theologians was great. Many took the Pope to be trying to turn back the clock to the times before Vatican II. Others just rejected the whole idea as a feeble attempt on the part of the papacy to flog the dead horse of birth control. For example, Fr. Bernard Haring says:

> After reading the new papal encyclical carefully, I felt greatly discouraged. Several hours later I suffered long-lasting seizures of the brain, and looked forward hopefully to leaving the Church on earth for the Church in heaven. After regaining my normal brain function, however, I have a new feeling of confidence, without blinding my eyes and heart to the pain and brain-convulsions that are likely to ensue in the immediate future.[3]

It is no great secret that it was the papal teaching on birth control which was the original source of the rejection of moral absolutes. Moralists have been dancing a tightrope since 1968 trying to show how *Humanae Vitae* could be wrong and yet preserve some sense of moral order in the universe and in human society. When confronted with their destructive opinions, their usual retort is that no one understands what they are actually saying. Richard McCormick says: "The vast majority of moral theologians known as proportionalists will rightly say that they do not hold or teach what the encyclical attributes to them. . . . *Veritatis Splendor* at key points attributes to theologians positions that they do not hold."[4]

The sad truth is that *Humanae Vitae* was just the tip of the iceberg. Contemporary theology has rejected the traditional *philosophia perrenis* of the scholastic theologians across the board. This is not only true of those who dissent from *Humanae Vitae*, but also of those who defend it. Dr. Germain Grisez, a very strong defender of the Church's teaching on contraception, gave a lecture at Holy Apostles Seminary, in Cromwell, Connecticut, in which he strongly advocated the position that the Pope should *ex cathedra* define every single moral teaching. Presumably, he took this position because he believes there are no natural law arguments based on analysis of the faculties which could support the teaching. The only basis for affirming the Church's teaching would be authority. Dr. Grisez has published a many-volume work on Christian ethics in which he tries to derive a moral theology without reference to traditional ideas about human nature. The rejection of the traditional teaching on the natural law is probably the most glaring difficulty for Catholic teaching in the last forty years.

Given all these difficulties, it is no wonder that the beginning student in moral theology is confused. I have heard students in many seminaries lament for years that there is no truly understandable moral theology textbook in which they can discern a systematic unity of the Magisterial teaching of the Popes, the emphasis on the human person in the Second Vatican Council, and the Scholastic tradition. In addition, many traditional Catholic moralists lament the lack of a complete teaching on the virtues and the inclusion of the ultimate end and the doctrine of grace in former manuals of moral theology. This should also be remedied in any new book written on fundamental moral theology. It is high time that such a book be written, especially since the publication of the *Catechism of the Catholic Church* and *Veritatis Splendor*.

The real difficulty in moral theology has always been to preserve a healthy respect for the law (the servant aspect) while also encouraging the interior formation in love which the truth of the law seeks to inculcate in human life (the aspect of freedom). Modern moralists have tried to play one off against the other. Moral theology, however, cannot be an either/or. Moral teaching, indeed all Catholic theology, must be a both/and. In this book, I will try to show the fullness of the Catholic synthesis which, based on an authentic picture of the human soul, seeks to direct man to a true experience of being both truthful and loving, both law-abiding and Spirit-filled, both obedient to absolute moral norms and freely pursuing heaven, BOTH A SERVANT AND FREE!

CHAPTER ONE
THE HUMAN SOUL

INTRODUCTION

Action follows being. *Operari sequitur esse.* This is the famous Scholastic axiom which governs all discussions about nature. This is no less true of the nature of man. There has been much talk in Catholic circles concerning the proper foundation for a true moral theology. Most moralists today want to distance themselves from anything which remotely resembles the traditional faculty analysis of the human soul. They do not want to derive moral obligations from the various powers present in the human soul. Many current moral theologians believe they must find another foundation than a faculty analysis of the human soul. These other sources range from a consensus about the greatest good which can be achieved or possessed from the consequences of the action to the authority of the Church without reference to natural law. Yet, Pope John Paul II reiterated again in *Veritatis Splendor*, "The Church has often made reference to the Thomistic doctrine of natural law, including it in her own teaching on morality."

"Man stands in the middle of creation, on the horizon of being, between flesh and spirit, between time and eternity." This quote expresses the fundamental thesis of this book and certainly expresses the metaphysical foundation of the natural law. It is a text from the *Book of Causes (Liber de Causis)*, attributed to an early neo-Platonist philosopher, Proclus, and quoted many times by the Scholastic theologians, including St. Albert the Great and St. Thomas Aquinas. It expresses the fact that the human person is a spiritual being. It also demonstrates that the body is an essential component of the human person. The relation of the supernatural order to man composed of body and soul is the next logical question following on the determination of his destiny. His destiny must relate to both aspects of his being: the spiritual and the material. These must not be divorced from each other in man's relationship with God.

Since man is an individual substance[7], there is only one human soul. This human soul underlies all human powers. In this truth, the Church accepts the philosophical explanation of Aristotle that there is only one form in man, the soul which is in a substantial unity with the body. The substance of man demands the union of both the soul and the body.

ANCIENT APPROACH OF THE PLATONISTS

There are several kinds of human experience that we can perceive on an everyday level with our common sense knowledge. Common sense knowledge does not presume a special experimental method open to only a few savants, but rather a knowledge open to ordinary, everyday experience. Man shares physical movement with the rocks. If the human body is dropped, it falls. Man also shares growth and nutritional life with the plants. Man's body is an organism and manifests the characteristics of all organisms. Man also shares the life of the senses with the animals. If I am hungry, I am drawn to the smell, sight and taste of food. If I am sick, I am repelled by the same. But man is unique among corporeal beings. He can also know and love spiritually. Man is then a microcosm because he summarizes in himself the whole universe from the angels to the planets.

These perceptions led Platonists to posit that there were several souls in man. Plato thought that universal ideas were the only real things. There was no reality to individual things. They were shadows. Each kind of action found in man must be merely a reflection of a universal idea. The human individual was a union of actions which reflected these real universal ideas. The vegetative soul governing nutrition and growth differed from the animal soul which was expressed in sense knowledge. This in turn differed from the world of the mind. He maintained that the unity of the human person was merely an external unity in acting, but not a unity in being. As a result, he did not believe the soul in man was one, but many. It was thus a mover, but not a form. The body has as many different movers as there were types of action in man. Their union was merely a forensic or a moral union and not a real union. Each of the various powers of the human soul represented a soul and they were joined together in moving man like sailors who, exercising different actions, move a ship.

According to Plato's position, neither man nor animal would experience a union in being by nature. They would only experience a union in acting. Each individual would be animal as participating in the idea of animal by sense knowledge; plant as participating in the idea of plant and man as participating in spiritual knowledge and love. If man were a unity of really diverse principles joined only in acting, there would be no need to posit the existence of a substantially unifying principle.

MODERN PHILOSOPHY AND THE SOUL

In modern philosophy, a similar divorce of the various ways of acting in man was begun by Descartes who viewed the soul as the "ghost in the machine," also merely the mover of the body. This led to a divorce of spirit from the senses which in ethics resulted in either the exaggerated empiricist school of Hume where man's good is only in pleasure or in the exaggerated idealism school of Kant where morality has no reference at all to either sense knowledge or passion.

THE CHURCH AND ARISTOTLE

The Church has followed a middle course affirming both, which is the way of looking at the soul/body composite as expressed by Aristotle. Man's one soul is the form of his body. The soul, which is rational, sensing and vegetal is substantially one only.

> Man, though made of body and soul, is a unity. Through his very bodily condition he sums up in himself the elements of the material world. Through him they are thus brought to their highest perfection and can raise their voice in praise freely given to the Creator. For this reason man may not despise his bodily life. Rather he is obliged to regard his body as good and to hold it in honor since God has created it and will raise it up on the last day.[8]
>
> The unity of soul and body is so profound that one has to consider the soul to be the 'form' of the body: i.e. it is because of its spiritual soul that the body made up of matter becomes a living, human body; spirit and matter, in man, are not two natures united, but rather their union forms a single nature.

The reasoning soul in man underlies all his powers and gives to the human body everything the sensitive soul gives to the irrational animal and the vegetal soul gives to the plant. It also contributes something over and above this. The one soul forms the bedrock on which all the powers act. There is no physical material principle necessary for the soul to act, but the body is necessary for the soul to exist. Man therefore has both an aspect which transcends matter and an aspect which is immanent to matter.

Again, the one spiritual soul underlies all the powers in man. Though man's passions, for example, are the same in nature as animal passions because they are derived from a sensing, physical body, they are nobler in man than they are in animals. The sensing part of the soul is immortal because the principle which underlies it is immortal.

One further distinction is necessary before the powers which go to make up the human act are treated. The soul is not the same as its powers. The powers of the soul derive from the substance of man, but they are accidents. The substance performs actions by means of the accidental principles. If the intellect were the soul, for example, a man would always be as much in the act of understanding as he is in the act of existing. In fact, a man only actually understands when he is performing an action of reasoning.

POWERS OF THE SOUL

The powers of the soul are not simple accidents. If they were, they would not be important to understanding human acts. In fact, they are properties. These are accidents which are not incidental to the existence or understanding of a given thing, but necessary to understanding a being fully because they are always found wherever that being is present. To be social or capable of a sense of humor is an example of a human property.

There are two kinds of properties in a being: those which reflect the species (e.g., the social character of man); and those which reflect the individual. Masculinity and femininity would be an example of the latter.

For example, the intellect in man is a power of the soul, not the substance. So it is a property. Man is considered to be intellect, not because the essence of the soul is the intellect, but because the highest power in man is the intellect. The powers of the soul are distinguished by their activity. Since the acts which the soul performs differ from each other (e.g. understanding, willing, loving, hating, tasting), the powers are distinct also. Each action which distinguishes a power of the soul has a different object or being which completes or brings this power into action. Differences in object are the sources of difference in action and so difference in powers.

There are three grades of action in the soul. Each is less dependent on matter for its action. Organic life completely depends on matter. The life of the senses is the beginning of the removal from dependence on matter. Men and animals experience the fact that they can receive things in the soul without their material extension, but with singularity and individuality which result from material extension. For example, they can experience an image of a tree in the eye, but the tree is not growing in the eye. This experience of an object of knowledge or desire without its proper matter is called an intention. This experience forms the basis for positing sense powers of knowing and distinguishing things in bodily organs like the eye.

In spiritual action, there is even really no dependence on matter except for input. Men experience the fact that they can receive things in a spiritual way not only without material extension, but without singularity. Man can experience not just one tree, but in experiencing one tree, he can experience how all trees differ from all cats. This is the highest and most perfect grade of immateriality. This is characteristic of intellectual knowing.

There is a natural inclination to pursue a union by action with what is known either in the senses or the intellect. This is called appetite or desire. As this desire can be either sensitive or intellectual or both, this distinguishes a third sort of power which is not stilled in capturing the being of the other thing within, but goes out to experience that being on its own terms. This desiring power is expressed in the passions or in the will.

The intellect, the will and the passions are the three sorts of powers involved in morals and so each must be defined and treated. An understanding of these is the necessary preamble to determine the truth of morals and also to demonstrate the influence of the various powers of the soul on moral freedom.

The sense powers of knowing and desiring are shared with the animals but because of the unity of intellectual soul, men and animals experience them in different ways. Sensation is a living action which results from an object stimulating a sense organ: the eye, the ear, the nose, the tongue or touch. For example, light reflected from the red surface of an apple reaches the eye. The nerves in the eye respond and an animal or man becomes conscious of the color of the apple. Aristotle compares this experience to a seal forming its impression on wax. This experience also causes the first experience of knowledge.

SENSE POWERS OF KNOWING

As with the wax, the impression remains in the organ even when the object is withdrawn. Unlike the wax, the organ is a living thing and so has its own response to this experience.

The experience of union with the object, of taking the being of the object in (albeit on a very superficial level), without destroying the object is consciousness. The quality of the object is experienced by the subject and the being of the subject is expanded. The form or intention produced in the organ is neither completely immaterial since it involves a material object reaching a material sense, nor wholly material since the organ is living. What the person experiences through the organ is called the intention, or the insensate quality of an object. All intellectual knowledge demands observation in the outer senses first because this is the way exterior beings are first experienced interiorly.

In addition to those outer senses shared by men and animals there are also inner senses which one can distinguish by the method of introspection. These are four: the common sense, imagination, memory and the estimative sense. Each is important to have a complete picture of what is involved in human knowledge and willing.

The common sense does not mean the popular "horse sense". Rather, it refers here to the fact that one does not merely know sensible impressions, but objects through them. This is also called perception. One combines and divides yellow, smooth, spicy and fragrant, bitter and sour, and the result is knowledge of a lemon. Many kinds of sensations are unified or distinguished to know a thing. Perception could be defined as: "the power of perceiving objects here and now present to the outer senses."

The common sense is the place where our sensations are put together, worked over, refined and compared to form the unity of a thing. The eye knows the color of the lemon and tongue knows it is bitter or sour, so seeing and tasting are connected in the common sense to experience an object.

CHAPTER ONE THE HUMAN SOUL

One of the advantages of the common sense is that it addresses the whole subject of illusion. Illusion is "a mistake in judgment which arises when knowledge supplied by the senses of imagination has not been properly interpreted."[12] An example of this is the perception of the bent stick in the water or lines which appear unequal in a diagram but which in fact are equal when measured. This is distinguished from delusion which is "an error in judgment which has no basis in reality."[13] Illusions, a problem which bothered Descartes greatly, have led some to distrust knowledge gained from perception through the senses altogether and have led to a kind of spiritualism in knowledge. However, the origin of all our objective knowledge and desire is in fact in the senses. The common sense aids us to check our sense experiences and what may seem a mistake in one sense (the bent stick in the water as sight perceives it) can be checked by touch to determine that the stick is in fact straight. The influence of the common sense is greatly diminished in sleep and that is why there can be both a free flow of images in dreams and yet dreams can seem so real. In any case, the common sense forms objective images which prepare the mind to form ideas.

In addition to the common sense, animals and man exhibit the ability to experience a thing when it is absent from them, to have imagination. This ability means that an animal or man does not have to be physically present to a thing to experience it. Imagination has two functions: reproductive and creative.

Reproductive imagination involves the ability to experience things which have their origin in the actual experience of the knower. Both animals and men imagine in this way. The knower is limited to what has been actually sensed.

Creative imagination is more complex and reserved only to human beings. Because of the power of the intellect in the spiritual soul, a man can compose and divide images to create an image of something which one has never experienced in fact. For example, a man can combine the wings of a bird and the body of a horse and experience a mythical creature, Pegasus. In sleep, the outer senses are not acting in their usual way and the influence of the common sense is reduced and so images in dreams are very creative. In dreams, the person experiences something as real which is not. Nevertheless, both Aristotle and Thomas Aquinas referred to images as "thoughts in the making."[14]

A third inner knowing sense is the memory. This differs from common sense because, in it, one experiences a thing which is absent. It differs from imagination because in it one experiences a thing as past. What is the difference between imagination and memory? It is the difference between picturing an apple and picturing the last apple one has eaten. Time does not enter as a part of the first experience but does enter as a part of the second. As is the case with imagination, there are two different experiences of memory: simple recall and recollection.

Simple recall is an experience man shares with other animals. In this way of knowing, one can spontaneously bring something already experienced back into consciousness without the aid of another power. A dog that has been kicked bites the one who kicked him many years later. A bird always returns to the same nesting area because the bird "remembers" it as useful.

Recollection on the other hand is unique to human beings again because of the presence of the intellect. In recollection, one thing suggests another thing to someone. He experiences the second thing because of the help or guidance given by reason in knowing the first thing. Plato, for example, reminds me of Socrates because they were both philosophers and one was the student of the other.

The last interior power of sense knowledge is called estimation by St. Thomas and the usefulness judgment by some modern authors.[15] This is the most important sense power of knowing. It is like instinct in animals. Certain animals always return to the same nesting place every year; the beaver knows what materials to use to make its dam. A myriad of wondrous examples exist in nature of animals knowing what is necessary to pursue or avoid for their survival and advancement. St. Thomas defines this power as: "The ability of the animal to know, without any previous information, what is good and what is bad for the organism."[16] The traditional explanation of instinct in animals includes three things: "first, the recognition of the utility or harmfulness of certain objects; second, experience of emotion as a result of such knowledge; third, motor behavior (the motion of the body as a result)."[17] This ability to judge the harmfulness or usefulness of a given action is placed in animals by God. Aristotle was so impressed with this ability that he attributed a kind of prudence to animals.

Man has this same ability. Since man has a spiritual soul, he is confronted with an almost infinite variation of possibilities when it comes to judging things as harmful or useful. For this reason, though this sense exists in man, it is not naturally perfect from birth as in animals but must be developed over time. The presence and use of the intellect are the means by which the development occurs. God supplies man with a higher way of determining what is harmful and useful which depends on the progressive examination of his world. An animal's world is determined by only a few things. There is no freedom of action. Man's world is not determined to any good but the universal one of perfection because of the intellect.

The sense power of estimation plays a part in all human actions, but since it is not developed by instinct it must be developed in the young by education. Moral education plays a great part in this. The relation of this power to intelligence guided by teaching is of vital importance in emotional health. "A retarded or impaired penetration of this power by the intellect will result in a psychopathic personality; a precocious or excessive penetration will result in a repressive neurosis."[18]

SENSE POWERS OF DESIRING

The sense powers of desiring which man shares with the animals, also called sense appetites, correspond to the sense powers of knowing. Though these are not powers which in themselves make up moral choice in man, they are central to any consideration of morals and so it is important to understand them. One of the easiest ways to distinguish appetite or desire from knowledge is by comparing their respective objects. Knowing what an apple is, one can describe the shape, size, touch and color of an apple. But this will not satisfy one who is hungry. Only the actual experience of the apple in eating it will satisfy hunger pangs. The goal of knowledge is to experience the apple "in an intentional way", whereas the goal of desiring is to experience it "in a real way"[19] by eating it.

As a result, for complete experience of anything, being a lover is more complete than merely being a knower. In the sensory realm, this includes experiencing emotional joy often accompanied by physical pleasure in the fulfillment of desire. God himself attached pleasure for both men and animals to things which should be done for each.

Food tastes good because those who have bodies need it to live. Sexual activity feels good because it is necessary to propagate the species.

Certain Christian teachers, influenced by Stoicism, thought that pleasures must be caused by Satan as their desire often leads to sin. Therefore they must all be denied.

Catholic doctrine and authentic philosophy have always taught that God made the pleasures to encourage the action which follows being in men and animals. C.S. Lewis has Screwtape, the senior tempter in hell, tell his junior apprentice tempter Wormwood in *The Screwtape Letters*: "Never forget that when we are dealing with any pleasure in its healthy and normal and satisfying form, we are, in a sense, on the Enemy's (Christ's) ground. I know we have won many a soul through pleasure. All the same, it is His invention, not ours. He made the pleasures: all our research so far has not enabled us to produce one. All we can do is to encourage the humans to take the pleasures which our Enemy has produced, at times, or in ways, or in degrees, which He has forbidden."[20]

The sensitive appetite produces feelings which are physical and emotions which are in the soul. These differ in degree for emotions are much stronger and more deeply rooted in the character than feelings.

For Thomas Aquinas the generic term "passion" includes both feelings and emotions. Today the term "passion" is used in a rather more specialized way, but for the purposes of morals the Thomistic use will be maintained in this book because it belongs to the Christian patrimony and, coming as it does from the Latin word *pati* (to suffer or be acted upon), aptly expresses how sensitive desires move us.

Two other important points: Thomas Aquinas distinguishes between sense knowledge and desire in this way: "The work of a cognitive power is done when the object of knowledge is in the subject of knowledge. But the work of the appetitive power is done only when the subject of desire is carried towards the object of desire."[21]

In other words, there is a circularity in knowledge and desire even on the level of the senses. Knowledge goes from thing to knower and the goal is the object in the subject; desire goes from lover to thing and only rests in the object of desire itself. Just knowing about food does one no good in a state of hunger. Only eating completes the desire. So, nothing can be desired unless it is first known and it is knowledge which sets desire aflame. A child who has never tasted chocolate and so does not know what chocolate is cannot cry for it.

There are two different general experiences of desire or appetite which man and animals share. "First, the concupiscible appetite (also known as the pleasure appetite) which gives rise to what can be called, in a general way, 'the passions of desire'; second, the irascible appetite (also known as the usefulness appetite), from which springs the 'passions of conflict'."[22] The difference in the two appetites allows for distinguishing things which are pleasant from their unpleasant opposites and things which are useful (or harmful) and demand striving because of their difficulty to obtain (or avoid).

The dog finds food pleasant; the medical student finds passing exams pleasant; the victim of the mugger finds saving his life pleasant and the attack of the mugger unpleasant. The passions which are experienced in these reactions are the concupiscible or pleasure appetite. If obtaining the good is difficult for the dog, he will make a great effort to obtain it; the medical student may have to give up a weekend of fun and stay up all night to pass the exam; the victim may have to fight the mugger to save his life. The passions which come to aid all these three desires for experiencing pleasure and avoiding pain are the irascible or utility appetite.[23]

All sense desires are drawn to particular goods and this includes those of man. But because of the presence of the intellect in man, as was the case with sense knowledge, there is a further perfection for sense desires. This is based on the unity of the powers of the human soul. "It belongs to the perfection of the moral or human good that the passions be governed by reason."[24] Also, since the good itself precedes the good perceived as useful or harmful, the natural order of these two appetites is concupiscible-irascible-concupiscible. Freud divided emotional experience between libido and the death wish which in general terms reflects the traditional division of the concupiscible and irascible appetites.

Every passion has a corresponding experience in the body. These can be evident outward expressions like sorrow causing one to weep or hunger causing salivation in the presence of food. Each passion also has internal effects; for example, blood sugar levels can rise or fall depending on the strength of the passion. This is because of the union of the body and the soul in man.

Scientists and philosophers study the passions by examining the various objects of human experience when an animal or a man is in a passionate state. Each appetite has several passions which characterize it. Though the various passions may differ materially, they are unified in the same appetite because they are generally about the same experience. In the concupiscible appetite, this experience is the good in itself.

The primary experience of the good in itself is the attraction between things which is caused by their likeness in being. In both animals and men, this attraction is a response to the perceived good, either sensibly or intellectually of the being of another thing as desirable. This desirability is based on a likeness in being and gives rise to a contentment or "complacency in the object" (*complacentia appetibilis*).[25] This experience is the passion of love, "the most fundamental passion [...] aroused by the attraction of the good."[26] All the other passions line up based on the experience of love. Love creates desire for the good and joy in attaining it.

The opposite of love is hate which is emotional revulsion based on a perception of the unlikeness of a thing or evil of the one moved by the passion against the hated thing. This hatred causes aversion. The experience of an evil which cannot be avoided causes sorrow.

The irascible appetite is completely different from the concupiscible one because it is not based on the basic experience of likeness or unlikeness to the moved subject. Instead, the emotional responses in this appetite come into play when a given thing desired or reviled is difficult to obtain or avoid. Thus, the passions in this appetite serve the passions in the concupiscible appetite. This emotional experience involves "assertiveness and optimism, or their opposites."[27]

When seeking to obtain an arduous desired good or avoid an arduous evil, if the animal or man can do it, then the passion of hope comes into play. This passion is characteristic of an energetic personality. If the animal or man has the experience that they cannot do it, then the feeling of despair, dejection or weakness enters. If either the animal or the man senses optimism at overcoming the evil or obtaining the good then courage comes into play or, if not, fear.

Courage and hope then are passions which aid in the attainment of a desired good or an averted evil when the subject experiences a threat to what is loved or hated. Fear and despair are emotional states which arise when the subject finds attaining the arduous good or avoiding the arduous evil out of reach.

The final passion in the appetite has no opposite and involves frustration in obtaining a good or resisting a threatened evil. This is the passion of anger.

All of these passions — love, hate, desire, aversion, sorrow, joy, hope, despair, courage, fear and anger — are natural to both animals and men and all must be felt for a complete experience of well-being in both. In addition to finding these in many philosophers under other names, the Catholic tradition has made them its own and an understanding of these passions is essential to the moral life. The *Catechism of the Catholic Church* enumerates almost all of them in a basic catechetical source. "There are many passions. The most fundamental passion is love, aroused by the attraction of the good and the hope of obtaining it; this movement finds completion in the pleasure and joy of the good possessed. The apprehension of evil causes hatred, aversion, and fear of the impending evil; this movement ends in sadness at some present evil, or in anger that resists it."[28]

Emotional states are determined by reactions to particular goods and so they are constantly changing. The quick change from one state to another is especially prevalent in children because the influence of the intellect is diminished in them. Babies cry and immediately laugh. But this is not just true of children. In all those subjects who enjoy passions, these states constantly change. A positive or negative experience does not necessarily call forth the same emotional response in every person. Physical constitution, upbringing or environment may each play a part in the development of passionate responses.

An understanding of the life of the passions is central to any consideration of morals. Though all are necessary, the passions of love, anger, sorrow and fear are the most important for moral life and are greatly misunderstood. A good bit of moral development turns on the question of how one deals with the passions.

The passions stand in a kind of no man's land between the body and the intellect and will. They are found in the life of the senses and respond naturally to sense knowledge but, because they are present in a being with an intellect and will, they have a second tendency in addition to responding to the sense perception of individual goods. This tendency is that they are naturally born also to experience union with the higher and more universal direction of the intellect and will. "It belongs to the perfection of the moral or human good that the passions be governed by reason."[29]

SPIRITUAL POWERS

In addition to the sense powers of knowing and desiring which man shares with the animals, there are powers of the soul which are characterize human nature alone. These powers show that man is a separate and unique being in the material universe.

The highest power of man is the intellect. This power allows man to know not just an individual tree as is the case with sense knowledge, but through the process known as abstraction, by a divinely-given light known as reason, man is able from an individual experience of this tree to participate in the beings of all trees that have existed, now exist or ever will exist. The means by which this action is accomplished is the intellectual image or concept which has a two-fold nature. Since the concept is tied to the senses because man has a body, it truly expresses the individual material thing of which it is the image. As a concept in which the nature of this individual thing is received is a spiritual soul, it is a universal idea which both expresses and transcends the individual thing. It is at one and the same time ideal because it is received by the spiritual soul and real and objective because it is a true participation in the being of each material individual thing which it represents. Through the intellectual concept or idea, the soul can become all things by a participation in their being. Of course, this presupposes that the concept is true. This means it truly represents the being it expresses. Truth is the equality of the mind with the thing. The concept in the mind must truly express the thing outside the mind it captures.

There are many powers of knowing in the senses because sense knowledge expresses only the individual things as individual and so there may be many different experiences of this: the five exterior senses, the common sense, imagination, memory and estimation. But because the intellect experiences the thing through a universal idea, there is only one power of spiritual knowledge: the intellect.

In the universal idea, the intellect allows man to be a part of his exterior world and to expand his horizons through real participation in the objective natures of things. By means of spiritual ideas, man receives the being of things outside of him in the secret recesses of

CHAPTER ONE THE HUMAN SOUL

his soul. The things outside him truly become like him. Knowledge is the window of the soul. Without knowledge, the person is blind and cannot act for no one can act for a purpose which he has not yet known is possible or exists, nor can someone love something he does not know exists.

There are two basic intellectual experiences of the thing known. They are not two different powers in the soul, but one power with two different applications: One is of its truth as such. The other is the relationship of this object to some action to be performed or its useful good. The first kind of knowledge is called the speculative intellect; the second, the practical intellect. Once man truly participates through the concept in the object known, then the quest of the intellect for truth about that particular thing comes to an end and the intellect rests.

But man does not rest for, as is the case with the life of the senses, knowledge is not enough for the complete experience of a thing. Knowledge is completed in the manner of being of the knower. Though this is a true union with the object, it is not the complete experience because, once the knower knows a thing, the knower is driven out of himself to participate in the object as it is in itself. Thus spiritual knowledge seeks to pour itself out in desire. The faculty in which this spiritual desire is expressed is the will, which is the central power in morals. The will is only one faculty. In sense desire there were eleven different passions because sense desire is drawn to individual things as individual. The will on the other hand is governed by the intellect and therefore is drawn to the universal so there is only one power of spiritual desire.

If the intellect is like the eyes of the soul, the will is like the feet. Both are necessary to a complete experience of a thing. Knowledge is necessary for love; but knowledge without love is incomplete. Nothing is willed unless it is first foreknown. The movement of the will according to the truth of human nature for a particular object is called love. The difference between sensual love and spiritual love is that one is drawn to a particular good and the other to a universal good. Animals are determined to what they love; men are not because of the presence of the intellect.

This lack of determination is caused by the fact that for every individual good, the intellect can see some undesirable aspect and so the intellect is the foundation of the freedom of the will. Freedom born from love completes the circle of the experience of a thing which man needs. "Accordingly both in us and in God there is a certain circularity in the acts of the intellect and will: for the will returns to that whence came the beginning of understanding: [...] in us the circle ends in that which is external, the external good moving the intellect and the intellect moving the will, and the will by appetite and love tending to the external good."[30]

Acts of will are called volitions and are of two kinds. There is the natural movement of the will towards anything which is perfecting of man or the universal good. Whatever a person wills he must will under the aspect of good. This does not mean it actually is the true good, but the subject must will it as something which perfects his being on some level. Then there is the freedom of choice which involves knowledge of some particular good and resultant movement towards that good under the aspect of perfection. In this latter act, the will uses means to obtain the ultimate end of perfection.

ETHICS AND HUMAN NATURE

The picture of the soul heretofore described has often been greatly questioned in the history of philosophy and those philosophical doubts affect faith. Before examining the nature of moral theology it would seem good to make some brief clarifications about people and ideas which affect the present climate. Since Pope John Paul II has often been invoked as the authority for an approach to the human person which is phenomenological and therefore not traditional, many of the ideas summarized here will be drawn from his lectures as a philosophy professor which have yet to be published in English.

According to John Paul II, in these lectures, the most important point is to state that "a strict link exists between ethics and anthropology."[31] Anthropology here refers to the ability to abstract by induction which is central to traditional Catholic philosophy and by examining human acts to come to a knowledge of the powers which all men share. Since knowledge comes through the senses, by induction one postulates what a person ought to do based on the goods which fulfill the human powers of the soul. These can be known by ordinary observations in the senses. "This is not the method of generalization of a certain thesis (as is the case with John Stuart Mill and the positivists) but only a method of directly seizing a general truth from particular facts (Aristotle)."[32] This connection recognizes the dependence of ethics, and hence moral theology, on a realistic metaphysics[33] and epistemology.[34] One truly participates in man from the idea of man and the soul gained from ordinary sense experience open to everyone. The idea of man is both material as it comes through the senses and expresses a being with a body and spiritual as it is formed as a universal in the mind at the same time. It is precisely this truth that is denied in modern philosophy which in turn has led to the destruction of morals.

Beginning with Descartes who wished to preserve certainty in knowledge in the face of the skepticism introduced by the Reformation and modern science into philosophy, there was a "turn to the subject" instead of the object as the source of truth. This led to a divorce between sense experience and intellectual ideas. The experience of man became either totally limited to the sensible world, so there was no idea of a universal nature, or preceded any common sense experience of how man acts and so was divorced from everyday sensible experience.

Hume is the great representative of the former tendency which actually is quite prevalent in the climate of the 21st Century world. "In his opinion, one can reduce the morality of man to a particular sense which allows us to distinguish virtue from sin beginning from the pleasure which accompanies the first and the pain which we find in the second."[35] Morality becomes experiencing the greatest pleasure and reducing pain as far as possible. Though Hume tempered his philosophy from the extreme conclusion that pleasure is the only good, this general attitude gave rise to a completely utilitarian ethics and can be summarized today in the common aphorisms "if it feels good, do it" and "how can it be so wrong when it feels so right."

Kant rightly reacted against this way of looking at ethics which reduced ethical experiences to mere descriptions of pleasure and pain. Kant accepted the general understanding of the Enlightenment that it was impossible to arrive at universal truths like moral laws or human nature through abstraction from the senses. Sense knowledge could not lead one there. Since he firmly believed there were such laws, he decided that they could not be derived from an objective metaphysics based on sense experience, a pure reason. Instead, since these laws were about human practice, they must be derived from need or practical reason.

Human need creates the nature of God and the common nature of man *a priori*, in other words, not as a result of everyday experience but according to the needs of the subject. "Kantian ethics and anthropology in which the moral sense is radically cancelled and morality must find its roots in the categorical imperative which forms a priori in practical reason are opposed to these ideas (Hume)."[36]

Kant therefore reduced ethics to pure duty based on a human nature which really could not be defined from anything which was observable. He also left emotions and sense experience completely out of the picture where ethics is concerned. Since there was no nature of man which could objectively be verified as a basis for determining right and wrong, there was no determination of man outside his own conscience. "The experience of the imperative is linked in the understanding of Kant, to the experience of freedom. The true negation of freedom of will is constituted by any type of determinism."[37] This would include a determinism caused by a prior existing objective nature.

So, for Hume morality was pure sentiment, for Kant it was pure duty. In the 20th Century, Max Scheler, a phenomenologist, sought to correct the excessive intellectualism of Kant by returning to the influence of the senses on ethical reasoning. Common-sense based on everyday experience leads one to the conclusion that the passions must be involved in morals. "One cannot deny that human acts are accompanied—just for their moral value, for the good and evil contained in them—by a very profound emotional experience. [...] Nevertheless the reduction of this experience of these sentiments to the category of sensible pleasure and pain is a gross simplification."[38]

Scheler sought to resolve the problems of Kant's *a priori* ideas about ethics based on subjective need with an *a priori* idea based on objective emotional feeling. "Above all it is necessary to affirm that if for Kant conscience had an eminently intellectual character—which was reason—for Scheler on the other hand it had above all an emotional character."[39] This attempt to return to the place of objectivity and the senses in morals was a very important corrective made on Kant, but it had the disadvantage of still not recognizing a real objective universal human nature. If one is to truly perform human actions, this must be based on a prior understanding of human nature. "Nevertheless, an accurate analysis of the Scheler's system demonstrates that the associations causing perfection are not wholly justified. This is because the person in the conception of Scheler, is not a being at all, but is only a unity of experiences."[40]

As a basis for the study of morals then, any attempt to separate man into two distinct and perhaps even contradictory experiences will fail. The actions of man must be based on a realistic objective metaphysics of man which recognizes a true human nature. This is the starting point for moral reflection. The traditional treatment of St. Thomas Aquinas and Aristotle forms this solid basis and while personalist philosophy may add the richness of everyday lived experience to this, ultimately it is the picture of the soul which has been described this chapter which must be its basis.

The real issue in this foundation seems to be the problem of determinism in relationship to freedom. There have been two extreme positions in examining determinism in the past. The one is physical determinism which is characteristic of thinkers like Democritus in the ancient world and Hume and Freud in the modern world. This results from the position of extreme positivism and materialism in which the will is reduced to mere materialist forces much like instinct in animals. Morals would then just involve a question of behavior but have no interior perfection as a part of it. In fact, as was shown above not only is the will not a material power and so is not determined to act for any particular good, but the human will even communicates some of its freedom to lower powers like the passions. Even if a man's body is tied up or by some sort of mind manipulation is forced to perform some action, he cannot be forced to love this action or will it. "He may be tied hand and foot, so that he cannot budge an inch; still, he remains essentially free in the sanctuary of his soul."[41]

The other kind of determinism is intellectual determinism in which knowledge forces the will to act in a certain way. This is somewhat like Plato's opinion that the wise man is always the good man. This opinion looks upon the will as forced to always choose the perceived greatest good. St. Thomas and the Catholic tradition have generally held with common sense experience that people often act against their own perceived best interests. In his letter to the Romans, St. Paul observed a fundamental experience of human nature that: "I do not understand my own actions. For I do not do what I want, but I do the very thing that I hate." (Rom. 7:15)

Instead, Catholic moral teaching has always supported a theory of moderate determinism. Both matter through the passions and the intellect have an influence over the will by presenting it with goods. But neither one of these influences can force the will to act if the person does not want to act. The intellect directs the will but cannot force the actions of the will. This is because since the intellect directs the will to particular goods based on the universal idea of human nature, each of these goods can always be examined in relationship to other goods in human nature which would turn those goods into evils in the context. For example, the intellect can present the love of God to the person as a good to be willed, but if that love leads to a person denying some pleasure because it conflicts with the law of God then from that point of view, the love of God in that individual action and context would be viewed as an evil if he thinks pleasure is always to be pursued.

Both intellect and will must cooperate together for human perfection and this is the reason why virtues must be found in both. The intellect moves the will without denying freedom because it is like the eyes of the soul. If one merely acted from impulse this would be like a man trying to walk blind. By the same token, the will cannot be forced to move. The eyes direct the steps but do not force the feet. If the eyes were to present a goal, but one were never to begin to walk, then one could not arrive at his destination. Still, if one is lame or chooses to walk blindly then one cannot attain the goal or one could walk over a cliff. The passions are not in themselves a part of this motive, but since they are there, to seek to act without considering their influence is unreasonable. Good passions make the journey easier, like taking a car. Bad passions make the journey more difficult.

Many modern thinkers emphasize that freedom is an innate quality of the will with no reference to any other power of the soul. Pope Benedict finds a source for this error in the thinking of Duns Scotus. Again, this would not in Scotus as such, but in those thinkers who uncritically expanded on some of his principles.

> Lastly, Duns Scotus has developed a point to which modernity is very sensitive. It is the topic of freedom and its relationship with the will and with the intellect. Our author underlines freedom as a fundamental quality of the will, introducing an approach

that lays greater emphasis on the will. Un[i]
in later authors, this line of thinking tur[ned] [ulti]ately,
voluntarism, in contrast to the so-called ['O'a]
ian and Thomist intellectualism'. For St[.]
Aquinas, who follows St. Augustine, freedo[m]
be considered an innate quality of the will,
fruit of the collaboration of the will and th[e]
Indeed, an idea of innate and absolute freed[om]
it evolved, precisely, after Duns Scotus — p[...]
the will that precedes the intellect, both in G[od]
in man, risks leading to the idea of a God who
not even be bound to truth and good.[42]

The rationalist seeks to reduce morals to pure reason[...]
voluntarist seeks to reduce morals to mere will power
without considering truth or passions. The hedonist se[eks]
morals to sentiment. Feelings are all that matters again[...]
really against the idea of moral responsibility entailed in[...]
Each of these ways of looking at morals is seriously deficient [...]
the intellect, the will and the passions are all involved in one w[ay or]
another in human freedom.

Moral theology demands a combination of all the powers of the human soul involved in willing: the intellect which presents the object to be loved; the will which loves it; and the passions which make love spontaneous and whole. This science is not limited to any one of these powers but is wholistic.

CHAPTER TWO
THE NATURE OF MORAL THEOLOGY

TOWARDS A DEFINITION

For many centuries there has been debate over the nature of moral science and this is due to disagreements about what is involved in human good. The determination of what the science of morals entails for a Christian in turn must take revelation into account. A related issue is that the method of the science is determined by what it is about. Fr. Servais Pinckaers, O.P., one of the most important contemporary authorities in Catholic moral theology, has given a detailed analysis of the difficulties people have had in developing a definition of moral theology.[43]

Fr. Pinckaers points out that the fundamental difficulty is related to whether one looks on moral science as a matter of perfection and happiness (like Aristotle, St. Thomas and St. Augustine) or one looks on it as a matter of obligation (like the many of the traditional manualists). One of the causes of this disagreement was the divorce of speculative and spiritual considerations in human actions from the more practical aspects needed by confessors. This long and complicated history is very well examined and researched by Pinckaers. For the purposes of this book, one should note that there should be no divorce in the treatment of happiness from obligation. The implications of this question and the various approaches to it will be briefly examined in Chapter Three.

In the post-Vatican II Church the Council fathers sought a renewal of moral theology and especially an evident reconnection of the Scriptures with questions of virtue as well as sins. In this book, it is presumed that the original division of St. Thomas in his famous *Summa Theologiae* is the only correct order for the treatment of morals. St. Thomas placed his moral teaching in the section of the *Summa* which examines the nature of the actions characteristic of "man made in the image of God."[44] Man, made in the divine image, is examined there as he reflects God and, since the intellect and will are the primary powers which reflect God, all the principles and actions involved in these two powers must be a part of this study. Though cases will be interspersed throughout the work, this work is primarily about principles. Since this treatment is made under the aspect of man as he reflects God in his freedom, it must include both reason and revelation.

Moral theology then is not really a separate study involving merely obligation, laws or cases, though all of these are a part of it and rooted in the more central principles. It is the application of what can be presumed by the rest of theology in the free acts by which a person freely makes choices by which he can arrive at his final perfection.

The "moral" part then of the term "moral theology" refers to what the Scholastics call the material object or the subject matter of the science which is the free acts of man by which he can realize the perfection of the powers of his soul. It thus has the same subject matter as ethics, the science of human choice open to reason alone based in the natural law. The "theology" part of the term "moral theology" refers to what the Scholastics call the formal object of the science, which is the light under which this subject matter is treated. This is divine revelation and includes all the traditional sources of this revelation. Faith plays an essential role.[45]

Moral theology could thus be defined as "the study of the free actions of man as an image of God viewed under the aspect of divine revelation." Pope John Paul II specified moral science in this way in his encyclical, *Veritatis Splendor*:

> [...] in the specific form of the theological science called 'Moral Theology', a science which accepts and examines Divine Revelation while at the same time responding to the demands of human reason. Moral Theology is a reflection concerned with 'morality', with the good and evil of human acts and of the person who performs them; in this sense it is accessible to all people. But it is also 'theology', is as much as it acknowledges that the origin and end of moral action are found in the One who 'alone is good' and who, by giving himself to man in Christ, offers him the happiness of divine life.[46]

The method of every science is determined by its nature. Since this science has to do with human acts, the entire science of ethics as described by Aristotle can certainly be a part of it. However, since the light under which these actions are viewed is divine revelation, this means that the method is first of all based on authority because in matters of faith authority is the strongest argument.

SCRIPTURE AND TRADITION

Vatican II was clear that, when it came to any science based on revelation, the Word of God was its source and the fonts by which this Word is known are equally Scripture and Tradition. Scripture is the Word of God written; Tradition is the Word of God spoken. Both are equally important sources for moral doctrine in Catholicism. "Sacred Tradition and Sacred Scripture, then, are bound closely together and communicate one with the other. For both of them, flowing out from the same divine well-spring, come together in some fashion to form one thing and move towards the same goal."[47] Scripture, however, is *norma normans non normata* (the norm which gives the norm but takes its norm from nothing else) and holds special place.

ROLE OF THE MAGISTERIUM

If there is a question concerning what faith teaches about morals in Scripture and Tradition, then this question must be authoritatively settled by the magisterium which is the servant of Scripture and Tradition. The magisterium does not create doctrines, but merely seeks to express what is contained in Scripture and Tradition. Examples abound in both sources of this truth.

In Scripture one can find such texts as: "The message is altogether reliable" (2 Peter 1:19); "Go, therefore, and make disciples of all nations, baptizing them in the name of the Father, and of the Son and of the Holy Spirit, teaching them to observe all that I have commanded you; and lo, I am with you always, to the close of the age," (Matt. 28: 18-20); and "When the Spirit comes, he will guide you to all truth." (John 16: 13) Tradition is equally clear: "'The task of giving an authentic interpretation of the Word of God, whether in its written form or in the form of Tradition, has been entrusted to the living teaching office of the Church alone. Its authority in this matter is exercised in the name of Jesus Christ'."[48] This means that the task of interpretation has been entrusted to the bishops in communion with the successor of Peter, the Bishop of Rome."⁴⁹

An example of this verification and the manner in which it is employed can be found in the encyclical, *Evangelium Vitae*, where John Paul II uses a very distinct formula in clarifying the fact that abortion and euthanasia are always wrong: "Therefore, by the authority which Christ conferred upon Peter and his Successors, and in communion with the Bishops—who on various occasions have condemned abortion and who in the aforementioned consultation, albeit dispersed throughout the world, have shown unanimous agreement concerning this doctrine—I declare...."⁵⁰

The language here invokes not the infallibility of the papal magisterium as described in Vatican I, but rather the infallibility of the bishops' magisterium as described in Vatican II when the bishops teach in a collegial act with the Pope as their head. Cardinal Ratzinger as head of the Congregation for the Doctrine of the Faith specifically cited the teaching on the evil of euthanasia in the Doctrinal Commentary of the Concluding Formula for the *Professio Fidei*, issued by this Congregation on June 29, 1998. He stated that teachings about these sorts of things fall under the second area of assent which are things "definitively taught but not in a solemn manner. The object taught by this formula includes all those teachings belonging to the dogmatic and moral area, which are necessary for faithfully keeping and expounding the deposit of faith, even if they have not been proposed by the Magisterium of the Church as formally revealed."⁵¹ Among other examples of this teaching he invokes: "... the illicitness of euthanasia [...] the illicitness of prostitution and of fornication [...]."⁵² The teaching on artificial birth control in *Humanae Vitae* can be included in this kind of infallible teaching because though Paul VI excluded an *ex cathedra* definition in this encyclical he was obviously deciding a truth about morals to be definitively taught as necessary to preserve the deposit of faith.

The Church does not establish or create good and evil. It rather clarifies and teaches those actions which accord with truth in doctrine. This is for the moral welfare and guidance of Christ's disciples. For this purpose, Christ also gave the Magisterium the charism to teach right conduct as implementing right teaching. The magisterium of the Church has the right to define the nature of moral acts whether by extraordinary or ordinary magisterium. In doing so, the Church does not establish the truth of these acts. Human nature and divine revelation do this. Rather the Church clarifies how and why these acts can or cannot lead to heaven. Since the teaching of the Church does not establish good or evil, but merely clarifies it, something which has always been taught as intrinsically evil cannot be now taught as good. "Yet, this Magisterium is not superior to the Word of God, but is its servant. It teaches only what has been handed down. At the divine command and with the help of the Holy Spirit, it listens to this devotedly, guards it with dedication, and expounds it faithfully. All that it proposes for belief as being divinely revealed is drawn from this single deposit of faith."[53]

INTRINSIC EVIL

This is an important clarification because in recent years there have been many otherwise credible Catholic authors who have maintained that the Church has changed her moral teaching several times in history, thus suggesting that this can occur with teachings definitively held by the Church. The opinion has been common that something always considered evil in itself can now be embraced as a good. This is the case with birth control. By the same token, the suggestion is made that something which has always been considered a good in itself is now an intrinsic evil. There are other moral teachings also which in the view of some have completely changed in time. For example, capital punishment. Before some said it was good but now it is intrinsically evil. One must be clear. Terminating a human life is not a moral good as such. The state has always had and continues to have a right to do this only in the context of heinous attacks on the right of innocent life in the society as a whole such as is the case with an obstinate capital murderer. There are many nuances in this teaching which will be taken up later, but it is important not lightly to state that the Church's teaching has altered so as to contradict previous teaching merely under the influence of the culture.

As an example of those who hold that the Church has changed her teaching, the famous Catholic legal scholar John T. Noonan has been of the opinion that the Church has done so at least four times in history. He summarizes this attitude: "That the moral teachings of the Catholic Church have changed over time will, I suppose, be denied by almost no one today."[54] The four areas where he holds

Church teaching has changed can certainly be disputed. What cannot be disputed is that his conclusion about theological methodology in morals simply does not square up with the nature of the science itself as involving both unchanging human nature known by reason and the unchanging deposit of faith as revealed definitively by Christ.

According to Noonan, cultural confrontation is what leads the Church to change moral teaching. Here he summarizes the work of the moralist Louis Vereecke: "Moral theology is where the unchanged gospel encounters changing cultures."[55] As an example of this principle he says: "The gospel as interpreted by Protestants and as mediated by Rousseau and the revolutionaries achieved much."[56] The changing times and climates of cultures led the Church to discover what was truly contained in the commands of Christ and the Old and New implicitly even against what the Church has taught in former ages. "All these factors, plus re-evaluation of the words of Christ, created a new moral doctrine."[57]

The implication is that the true nature of the gospel can never be discovered in any definitive way and that all is continually evolving, especially about those things which are intrinsically evil. All attempts then to express unchanging moral norms would be vain. "All will be judged by the demands of the day in which they live."[58] Noonan ends by suggesting that this ever evolving norm must lead back to the idea that the moralist is still dealing with the same Gospel. "Must not the traditional motto *semper idem* be modified however unsettling that might be, in the direction of *plus ça change, plus c'est la meme chose* (The more things change, the more they are the same)?"[59]

Regarding the idea that the culture is a part of the method of moral theology, one can admit this as a part of reason which examines human nature. Some of the norms of the natural law, for example, things which have to do with property rights in families can be culturally conditioned. But to maintain this of every moral norm is certainly contrary to the traditional teaching on the natural law and to common sense as it makes nonsense of the idea that there is an objective human nature which at least in general terms can be known by anyone with a modicum of intelligence. The conclusion that the culture is necessary to analyze moral norms, especially about things which are intrinsically evil, would fly in the face of the teaching of John Paul II in *Veritatis Splendor*: "Consequently, respect for norms which prohibit such acts and oblige *semper et pro semper*, that is, without any exception, not only does not inhibit a good intention, but actually represents its basic expression."[60] Those moral teachings which might be culturally conditioned would be so under the rubric of circumstances which cannot make an intrinsically evil act good.

A similar thing would be true of the idea that something always considered to be good in object could become evil. Later in the text, one will discover that there are actions which intrinsically accord with the nature of man, but which demand circumstances which correspond to this accord or must be reasonable. Recently a number of Church authorities have maintained that because of *Evangelium Vitae*, capital punishment has been demonstrated to be as evil as abortion. In fact, if one is going to be against abortion, one must also be against capital punishment because both involve the death of a man. This is called the "seamless garment" theory invoking the robe of Christ which was not torn by the Romans playing dice for it at the foot of the Cross.

The *Catechism of the Catholic Church* reflecting Pope John Paul II's teaching in *Evangelium Vitae* summarizes Church teaching on the death penalty by maintaining: "Assuming that the guilty party's identity and responsibility have been fully determined, the traditional teaching of the Church does not exclude recourse to the death penalty, if this is the only possible way of effectively defending human lives against the unjust aggressor."[61] It goes on to clarify: "Today, in fact, as a consequence of the possibilities which the state has for effectively preventing crime, by rendering one who has committed an offense incapable of doing harm—without definitively taking away from him the possibility of redeeming himself—the cases in which the execution of the offender is an absolute necessity 'are very rare, if not practically non-existent.'"[62] This would seem to be a clear case in which the teaching of the Church has changed according to the culture. If one looks closely though, one can see that the traditional teaching of the Church is affirmed that capital punishment accords with the natural law and is in fact in accord with human nature if properly applied. The issue raised by John Paul II is the issue of the circumstances inherent in modern prison systems which may make this an unreasonable means for affirming the right of innocent life if the prison system is an adequate defense of the right to life of innocent citizens. This, in fact, does change and also can be an object of debate.

To summarize: the methodology of moral science is affirmed which bases moral teaching on the authority of reason and faith experiencing an unchanging human nature. If the death penalty need not be applied any longer, this is not because the culture has given us a new insight into human nature which the Church never understood. It is rather because the circumstances of prison systems have made this penalty unnecessary for what its objective purpose has always been.

INFALLIBLE TEACHING?

One further point before summarizing what moral science is. Since moral theology is "theology" and involves the science of faith, there are those who maintain that the magisterium should *ex cathedra* define every moral teaching. Only thus can obedience to Church teaching be preserved. The clarification of Cardinal Ratzinger on what teaching may be made *ex cathedra* should be kept in mind here. "These doctrines are contained in the word of God, written or handed down and defined with a solemn judgment as divinely revealed truths either by the Roman Pontiff when he speaks *ex cathedra* or by the college of bishops gathered in council, or infallibly proposed for belief by the ordinary and universal Magisterium."[63] These are teachings directly found in the deposit of faith, not truths which are connected to these "by logical necessity"[64] such as *Humanae Vitae* or the teaching on euthanasia, already invoked.

Ex cathedra definitions are not possible for every Church teaching because not every one is found directly in Scripture and Tradition but many follow by logical necessity. Still these other teachings if defined partake in the infallibility by logical necessity, such as the teaching on euthanasia. Moreover, there are many moral teachings which can be effectively demonstrated using the natural law of human reason. Many human reasons can be used to demonstrate that something like artificial birth control is contrary to reason and so to arriving at heaven. A methodology in moral theology which refuses to incorporate effective arguments from reason would be like boxing with one hand tied behind one's back.

Though the magisterium can certainly define these things too it would be methodologically deficient not to use available arguments from reason alone. This would seriously limit an explanation of the magisterium's reason for so defining. Church teachings are of two kinds. Some in addition to being revealed to us by faith can be also proven with demonstrative arguments from reason. These are teachings like the evil of birth control or the existence of God. Others like the Trinity and the Incarnation can only be proven using probable arguments from reason like the divinity of Christ. The latter would demand magisterial intervention if questioned as these kinds of truths can only held by faith; the former can also be held by reason. Most moral teachings are truths of faith open to definitive arguments from reason alone.

So, this is the definition to which we have been building: moral theology is the study of those free acts of man in which he reflects being made in the image of God from the point of view of the divine revelation of the Old and New Testament. The methodology would entail use of both Scripture and Tradition as served by the magisterium. Truths from moral philosophy and ethics can be brought in to support and expand knowledge of these truths. Among the prime theological authorities invoked by the magisterium as a source for a correct exposition of moral theology is St. Thomas Aquinas. Christoph Cardinal Schönborn, O.P., who was the head of the theological committee responsible for the *Catechism of the Catholic Church*, confirmed this in his Introduction: "The structure of this 'fundamental moral theology' follows the great intuition of the *Summa* of St. Thomas. Is this the choice of a particular theological school? The commission was convinced that it should take the *doctor communis* as guide, not as the founder of a school, but as the great teacher of Christian morality."[65] So, it is clear that the Church has given a special place to St. Thomas in the arena of moral theology. The Church has accepted St. Thomas' teaching as her own especially in this field. One should therefore study and understand St. Thomas' moral theology to be able to give a realistic explanation of Catholic moral theology.

In this book, the order of St. Thomas in the *Summa*, also used in the *Catechism of the Catholic Church*, will be used as a guide. Thus the treatment of the subject will be in this order: the ultimate end, the will and responsibility, the intellect and law, the passions, the conscience, virtues, sins, law and grace.

CHAPTER THREE
HUMAN HAPPINESS

ACTING FOR AN END

There are some moral theologians today who express the opinion that moral theology should only be about obligation and not about acting for happiness. They think that all the arguments which emphasize acting according to a prior existing nature are not really valid in morals and perhaps actually detract from the science. For them the commandments with their accompanying obligations fall out of heaven and have no relation to fulfilling the powers of the human soul. For these theologians, desiring one's own happiness or salvation is at best unimportant; at worst, selfish and utilitarian.

The Catholic tradition following St. Thomas Aquinas and St. Augustine has never been of this opinion. Concerning the derivation of morals from nature, Pope John Paul II has gone so far as to teach in *Veritatis Splendor*: "The Church has often made reference to the Thomistic doctrine of natural law, including it in her own teaching on morality." (n. 44) Though one can examine morals from many different points of view, the most logical, conforming to the subject matter, would be to begin with what sets human actions apart from all the actions of other beings in the universe. Since actions are the implementation of powers, one must ask which action fulfills the highest power in the human soul. This is the end or purpose one should seek. Acting for happiness is to act for the sake of a purpose in which the soul becomes more perfect by participating in the good of things outside of it.

The reason moral theological reflection must begin with questions of ends is that nature is about the kind of activity which fulfills the powers of a given being. The existence of a thing and its further perfection in activity are distinct in everything. This is because God can gain nothing by acting, since he is infinite. Also, in him, what he is and that he is, are one thing. He gains nothing he does not possess by acting. He is Pure Act in Aristotle's way of putting it. In the case of all beings which do not have a reasoning soul, their powers are completely determined to a very limited number and kind of acts. The question is how can one determine which acts are perfecting of man unless one knows in what the ultimate perfection and satisfaction of human powers consists?

The Catholic tradition begins reflection on human acts then with a designation of what distinguishes human acts from all other actions, including those human acts shared with other beings.

> Of those actions done by man those alone are properly called human, which are proper to man as man. Now man differs from irrational animals in this, that he is master of his actions. Wherefore those actions are properly called human of which man is master. Now man is master of his actions through reason and will; whence too, the free-will is defined as the faculty of reason and will.[66]

One must distinguish between two types of acts in man: the first type are acts which result from intellect and will and are called human acts. The other type are acts which may be done by a human being, but do not involve reflection or choice. These are called acts of man. They would be things like absentmindedly shifting the feet or blushing.

Actions which are done with deliberation are actions which also are properly personal acts because they are done with intellect and will and the person is "an individual substance of rational nature." John Paul II expresses this character of man as a person, which he calls original solitude (Adam's awareness that he is not like the rest of creation) when he says: "The concept of original solitude includes both self-consciousness (intellect) and self-determination (will)."[67] One should notice at once that the concept of free will, so characteristic of persons includes BOTH intellect and will. Both of these powers of the soul must participate in any moral choice and so actions of self-determination or freedom involve the presence and perfection of both.

Reasoning persons also must first determine what the ultimate goal of their actions is and then begin to implement these goals. The determination of the destination is called the order of intention. The intellect takes first place here because one cannot begin the journey of life or any other journey for that matter until one has determined the destination. Without a determined destination, one cannot take the first step. The actual arrival at the destination is called the order of execution. The will has first place here because it is through choices that a person attains those goods which are his further perfection. If one endlessly examined possible courses of action or, having decided on one as the best, simply failed to choose it, one would spend his life spinning his wheels. If one just chose blindly, but never investigated to discover where one was going, one would also never arrive and might fall into a ditch. The same is true in life. One must investigate and decide on an ultimate destination and pursue it.

In fact, everything on earth has a destiny. It is the same ultimate destiny. Only man pursues his destiny with awareness and choice. All other things are like tools of God who are drawn to their destiny without participating in realizing it. Man, on the other hand, is what John Paul II calls a "partner with the Absolute." This is demonstrated in the very first human act in which man is given the commandment not to eat of the tree of the knowledge of good and evil. "The peculiarity of reasoning creatures is not that they pursue goals, but that they do so by directing themselves there; whereas non-reasoning creatures are directed by another to goals of which they themselves, unless they are animals, are quite unaware."[68]

In pursuing such a destination the will also has two sorts of acts. The one is within the very action of the will itself, the secret place where the person is most fully himself. This is called the elicited act. The other is an action which issues from the will commanding either itself to a further act or one of the other powers of man from the physical limbs to the passions to the thoughts of the mind. These are called imperated acts. Both are means by which a person wills and pursues his destiny.

Since human nature is realized by what is willed, praise or blame is attached to actions depending on whether they truly realize human nature or not. The ultimate end is obviously very important here as are all intermediate ends because, like a journey, all these intermediate ends contribute to or detract from attaining the final goal. The contribution of each of these acts is not just determined by their physical nature. Their physical nature must be considered in relationship to all the powers of the soul. Only human reason can do this.

The result is that acts which are distinct can morally be considered as one in so far as their goals relate to the final goal of an action. For example, buying a gun, walking, talking, driving a car, entering a bank, talking to the teller are physically all different actions, but if their final purpose is robbery, they all participate in the same moral dimension.

The same is true of one physical action which may look the same as another but have a whole different moral meaning because of its relation to the human soul in general. Killing in war, killing in capital punishment and killing the innocent all physically look the same because they all involve the death of human beings. Morally the first two differ from the last because they involve the death of the guilty, whereas the third involves the death of the innocent. This distinction is reflected in Scripture. "Scripture specifies the prohibition contained in the fifth commandment: Do not slay the innocent and the righteous. The deliberate murder of an *innocent* (Italics added) human person is gravely contrary to the dignity of the human being, to the golden rule, and to the holiness of the Creator. The law forbidding it is universally valid: it obliges each and everyone, always and everywhere."[69]

The ultimate goal of human action must be one in the same way that there cannot be two final destinations of a journey. As the final destination changes, the roads by which it is reached may change also. There can only be one final purpose in every human action. Each action also has a relationship to that purpose in the same way that each milestone and crossroads has a relation to the arrival at a final destination on a journey. For human beings, the general primary idea to grasp is that being seeks perfection. In every action, the general purpose is the fulfillment of some human power by a greater or further participation in being than that conferred on man from birth. As the eye seeks sight, the mind seeks truth and the will seeks good or perfection. So, the first principle of all moral reasoning is: Do good and avoid evil.

PERFECTION AND THE WILL

When one participates in the good, this is a further experience of being. This further participation is also a realization of a power in act. This is what everyone wills. This is called the formal end of the will. The formal nature of the ultimate end is present in every choice and a person does not have to be actively thinking about it just as one is not always thinking of the final destination in a journey with every step taken. Still, at certain crossroads or milestones, affirming the ultimate goal is necessary in order to arrive at the destination.

Though all men agree in acting to participate in the perfecting good, not everyone agrees on what the final good should be. The actual good which is the perfection of the human race is called the material end. This is the object which truly can complete man. "So all men agree in pursuing an ultimate goal and seeking their own fulfillment, but they disagree as to where this fulfillment can be found; just as all men like their food tasty, yet disagree as to which food is the tastiest."[70] One could say then that all men concur in the formal end of human action: experiencing the final perfection of all human powers (what Aristotle calls happiness and Christians call beatitude) but not everyone agrees on what good can cause this final perfection (the material end).

Even sinners act for the sake of good. However, they seek that good in something which cannot truly and objectively cause the perfect act of all human powers. "Sinners turn away from the true ultimate goal as such, since this is what they seek falsely in other things."[71] Regarding the formal end, all men agree when they act, but regarding the material end there is much disagreement. Everyone wants to be happy but the actual good which can objectively bring about this happiness is not sought by everyone.

Still, since everything that exists has its origin in the Trinity and is supported by an act of continuous creation on the part of the Trinity, each thing that exists, acting according to its nature, seeks to return to the unity of being itself found in God. God's presence as an intimate presence in all that is occurs not only in the existence of these things but in their action.

Fulton Sheen gave a masterful summary of this presence in an early work of his:

> God is the efficient, the final and the exemplary cause of all things in the universe. He is the Cause of all being, the Exemplar of all being and the End of all being. Thus it is that, from the point of view of the creature, everything has being in virtue of God as Efficient Cause, everything is good in virtue of God as Final Cause, and everything is true in virtue of God as Exemplary Cause. The transcendentals consequently attach themselves to God in virtue of the real relation between creature and God. *Ex Ipso, per Ipsum, et*

in Ipso. From Him, because of His Creative power; by Him, inasmuch as He made all things according to His Wisdom; in Him, inasmuch as all things are conserved in His Goodness. [...] All things lead to God, as all things come from God. There is nothing intelligible without Him, as there is nothing unintelligible with Him. He is the Alpha and Omega, the beginning and the end of all things.[72]

Regarding the ultimate end then, the actual material end of all things is God and all things concur with man in seeking this in their actions. Things come from God and seek to return to him. The good of the Trinity is the final purpose which moves the whole creation. Only man and the angels, though, can arrive at this final good because they are spiritual and transcend matter and so only man can properly speaking be called happy. "Men attain their goal by coming to know God and love him; other creatures are incapable of this, but attain to their goal by existing and being alive and aware, and so imitating God. We call man's way of attaining his goal being happy."[73]

The most important distinction to make about willed acts is that between what the end is and the actual attainment of the end. Happiness is attaining the end. Some moral manuals have been accustomed to make distinctions between material and formal happiness. Such a distinction is possible about ends. It is not possible about happiness. This is because the term happiness itself has to do with the enjoyment and rest in the end. In the case of a thirsty man, for example, the water is the material end, but slaking his thirst is the formal end. He can desire water all he wants and if he cannot drink it he cannot be happy. The mere identification of the end is not happiness. It is only in the arrival or the tasting that he can be said to be happy. Happiness is found only in the attainment of the goal.

WHAT IS HAPPINESS?

Once one has determined the fact and characteristics of the human beings' origin in action, then one must discuss what the basic good is in which this ultimate end consists. One must also determine how the attainment of this end relates to nature. There were two basic heresies about this end in the history of the Church. Pelagianism maintained that the nature of man was sufficient in itself to arrive at the final destiny of man. Grace only made this arrival easier. So the human will was sufficient in itself. The Calvinists and Jansenists maintained that grace overcame the human will and the arrival at the ultimate destiny of man was completely apart from any natural perfection of the human will. The issue of what the end of man is then is central to the issue of how one attains the ultimate end.

One important point must be observed in this discussion. The determination of the end is an ontological one. The practical nature of how one attains it or beatitude is a separate, though not unrelated question. Unfortunately many people have begun their discussion of this question with the issue of its attainment in the will. The first question must not be the actual attainment but the identification of that end which can fulfill the highest human powers of the soul.

Many ethical discussions have begun with the same question and certain material goods in which people find their happiness have been examined as to whether they can bring about human fulfillment.[74] Though revelation is clear about what the final purpose of human life is, reason can still investigate this by examining the powers of the human soul themselves.

In his *Summa Theologiae*, St. Thomas goes through the list of what people think is their final happiness. To briefly summarize his teaching, each answer of the human race must be taken in order.

Many people think they can find their happiness in wealth. In wealth there is a distinction between natural wealth like food and drink and artificial wealth, like money. Natural wealth cannot be the final destiny of human life because it only supports the material body and the more one has of this wealth, the more one wants. The body rebels against too much food and drink and produces ill health. Many people think artificial wealth can bring them ultimate happiness, but there is a peculiar psychology about this wealth. The more one has, the less sufficient it seems. Also, both kinds of wealth have further things as their purpose. Artificial wealth like money leads to power and what it can buy as its purpose and natural wealth has the human body as its purpose. Wealth then is only a means. There is something attractive about buying power because it seems to guarantee security in life. Yet this is deceptive. This security can end with a natural disaster or a change in the market. "All material things obey money as far as the multitude of fools are concerned, who know no other than material goods which can be obtained by money."[75]

Many people seek honors and glory as their ultimate destiny. Both of these are inadequate to finally implement the powers of the human soul. First, honors cannot be a final purpose because honors are the recognition of another good possessed by the honoree. As a result, they are a means also, never an end. Regarding honor many people are honored who should not be because of human error, so even the recognition of the good may not be true. Glory is the fame which one possesses through goods known, recognized and praised by others. The trouble is that fame is very fleeting. Today one is a star and one's name is a household word. Tomorrow, no one remembers. Also, the value of recognition depends on the worth and true estimate of the person making the recognition. The only one who cannot make a mistake and whose appreciation is without error is God. So, the only recognition or glory that ultimately matters comes from God.

There are four basic reasons why human destiny cannot consist in exterior goods. First, both good and evil men have them. Second, possessing one of these goods leaves one without other necessary goods. For example, one may have lots of money but no love. Third, final and perfect goods should not lead to any evil, yet riches are often possessed to a person's harm. For example, one may often enjoy the pleasures of food and drink but harm one's health. Finally, most people think they cannot be finally happy without absolute security in the possession of these goods. People often go to extremes to safeguard these goods. Yet, all of them are easily lost by chance happenings.

Since external goods cannot be the final purpose of human life, what about the goods of body? Sometimes in the history of Christian thought one gets the impression that the body is evil or that goods of the body are to be shunned as unworthy. St. Thomas, and indeed traditional Christian teaching, was not of this opinion which actually reflects Manichaeism and Stoicism. Goods of the body serve the soul. Pope John Paul II goes so far in his Theology of the Body as to teach that the body is a means by which man gives the good of his soul. "The body, and it alone, is capable of making visible what is invisible: the spiritual and the divine. It was created to transfer into the visible reality of the world the mystery hidden since time immemorial in God, and thus be a sign of it."[76]

When Christ speaks about looking at a woman with lust in the Sermon on the Mount (Mt. 5:28), he does not hold the body in suspicion as though it were something evil. The same is true of the pleasures attached to the sexual experience. When Christ speaks about looking at a woman with lust in the heart as being adultery, he is not holding the body in suspicion as a thing. Rather, he is pointing out that the original value of the body as a place where the prior union of hearts was given physical expression by Adam and Eve was spoiled because of the sin. The body was reduced from being a tool where people gave themselves to a tool where the tendency for extortion and domination was only too prevalent. Christ came to call man back to this original gift nature of the body. "For the Manichaean mentality, the body and sexuality constitute an 'anti-value'. For Christianity, on the contrary, they always remain as a value not sufficiently appreciated."[77]

The goods of the body are important and necessary, but they exist to support and express the good of the soul. To make the body an ultimate purpose would be like making the ship rather than the journey the ultimate goal of sailing. The passions are also important, but all of them are adjunct goods which accompany other goods, so those prior goods must be more central. When I take pleasure in eating, for example, it is the food which is the good. The pleasure is a physical accompanying good. The food is what causes the pleasure, not the other way around. To make pleasure the end of any human activity is like throwing the fruit of the banana away and eating the peel.

Happiness, in fact, is a good of the soul. It is such a good, however, because it is experienced in the soul, not because the soul is the object of happiness. If happiness is an internal good of soul, it is certainly not found in the will as such because the will merely desires good in general and, though the will unites man to the good object, it is not the faculty in which objects from outside man are experienced. Man arrives at all the goods through the will but actually participates in those goods through other powers. So the will can be satisfied by many different kinds of good, though the will is the faculty where man desires and pursues happiness. Happiness cannot be found in the moral virtues because virtues are dispositions of powers to actions not actions themselves. These may prepare a person for happiness and assure that one is on the right road, but they are dispositions for the further experience of the good.

In answer then to the question of what object can alone complete human powers, one is led to the desire for truth in the intellect. The intellect as a power is oriented to receiving the natures of things outside the intellect and so to experiencing union with these things within the soul. These would be the truths of nature and their explanations. When the intellect understands these natures, man participates in the being of these things within himself and his character is expanded. The intellect is oriented to explanations. The more the mind understands the relationships of the various things in the world to each other, the more man's character is expanded to take in the whole universe. The deeper the explanation the more the mind seeks further truths. The only explanation which will finally satisfy the mind is the ultimate explanation for the world as such.

Aristotle observed that one experience of an effect leads one to seek the causes of this effect; this is the beginning of philosophy. He thought that one arrived at the necessity of the science of metaphysics, or "being as being," by the discovery that the existence of physical, material beings demanded the existence of a being which is not material, physical or changeable. In other words, physics led to metaphysics.

> That this [metaphysics] is not a science of production is clear even from the history of the earliest philosophers. For it is owing to their wonder that men both now begin and at first began to philosophize; they wondered originally at the obvious difficulties, then advanced little by little and stated difficulties about greater matters. [...] It is evident, then, that one must acquire scientific knowledge of those causes which stand at the beginning; for we say that we have scientific knowledge of each thing when we think we comprehend its first cause.[78]

The first cause here does not mean first in a series in time but the ultimate explanation for the whole cosmos. The first cause is like the foundation of the building which underlies the whole structure. It is true that this is the first thing built, but in the case of a first cause which is eternal, outside time, this is the basis for time and change and is equally present wherever time and change are present. So it would not be first in a series of changing things, but first in the sense of foundational to all.

When St. Thomas comes to examine the final purpose of human life, he uses almost exactly the same language as Aristotle.

> Besides, there is naturally present in all men the desire to know the causes of whatever things are observed. Hence, because of wondering about things that were seen but whose causes were hidden, men first began to think philosophically; when they found the cause, they were satisfied. But the search did not stop until it reached the first cause, for 'then do we think that we know perfectly, when we know the first cause.' (Aristotle, *Metaphysics*, I, 3, 983a 25) Therefore, man naturally desires, as his ultimate end, to know the first cause. But the first cause of all things is God. Therefore, the ultimate end of man is to know God.[79]

Since the intellect cannot be brought completely into act except through knowledge and St. Thomas says there is a natural desire in the intellect to know God, the next question is: What sort of knowledge can alone still the quest of the intellect? The knowledge which reduces the power of the intellect to complete knowledge must be knowledge of something which leaves nothing left to know.

Before answering this question, several points must be made. Many theologians have had difficulty with the concept of the natural desire to see God. Cardinal Thomas de Vio Cajetan[80] (1469-1534) was one of the most important. His commentary on the *Summa Theologiae* exercised such great influence that, when the critical edition of the *Summa* was originally done at the end of the 19th Century, his commentary was printed at the bottom of the page.

Cajetan took the term "desire" to be an appetite of the will. He therefore was very concerned that to say that if there were a natural desire for God in the will God would be obliged to give man grace to will heaven in creation by justice. This has a Pelagian tinge to it. It would compromise the gratuity of grace. Cajetan therefore developed a two end theory which highly affected both spiritual and moral theology for several hundred years. He maintained that man's intellect in the state of "pure nature" could have been happy with only knowing the existence of God as the cause of the effects of the world.

Hypothetically then, the knowledge of the existence and nature of the first cause Aristotle speaks about would only be the knowledge of the existence and some of the properties but not the essence of the first cause. Yet, the Catholic Church has always taught with Christ that beatitude or happiness consists in the vision of God in heaven which is a direct knowledge of the divine essence without concept or medium. Cajetan escaped this dilemma by maintaining that since man was created in grace, as the Council of Trent teaches, this gave man another ultimate destiny than the one he would have had in the hypothetical state of "pure nature." As a result, man cannot now be happy with just knowing the existence of God as the cause for the effect of the world, but now must know him as he is in himself.

This solution contributed much difficulty in trying to determine just how grace and nature related to each other and the relationship of moral theology to spiritual theology. There was a laicist attitude which grew among many moralists who followed Cajetan and held that the laity was called only to acquired contemplation and the living of the moral virtues, but religious and priests were called to the perfection of the virtues. Vatican II effectively did away with this attitude with its teaching on the universal call to holiness. This was not an innovation but a clarification.

Many theologians in the 20th Century found this solution very strange. For one thing there cannot be two ultimate ends to a nature. So, either grace destroys nature or there is no relation between the two or some hybrid being is produced that is neither one nor the other. The problem was characterized well by Etienne Gilson[81] in a letter to Henri de Lubac[82] in which he quoted Dominic Soto[83], a contemporary Dominican theologian of Cajetan: "This commentary destroys the text, it is full of turns and windings."[84]

Strangely, though St. Thomas identified happiness with the vision of God, many otherwise orthodox moralists disagree with him. The famous moralist Germain Grisez[85] goes even so far as to say that both St. Augustine and St. Thomas blundered when Augustine said that: "Our hearts are restless until they rest in thee" and St. Thomas approved this answer. In an unpublished talk he gave in 2005, Grisez not only maintains that these theologians blundered but he says: "For this and other reasons, I believe that the classical restless-heart thesis is at odds with the Catholic faith. Our hearts do not naturally tend toward complete fulfillment in God."[86] He gives the various solutions of St. Thomas to difficulties about this thesis and finds them all wanting. So, it seems imperative to clarify this problem.

These theologians have their own difficulties in their attempt at a solution to this problem and the reason is that they, like Cajetan, identified the "natural desire" with an appetite of the will. Thus the moral question of *how* one arrives at the end which is certainly a question of the will in the order of execution is treated before the more ontological question of the ultimate destiny itself. The solution of St. Thomas to this problem will be clear if one keeps in mind that "natural desire" here does not refer to an appetite of the will which is treated in morals, but to the object which alone can satisfy the intellect as a power. Thus the intellect "naturally desires" knowledge of the first cause like a stone "naturally desires" rest on the earth or potency "naturally desires" act. None of these "desires" involve will or freedom. The term "desire" merely expresses a power in relationship to its perfect act. The first question must be what that object is. The next question would be how one attains it or its possibility. Once these two things are determined, then and only then can the issue of whether the will is stilled in the experience of this object or happiness be considered.

St. Thomas identified the final destiny of man with the knowledge of God because of the intellect. The question is: Is knowledge of God by reason or faith a sufficient knowledge of the nature of God as the first cause of all the effects in the world to still the quest of the intellect? St. Thomas maintains that this is not possible for the intellect as such and has nothing to do with some hypothetical state of "pure nature,"

> Moreover, the will rests its desire when it has attained the ultimate end. But the ultimate end of all human knowledge is felicity. So, that knowledge of God which, when acquired, leaves no knowledge of the knowable object to be desired is essentially this felicity. But this is not the kind of knowledge about God that the philosophers were able to get through demonstrations, because, even when we acquire this knowledge, we still desire to know other things that are not known through this knowledge. Therefore, felicity is not found in such knowledge of God.[87]

No natural knowledge of God can satisfy the power of the intellect and reduce it completely to act. Faith is a further knowledge of God which deepens the knowledge of God that man has by reason. If man cannot be happy just knowing God as the cause of all the effects known by him, the next logical question is: Would the knowledge of God communicated through the light of faith satisfy the power of the intellect? St. Thomas maintains that not only does such knowledge not satisfy the intellect, but actually makes the desire for such knowledge more urgent. "Moreover, through felicity, because it is the ultimate end, natural desire comes to rest. Now, the knowledge of faith does not bring rest to desire but rather sets it aflame, since every man desires to see what he believes. So, man's ultimate felicity does not lie in the knowledge of faith."[88]

The only conclusion possible from these reflections is that it is possible to know that the ultimate happiness of man cannot consist in the knowledge of this life. St. Thomas explains:

> Although this mirror, which is the human mind reflects the likeness of God in a closer way than lower creatures do, the knowledge of God which can be taken in by the human mind does not go beyond the type of knowledge derived from sensible things, since even the soul itself knows what it is itself as a result of understanding the natures of sensible things. [...] Hence, throughout this life God can be known in no higher way than that whereby a cause is known through its effect.[89]

It is this fact which leads to the darkness of the mystical life. In the life of faith, since the object can never be understood by us here on earth as we are limited to sensible knowledge both assent and inquiry run together. This is the only kind of theoretical or speculative knowledge in which the will plays an active part because the will must be drawn to the one revealing as trustworthy. The prime revealer and prime revelation is Christ. Through his physical nature man enters as much into the life of the Trinity as is possible here on earth, but the direct knowledge of God, the cause through the cause, still eludes man here. This is why Teresa of Avila could cry: "*Muero porque no muero.*" (I am dying because I do not die). Love for God leads the way here on earth, but the object is never evident to us because the intellect as a power is oriented to know the cause in itself.

These facts led many philosophers either to teach that happiness cannot be experienced directly by man but through a separate substance like an angel or an idea (Alexander and Averroes) or with Aristotle to teach that only limited happiness was possible.[90] If Aristotle was so astute about the fact that the intellect could not be perfected as a power without participating directly in the first cause, why did he maintain that only limited happiness was possible, a very sobering and sad conclusion? This was because he thought the nature which was open to his sense experience was human nature as it ought to be. In fact, Christianity teaches that this is fallen nature, without grace. Aristotle did not know about revelation and was too good a scientist to posit the possibility of something for which there was obviously no means of attainment in nature. St. Thomas concludes therefore:

> On this point there is abundant evidence of how even the brilliant minds of these men suffered from the narrowness of their viewpoint. From which narrow attitudes we shall be freed if we grant in accord with the foregoing proofs that man can reach true felicity after this life, when man's soul is existing immortally; in which state the soul will understand in the way that separate substances understand (angels and the soul separated from the body)."[91]

St. Thomas then clarifies that even the angels cannot have the power of their intellects stilled by knowing God through his effects. They know God through themselves as his effects, but even this knowledge does not still their intellect. This should put Cajetan's theory of "pure nature" to rest for two reasons. If the intellect can be finally fulfilled in knowing God through his effects, this would be especially true of the angels who have a much more powerful and immediate theoretical knowledge by nature than man. In fact, the angels desire to know is not stilled in the kind of knowledge they have of God through their own natures, but drives them even more than us to want to know God's nature. Also, if the orientation to heaven was due to man's creation in grace, this must be true of the angels also. But they have no common nature which could be given another purpose than nature would have left without grace. Each angel is its own special nature.

St. Thomas summarizes his conclusion with six arguments in the *Summa Contra Gentiles*, III, 50 drawn from the nature of the intellect in which no state of pure nature is mentioned and the angels are made equivalent to men regarding their happiness. I will summarize these with six syllogisms. The similarity between this language and Aristotle should be noted. The necessity of grace for human moral perfection is a truth of faith open to reason:

> 1. What is imperfect desires perfection. The knowledge of God the angels have through themselves is imperfect. Therefore, the angels seek to flee this imperfection and know God as he is in himself.
>
> 2. One who knows an effect desires to know its cause. The angels know they are effects of God. Therefore the angels desire to know God in himself.
>
> 3. One who knows the existence of something desires to know its essence. The angels know that God exists. Therefore they desire to know his essence.
>
> 4. Nothing finite fulfills the power of the intellect. The angels know their conception of God is finite. Therefore they desire to know God in himself.
>
> 5. One who wishes knowledge desires to flee ignorance. The angels know God surpasses their natural knowledge. Therefore they desire to flee their ignorance and know his essence.
>
> 6. The closer a thing comes to its goal, the more it desires it. The angels are closer to God in being than the rest of creation. Therefore they desire God more.

St. Thomas concludes from this that the intellect of man as a power is naturally only fulfilled by the direct perception of God without medium.

> Quite apparent in this conclusion is the fact that ultimate felicity is to be sought in nothing other than an operation of the intellect, since no desire

carries on to such sublime heights as the desire to understand the truth. Indeed, all our desires for pleasure, or other things of this sort that are craved by men, can be satisfied with other things, but the aforementioned desire does not rest until it reaches God, the highest reference point for, and the maker of things. [...] Let those men be ashamed, then, who seek man's felicity in the most inferior things, when it is so highly situated."[92]

"Final and perfect happiness can consist in nothing else that the vision of the Divine Essence. [...] Consequently, for perfect happiness the intellect needs to reach the very essence of the first cause. Thus it will have its perfection through union with God as an object, in which the happiness of man alone consists."[93]

The fact that happiness is essentially an action of the intellect does not mean that there are no other accompanying goods which are present with happiness or necessary to attain it. Happiness certainly leads to joy and delight in the vision once it is experienced. "Since happiness is achievement of our highest good it must bring with it delight. The delight however is secondary to the achievement."[94]

Once it is clear what the final destiny of man is, then the moral question about how and when one arrives at this destiny or the question of its possibility can be answered. Though happiness essentially consists in an action of the intellect or contemplation, this does not mean the will is not involved. "Right willing must precede and accompany happiness. For we will rightly when we are properly adapted to our ultimate goal. [...] Nobody then can achieve happiness unless he wills rightly."[95] This is the foundation of morals.

Though happiness is an activity of soul, this does not mean the body is not involved. The disembodied soul is not man. Man after death before the general resurrection is a disembodied spirit. The soul experiences perfect act in the vision of God. The soul, however is not man. Man is a substantial unity of body and soul. If the body could not experience the effects of this happiness by a kind of overflow through the resurrected and glorified body, then man in his nature could not experience happiness. St. Thomas is clear that this does not add to happiness regarding the satisfaction which man seeks, but rather adds the dimension of all the natural powers of man experiencing happiness. "For although the disembodied soul's desire for an object is wholly satisfied in God (for it now possesses what fulfills it), nevertheless it does not possess its object in every way that it could wish; and so when it regains its body its happiness will grow in breadth, though not in depth."[96]

Exterior goods are necessary for the limited happiness which one can experience in this life so that one can pursue the path of virtue. A modicum of exterior goods are necessary as tools to this. But in heaven, such goods will not longer be needed.

By the same token the fellowship of friends is also an accompanying good to the partial happiness man can experience in this life. But this is not because virtue and union with God by grace are not sufficient for this. Every person needs the companionship of friends but more as an encouragement to the virtuous life. This is the basis for friendship which is spiritual. One does not need friends like a drowning man who experiences no affection and no love. The normal love of parents and the eternal love of God should make one feel sufficiently loved. Rather, in both the active and contemplative life, friends are companions on the journey to heaven encouraging and correcting one's outlook to be sure one keeps the final goal pure and unclouded in one's mind and intention.

> The happy man in this life needs friends, not for their external usefulness, since his happiness is from within, nor for pleasure, since his perfect pleasure comes from the activity of virtue, but as contributing to that activity itself. He does good to them, he delights in seeing them do good, and in turn they help him do good to him.[97]

In heaven strictly speaking friends are not necessary at all because one can be fulfilled completely in God as the alone with the alone. Still, because heaven is peopled with angels and human beings, all of whom are enjoying God, this cannot help but overflow to be the basis for true and lasting friendship as an accompanying good.

It is both a truth of reason and of faith that one can possibly arrive at such an end. "Man's ultimate happiness consists in his highest activity, exercising his mind, and if created minds cannot see God then either men will never be happy or their happiness must lie elsewhere than in God. That is not only opposed to our faith but makes no natural sense."[98] One can only arrive at such a destination through grace. "For although man is naturally inclined to his final end, yet he cannot attain this end by nature but only by grace [...]."[99] One must always remember that this final purpose is identical with the action of the intellect and so is natural to man. In fact, in arriving at this ultimate end of the vision of God, the potential of the intellect to experience the causes of all things is finally completed. Aquinas quotes Augustine: "Unhappy is the one who knows all these things (namely created things), but does not know You; happy is the one who knows You even if he knows nothing else; and the one who know you and the other things is not any happier for knowing the created things than for knowing You alone."[100] To arrive at experiencing the object which is God Himself is not possible for the human will without the aid of grace. So, St. Thomas discusses the possibility of arriving at this vision as the last question after the fact that it is the ultimate end and that it is the happiness of man. His position is that it is not possible in this life, but must be possible in the next. It is also not possible in this life for the will of man to arrive at this, this can only be done by grace.

God never acts in anything against its nature and, as the analysis of the soul shows, acts of free choice set human nature apart from all the rest of material creation. Though the experience of happiness is supernatural and experienced in the intellect, God aids the will by giving a gift to human nature so that man might will heaven.

> Yet just as nature provides for man's needs, though denying him the weapons and covering natural to other animals, by giving him reason and his hands to make such things for himself, so too nature provides for man's needs, though denying him the resources to win happiness for himself—an impossibility—by giving him free will to turn to God who can make him happy. As Aristotle put it, what our friends enable us to do we have in some sort the power to do.[101]

The first point then in moral theology is that the ultimate end of man is the experience in the intellect of the Blessed Trinity, an experience in which the will rests. To arrive at this experience though, the constant choice and formation of the will is necessary. Since man cannot see God here on earth, the two great commandments of the law are not

"Know" but "Love." The formation of the will to receive and live the life of grace is the central purpose of the science of morals.

MAN IS FREE: THE GENUS OF MORALS

CHAPTER FOUR
MORAL RESPONSIBILITY: THE VOLUNTARY

THE VOLUNTARY

Man is both a servant and free. Since it is by acts of free will that man arrives at his ultimate happiness, the first moral question then must be to distinguish the primary characteristics of those acts by which man can arrive at heaven from all the other actions of nature. Only actions of free will deserve praise or blame because only actions which result from the will can move man towards and away from heaven. The actual ability to arrive at heaven always has its source in the Holy Spirit guiding, assisting and supporting right human moral decisions (God always acts first). In this discussion of what constitutes free human choices, one must first examine the characteristics of these actions of the human person which make him at one and the same time a servant and free.

The actions by which man cooperates in grace and which determine human responsible participation in God's grace join the order of intention which is determined by knowledge or truth to the order of execution which is determined by love or the will. The passions influence both orders. Thus those actions which do not include a correct order of intellect, will and passions are not worthy of praise or blame and so are not subject to moral responsibility. Such acts could not relate to man's cooperation in grace and so would not relate to his quest for heaven either by affirmation or denial.

The first requirement for moral responsibility is that the action result from a movement within and not from a movement outside man. If the stone seeks rest on the earth, the origin of its movement is due to the nature of the stone and the earth. If it is thrown up in the air, the hand which throws it is the origin of its motion and the movement is a violence done to the nature of the stone. "To some movements and activities, like bricks falling, there is a proneness within what moves or acts; other movements, like bricks rising, are externally forced."[102]

The next distinction is between things which move themselves from within their nature because of awareness of the goal of the action and others where the awareness of the goal is in something else which moves them albeit according to principles intrinsic to nature. This is distinction between animate and inanimate nature. Plants which synthesize all the elements and energy from the sun, water, and the soil to form organic tissue are examples of this.

The next distinction is between those beings which have some knowledge of the end but no understanding about why the end is the end or how the means fit into it. This is the level of consciousness and separates knowledge of animals and children before they have reached the age of reason from voluntary acts. Voluntary acts demand an interiority which is characterized by knowledge of the end and the reason why the end is the end and the means which is the result of intellectual knowledge. This way of acting is characteristic of human beings.

Therefore, that an action be in the genus of morals and subject to moral responsibility, there are four required qualities:

- it must be an action, not a passion;

- it must result from a principle intrinsic to the being;

- this principle involves some knowledge of the end and the means;

- this principle must include not just awareness of the end but also a knowledge of the ends and the means which includes why they express human nature.

This would be a complete and perfect knowledge of ends and means.

The first requirement distinguishes actions from passivity; the second, nature from violence; the third, animals and man from the rest of nature; the fourth, man from the animals. Unless all of these requirements are met, the action in question cannot be subject to moral responsibility and therefore cannot be a means by which a human being moves either to or against his ultimate end. Only actions which have all these characteristics fall within the genus of morals and are worthy of praise or blame. Only actions which have all these characteristics can be a means by which man arrives at or fails to arrive at heaven. The classic term for actions which include all these characteristics is: THE VOLUNTARY. "So men's actions are in the fullest sense voluntary: they deliberate about the goal of which they are aware and about what will lead to it, and are able to pursue it or not."[103] It is this voluntary aspect of human actions which makes man "lord of his own actions."[104]

In this teaching, St. Thomas argues against determinism, a moral philosophy which holds that man must act in a certain way because of some exterior factor like poverty or bad education. He also argues against absolute freedom which is license because freedom is based on knowledge which presupposes a certain objective metaphysics of human nature. The self-determination which characterizes human acts is not a freedom from all objective references to the real world as though man created himself by his free choices. "The important thing in human striving is its truthfulness—the striving must correspond to the true value of its object."[105]

A HUMAN ACTION OR OMISSION

The first evaluation of an action as good or evil, which can lead to heaven or not presupposes the judgment as to whether a human action has occurred at all. Though one of the requirements above was that there must be an act, this can also occur when an act which should be done by which a person can arrive at heaven but no such act has occurred; what is commonly called a sin of omission. The classic example of this type of sin is a captain whose ship goes on the rocks either because he just refuses to guide it or steer it or because he refuses to take the necessary precautions to prevent this. This could be because he just does not want to be bothered or because he got drunk and could not do his duty.

In examining the question of the sin of omission, St. Thomas asks if there must be an act connected with this sin. He says there are two opinions on this subject, each of which has some truth. One opinion states that in any sin, even one of omission, there must be either an interior act of the will or some connected exterior act which keeps the person from doing a deed he should do. The other opinion is that a sin of omission does not involve an act. To sin from omission is precisely to cease (*desistere*)[106] acting.

The latter opinion is true regarding the essence of sin which does not demand an act for a sin of omission. "Absolutely speaking (*per se*) the sin of omission consists in the very cessation or desistance from an act, i.e. a not-doing."[107] One is blamed in art if one does not observe the proper form or rule and measure and also if one does not arrive at the purpose for which the art exists. For example, one would fail in mathematics if he did not observe the proper method to attain the answer just as much as if he got the answer wrong. One can get the wrong answer even by using the proper method if there is some variable which is not known. St. Thomas uses the example of human digestion. One's digestion may work fine, but one may try to eat something the human digestion cannot pass, such as metal or a stone. By the same token, a doctor can prescribe a medicine and use his art, but the person is not cured either because the disease cannot be cured or the patient does not use the medicine properly.

St. Thomas maintains that one is more at fault for not choosing to use the correct method than merely to fail to achieve the desired result. The correct method is a reflection of the rule of reason about the particular discipline involved. In morals this is the natural or divine law which commands or forbids actions in accord or contrary to objective human nature.

The rule of reason entails both positive and negative precepts. Positive precepts would be expressed as "Thou shalt". Negative precepts would be expressed as "Thou shalt not." Acts which should not be done and are knowingly done are contrary to the negative precepts. Acts which should be done and are knowingly omitted are contrary to the positive precepts of the law. "So then, *per se*, i.e. absolutely speaking, there can be a sin for which an act, which is of the essence of sin, is not required."[108]

As to the cause of sin, the will is the cause of sin. From this point of view, an act is necessary for the existence of a sin whether it be of commission or omission. If the cause is something outside the will, this does not have the nature of a sin because it is completely extrinsic to man and as such does not fall under responsibility. The example St. Thomas uses is one who is injured by a falling rock and cannot go to church or is robbed and so cannot give alms. Another example would be a couple who cannot have children and so if they do not have children this is not due to contraception and so does not fall under responsibility. Only an omission which results from the interior act of the will is voluntary and so is responsible. So, if a person is to held responsible for the omission of an act, there must be some act of the will.

The act of the will may be either direct (*per se*) or indirect (*per accidens*). A direct act of the will is one in which the person intends the effect as when someone finds a treasure he is looking for. An indirect act of the will occurs when a person attains something apart from his intention as when a man goes into a field intending to dig a grave and finds a treasure while he is digging. When the will directly causes an omission, this does not mean that the person wills the omission as such. The will is always drawn to good.

However in the direct act of the will the person positively wills something knowing that it may lead to an omission. This is like the captain who gets drunk knowing that it might impair his ability to steer the ship. He is enticed by the pleasure of drink and wills that but with the effect that he knows he may omit something necessary to which he is obliged. This is also called the voluntary in cause (*voluntarium in causa*). Other examples of this would be an alcoholic who may not be able to control his drinking but knowingly omits to attend AA or some help program which can give him some control regarding the fact that he drinks. The same would be true of someone who drinks, drives and has a fatal accident while under the influence of drink. He does not intend the accident or the death that may result but he intends a condition from which such an accident or death could arise.

A person wills something indirectly when he omits to do something because he is so involved in something else. An example would be someone who is so delighted in reading a book when he should be going to sleep that he stays up all night and so he cannot go to Mass the next day. As to cause, then an act of the will is necessary.

The voluntary is the source of determining responsibility. "A thing is said to be voluntary not only because it falls under the act of the will, but also because it falls under the power of the will."[109] So if the action is in a person's power and he does not will it then such a lack of willing is voluntary and the person is responsible. "An action can be indirectly voluntary when it results from negligence regarding something one should have known or done: for example, an accident arising from ignorance of traffic laws."[110]

How does violence affect the will's act? Can one be forced to act against his will? Violence involves some action which has it origin completely outside the will and which corresponds to no natural tendency in the thing. A good example is the hand moving the stone upwards from the earth. The motion imparted to the stone is from the hand, not the stone. Should the hand move the stone downwards this would increase the natural attraction between the stone and the earth. Though, of course, stones have no will still the principle should be clear that any violent action be it natural or willed has its source completely outside the moving thing.

THE WILL

Within the purview of willed acts, there are those which are executed by the power of the will but involve a further act of some other power of the soul, such as walking and talking. These are called imperated or commanded acts of the will because these acts are not intrinsic to the will itself but result from the will using other powers. There are also acts of the will which are intrinsic to the will itself like intending, choosing and enjoying. These are the elicited or intrinsic acts of the will.

Someone can be forced against his will to do something which is a commanded act. No power on earth can force someone to will an elicited action. The only power which can move the will intrinsically, beside the individual person, is the Creator of the will who is God. Though God may move the will internally, this is never against man's freedom or nature and so such actions are not against the will. Someone cannot be blamed for something done as a result of force in the commanded actions.

One application of this would be demonic possession. The devil induces man to sin, but this is not by directly moving the will. "Not every power that is greater than man can move man's will. God alone can do this."[111] The will is moved by the object which is presented to it and it also moves itself. Satan can affect the will by affecting the manner in which the object is perceived. Since the devil is an angel, he can influence the sense perceptions in the imagination and memory which in turn have an influence on the passions and the intelligence and through them on the judgment and indirectly on the will. "Consequently the action of the devil seems to be confined to the imagination and the sense appetites so by moving either of them he can induce man to sin."[112]

CHAPTER FOUR MORAL RESPONSIBILITY: THE VOLUNTARY

In the case of possession, Satan can so bind the imagination and the memory as to almost force certain reactions in the commanded acts of the will. He cannot however enter the soul directly without being invited in. So in one who is a victim of possession through no fault of his own, what he does would not be imputable to him so he would not be blamed for it. In one who invites the devil in though, he would be guilty of whatever sin should result from this. All the sins of man cannot be attributed to the devil because man could still think up ways of evil if there were no devil and man alone can voluntarily agree to engage in the acts which result from the devil's suggestion. For that reason, St. Thomas calls the devil "the occasional and indirect cause of all our sins."[113]

DOUBLE EFFECT

The question of the indirect voluntary also gives rise to a famous moral principle developed in the 19th century by Joannes O. Gury, S.J.[114] Though the claim is often made that the origin of this principle is in St. Thomas', *Summa Theologiae*, I-II, 64, 7 and his teaching on self-defense, this claim does not seem sustainable. Still, the work of St. Thomas may have suggested the background for the development of this principle. The Church has made this principle her own. One should note that the treatment of this principle falls in the section of the *Catechism* which deals with moral responsibility and not with the object of moral acts.

A classic application of this principle is the surgical removal of a cancerous uterus of the woman who is also pregnant. This may involve the death of the child who could not be brought to term. The cancer would lead to her death unless the uterus was removed as soon as possible.

> The operation of hysterectomy is morally lawful, for this operation is permissible in itself as a normal means of saving the woman's life. She does not positively will the death of her child, but permits it as an unavoidable evil. Both the benefit to her health and the death of the child follow from the surgery with equal directness or immediacy in the order of causality, though the death of the child is prior in the order of time. The woman's chance of restoration

to health (the good effect) is sufficiently desirable to compensate for the death of the fetus (the bad effect), which would probably not survive even if the operation were not performed.[115]

There are traditionally four conditions which must be met for such an action to be morally good.

> The act itself must be morally good or at least indifferent.

> The agent may not positively will the bad effect but may merely permit it. If he could attain the good effect without the bad effect, he should do so. The bad effect is sometimes said to be indirectly voluntary.

> The good effect must flow from the action at least as immediately (in the order of causality, though not necessarily in the order of time) as the bad effect. In other words, the good effect must be produced directly by the action, not by the bad effect. Otherwise, the agent would be using a bad means to a good end, which is never allowed.

> The good effect must be sufficiently desirable to compensate for the allowing of the bad effect. In forming this decision many factors must be weighed and compared, with care and prudence proportionate to the importance of the case. Thus, an effect that benefits or harms society generally has more weight than one that affects only an individual; an effect sure to occur deserves greater consideration than one that is only probable; an effect of a moral nature has greater importance than one that deals only with material things.[116]

An action which meets all of these criteria would be one in which the good involved is directly willed by the agent and the evil tolerated is indirectly willed by the agent. In such a case, the person would not be morally responsible for the evil.

The *Catechism* reflects the same teaching. Although they use the example of self defense, the principle is clear.

An effect can be tolerated without being willed by its agent; for instance, a mother's exhaustion from tending her sick child. A bad effect is not imputable if it was not willed either as an end or as a means of an action, e.g. a death a person incurs in aiding someone in danger. For a bad effect to be imputable it must be foreseeable and the agent must have the possibility of avoiding it, as in the case of manslaughter caused by a drunken driver.[117]

The important point is that any action or lack of action which occurs from knowledge and will and is necessary for someone to do or avoid to attain heaven is imputable. "Every act directly willed is imputable to its author."[118]

One further distinction is important in determining the nature of the will in an action. One can be either actively voluntary or passively voluntary. "Behavior can be actively voluntary, when we want to do something, and passively voluntary, when we want something done to us."[119] If someone suffers something voluntarily, this is not violence to them even though it may involve a violent act. The person who suffers does not will the thing which is done to him, but wills to suffer it being done to him.

FEAR

One must remember that for an act to be imputable it must involve the intellect which presents the good to the will which then desires it. The passions are also involved in every act of freedom. As a result, no treatment of moral responsibility would be complete without an examination of the contribution of the passions and the intellect to the action of the will.

The passion which many people consider to diminish responsibility is fear. Actions done from fear have their origin much more outside the person than within. The fear in question is not neurotic or psychotic fear which would involve an arousal of the passions outside the order of the intellect. The consideration here would be of reasoned fear. If one is being shelled in a battle it is reasonable to be afraid. The classic example given by St. Thomas is the captain who throws his cargo overboard in a storm lest his ship sink. The question arises: Did he do this voluntarily so that he can be held morally responsible for this? An interesting application of this difficulty concerns contrition for sin. The Jansenists maintained that what is normally called "imperfect contrition" (sorrow for sin because of fear of the consequences on earth or fear of hell) would be an insufficient motive for repentance even coupled with confession. Jansenist confessors routinely refused people absolution if they manifested only this kind of contrition. Is such a contrition voluntary and therefore can it provide sufficient groundwork for absolution from sin?

To decide this question, St. Thomas makes use of an important distinction. He calls actions like the jettisoning of the cargo in the storm, the mixed voluntary. If one considers such an action in the abstract, no one would willingly jettison his cargo. But given the circumstance of the immediate danger to the ship because of the violence of the storm, one would voluntarily throw the cargo overboard to keep the ship from sinking and possibly drowning. Obviously the welfare of the ship which is directly connected to the lives of the crew is a more immediate human good than the possible profit which could be realized from the cargo. Unless the cargo is thrown overboard it is quite possible that the cargo, the ship and the crew would all be lost. So in the concrete circumstances, one would willingly lose the cargo.

These acts are strictly speaking voluntary and so one is responsible for them. "So, since actions are always individual here-and-now actions, what is done out of fear is simply speaking voluntary, and only in a certain respect—namely, when looked at in abstraction from the individual event—unwanted and involuntary."[120] So, though fear is not the best motivation for a moral deed, things done as a result of reasoning fear are voluntary and fall under responsibility.

This can be applied easily to the case of perfect and imperfect contrition. Though imperfect contrition which results from fear is not the best motivation for the ongoing conversion experienced in confession, still since one is responsible for sorrow for sin, this contrition coupled with sacramental confession is a sufficient motive for absolution and the forgiveness of sins. Perfect contrition is much better because since it is done from love, it is almost second nature and betokens a much deeper *metanoia* or conversion of heart to the Beloved. Sacramental confession is still necessary for this conversion because the forgiveness of sins always demands a community context.

> Contrition is 'sorrow of soul and detestation for the
> sin committed, together with the resolution not to

sin again.' When it arises from a love by which God is loved above all else, contrition is called 'perfect' (contrition of charity). Such contrition remits venial sins; it also obtains forgiveness of mortal sins if it includes the firm resolution to have recourse to sacramental confession as soon as possible. The contrition called 'imperfect' (or 'attrition') is also a gift of God, a prompting of the Holy Spirit. It is born of the consideration of sin's ugliness or the fear of eternal damnation and the other penalties threatening the sinner (contrition of fear). Such a stirring of conscience can initiate an interior process which, under the prompting of grace, will be brought to completion by sacramental absolution. By itself however, imperfect contrition cannot obtain the forgiveness of grave sins, but it disposes one to obtain forgiveness in the sacrament of Penance.[121]

MORALLY RESPONSIBLE PASSIONS

The introduction of the question of fear regarding the voluntary leads logically to the consideration of the place of the passions in general regarding the will. Are acts of passion voluntary and so fall under moral responsibility? If someone strikes a blow because he is exceedingly angry and kills someone, is he morally responsible? If someone gives alms merely from the sake of compassion because he is a bleeding heart and afraid someone will not think he is good, is he responsible?

Aquinas answers this question by distinguishing between passions which come before the action of the will can be brought to bear (antecedent passions) and passions which are caused by the action of the will (consequent passions). Passions in man are born to be obedient to reason. Thus ideally all passions should be consequent passions which only arise as a result of the judgment of the intellect about the truth which motivates the will to the good. This is because any action on the higher part of the soul ideally always has a corresponding movement in the lower part of the soul. Justice should also be accompanied by compassion; courage by the passion of courage. The passions are not automatic though and the reason is that there is a knowing life in the senses as well as the intellect. They always have the ability to resist the direction of the spirit or simply not to come along.

In the state of Original Justice which man enjoyed before he sinned all the passions were consequent. There was no resistance to the guidance of intellect and will. This was caused by the presence of grace in Adam and Eve without the presence of sin or moral weakness. Our first parents really enjoyed doing good. *Eros* (the passions) was naturally joined to *ethos* (the guidance of intellect and will). Our first parents had an easy practice of virtue. Pope John Paul expresses their experience of the passions at least regarding the sexual order as the "Original Nakedness". Adam and Eve experienced interpersonal communion in the soul which led them to use their bodies as a vehicle by which they gave the gift of themselves to each other without the possibility of extortion or domination. They really enjoyed sexuality as an expression of willed love. The body was for them a means of self-giving of one to another. The Pope calls this the Spousal Meaning of the body. They had a preternatural gift, given by God as a suitable accompaniment for grace, which led to complete spontaneity regarding the passions.

> In the state of original innocence, as we observed earlier, nakedness did not express a lack, but represented the full acceptance of the body in its whole human and thus personal truth. The body, as the expression of the person, was the first sign of the presence of man in the visible world.[122]

St. Thomas reflects this lack of concupiscence by explaining that in the state of innocence the passions would have followed reason and in fact been more intense rather than less intense.

> Beasts are without reason. In this way man becomes, as it were like them in coition, because he cannot moderate concupiscence. In the state of innocence nothing of this kind would have happened that was not regulated by reason, not because delight of sense was less, as some say (rather indeed would sense delight have been the greater in proportion to the greater purity of nature and the greater sensibility of body), but because the force of concupiscence would

> not have so inordinately thrown itself into such pleasure, being curbed by reason, whose place is not to lessen sensual pleasure, but to prevent the force of concupiscence from cleaving to it immoderately.[123]

So passions which result from the action of the will demonstrate a greater love for the good, a greater freedom in pursuing it and a greater integrity in action. They therefore increase voluntariness. "Virtue produces ordinate passions."[124]

After the Original Sin, man lives no longer in the state of Original Justice. Even after redemption and man receives grace again, certain weaknesses from the Original Sin remain. Among those is a weakness of the passions which causes them to arise before the will can be brought to bear on them. They color the judgment and make the real good appear only an apparent good to us and a real evil appear as only an apparent evil to us. The truly good becomes unattractive and the truly evil becomes attractive. John Paul II calls the man who experiences this weakness the "man of lust" and the present state as one characterized by the loss of the Original Nakedness and the Spousal Meaning of the body. This is the man who experiences the "lustful look" (Mt. 5: 28) and "hardness of heart" (Mt. 19:8)

> 'Concupiscence' removes the intentional dimension of the reciprocal existence of man and woman from the personal perspectives of 'communion,' which are proper to their perennial and reciprocal attraction, reducing this attraction and, so to speak, driving it toward utilitarian dimensions, in whose sphere of influence, one human being 'makes use' of another human being, 'using her' only to satisfy his own 'urges'.[125]

After the sin, all members of the human race become wounded in their nature, so that they lose the integrity which was a result of grace in the original creation of mankind. This is generally termed lust or concupiscence and according to Scripture is found in three basic areas: the lust of the flesh, the lust of the eyes and the pride of life. (1 Jn. 2: 16) The lust of the eyes is about material possessions and the seeming security and self-sufficiency they can bring. The lust of the flesh is about pleasure either of food and drink or sexuality. Our desires for these blind us often to real goods. The pride of life is about the desire to dominate and manipulate others which is especially characteristic of spiritual people. The other two lusts may be reduced to the desire to dominate others in the end. "For him, (Augustine) the over-riding tendency to iniquity was that powerful substitute for sex, which is the peculiar prerogative of the spiritually-minded, 'the desire to dominate'."[126]

The passions now enter into the equation because they have a tendency to arise before the judgment of reason can be brought to bear on a prospective act. Even if one judges an act evil, the passions can be a screen which colors this judgment and makes an evil appear as something desirable, or a good appear undesirable. Though the baptized have received back grace, they have not received back emotional integrity. Concupiscence or lust is still very much with the human race as is attested by St. Paul: "I can will what is right, but I cannot do it. For I do not do the good I want, but the evil I do not want is what I do. But I see in my members another law at war with the law in my mind and making me captive to the law of sin which dwells in my members." (Rom. 7: 18-19; 23)

Some like Socrates and Plato thought that when one has knowledge one cannot sin. They so revered the power of the intellect that they thought truth would always prevail even over passion. This was partly because they devalued the place of the senses in knowledge and also the fact that the passions contribute to human freedom and can even prevent knowledge from being applied in several ways. For example, one can know something theoretically or in a habitual way and not attend to it in a particular choice. Thomas Aquinas uses the common example of a person who is so concentrated on one thing that he does not pay attention to someone speaking to him. "And the reason for this is that all the soul's powers are rooted in a single soul, whose intention applies each power to its act; and therefore, when a person is resolutely intent on the act of one power, his attention to act in another power is reduced."[127]

This is also true because knowledge is primarily about universal propositions whereas passions are about particular things. Moral science is not about grand ideas, though not contrary to them. Rather, it is about particular action and so it is very possible for a person to be able to write a treatise on sexual ethics and commit sexual sins in his particular actions because distracted by his passions. The feeling may be so strong for the particular deed that reason is prevented from being brought to bear on the action in question.

Because man is composed of body and spirit and the passions share in both, strong passions often alter body chemistry and because man uses the body and the senses in reasoning, "a change may take place in the body in such a way that sometimes people have fallen into madness on account of anger or concupiscence or some other passion. And therefore when such passions are intense, by reason of the bodily change itself, such passions so to speak fetter the reason so that it does not exercise free judgment about particular acts to be done."[128]

In all these cases, freedom is altered because the ability to apply the judgment of knowledge to the will is altered. An action which results from the passions then is therefore less free than one which comes from the will.

So, one may formulate the general principle that one must make a distinction in human actions which are passionate. If the passions precede the action of the will and the person wills as a result of the passion, such actions are less voluntary. These are antecedent passions. Acts which result from passion adhere less in the soul and so if they are good, they are less meritorious and if they are evil, they are less demeritorious. Another way to put this is that they really do not relate strongly to either tending to heaven or away from it because the love of the will for either good or evil is diminished in them.

On the other hand, passionate acts which result from acts of the will are more voluntary. Actions which are performed by the passions moved by the will are more loving, more free and therefore if they are good, more meritorious, and if they are evil, more demeritorious. These are consequent passions. They show a stronger love and therefore are more efficacious in the journey towards or away from heaven.

The passions only enter into moral responsibility because they participate in the will.

> In themselves passions are neither good nor evil. They are morally qualified only to the extent that they effectively engage reason and will. Passions are said to be voluntary 'either because they are com-

manded by the will or because the will does not place obstacles in their way'."¹²⁹

The proper order then of judging moral freedom in relation to the passions would be as follows: 1) an act done merely from passion does not involve the will and therefore has little to do with morals either for good or for ill. Alms given merely from the feeling of compassion are not meritorious. Sins committed merely from antecedent passions would not arrive at the soul and so not be demeritorious. 2) Acts done from reason guiding will are those with which morals is primarily concerned. Almsgiving from love of the poor to alleviate suffering is very good and accords with the virtue of justice. 3) An act done with both will and consequent passion shows a greater freedom in the deed and so is more virtuous or more sinful. Alms given from love of the poor which inspires a feeling of compassion for them is the best of all. Murder caused by a nursed hatred is more deeply in the character than even cold-blooded murder.

The fact that antecedent passion can diminish moral responsibility is attested to in the *Catechism of the Catholic Church* in dealing with sexual sins like masturbation. "To form an equitable judgment about the subject's moral responsibility and to guide pastoral action, one must take into account the affective immaturity, force of acquired habit, conditions of anxiety, or other psychological or social factors that can lessen, if not reduce to a minimum, moral responsibility."¹³⁰ Sins like this are generally termed sins of weakness. One more easily repents of these sins because they are not as central to the formation of the character as sins of pure will (termed sins of malice).

IGNORANCE

The last important question which must be answered regarding freedom of will in an act has to do with ignorance. The point has already been made that nothing can be willed unless first known. (*Nihil volitum nisi praecognitum*). This is because the will cannot move towards anything unless this is first presented to the will and only the intellect can do this. Since this is the case, ignorance must affect moral responsibility. The fact that knowledge is necessary for action also introduces the role of the conscience. How does conscience relate to the exercise of moral responsibility?

Socrates and Plato rightly saw that knowledge was necessary for a person to act freely. However, since they down played the role of the senses in knowledge and that included the passions and their necessary place in human freedom, they thought that the wise man was always the good man. The philosopher would always naturally do the right thing. Later, this will affect the question of whether there must be other virtues than those in the intellect for a person to act rightly. St. Thomas says that their opinion would be correct if by knowledge one means a truth applied to action and carried through. But if one means merely speculative knowledge or even a right conclusion in the conscience about good and evil here and now, this does not correspond to human experience.

Some also argue that every moral choice of evil in which a person acts against conscience is a kind of ignorance. Ignorance would not seem to exclude moral responsibility then unless one wants to say that almost no one is responsible for evil.

As is the case with the passions, the key to the solution to this question is found in the ability of the will to control the presence or lack of knowledge. When Thomas Aquinas treats this question he first distinguishes between nescience, ignorance and error. "For nescience denotes a simple negation or absence of knowledge."[131] There is no judgment here about whether the knowledge which is absent is a knowledge someone ought to have.

"Ignorance is nothing else but a lack of knowledge which a person is designed by nature to have, for this is characteristic of any privation."[132] For a stone to lack eyes would not be considered to truly be a privation because a stone is not designed by nature to have eyes. For a dog to lack eyes would be a privation because of the nature of the dog.

Ignorance may be further distinguished between that which "results from a perverse frame of mind, for instance, when a person has a habit of false principles and false opinions by which he is impeded from knowledge of the truth"[133] and "error [which] is approval of the false as true."[134] The difference between these two concepts is that one can be in ignorance without making a judgment about truth but one cannot be in error without making a false judgment.

Error would certainly have the nature of sin because it requires an act of judgment in which the intellect is moved by the will. Simple nescience has no relationship to fault or sin as even the good angels do not have knowledge about all the worlds God possibly could have made for example. The ignorance the human race generally experiences is a punishment for the Original Sin. But such ignorance does not take on a moral significance for the human race inheriting this state and does not thus fall under responsibility unless one is obliged to know something before acting. This would fall under sin. St. Thomas maintains that "all men are obliged to know the truths of faith because faith directs intention, and they are obliged to know the Ten Commandments, which enable them to avoid sin and to do good."[135] More obscure conclusions from the Ten Commandments oblige only superiors whether ecclesiastical or civil.

Ignorance is a punishment because it is a lack in the subject of something which the subject needs to act. If the cause of this ignorance is simply failing to apply what a person knows in general to an action, this is a sin of omission if the action following from this ignorance is a sin. In theory a person would naturally desire to know the truth, but "on account of the hardship of learning or for fear that it is an impediment to a sin which he loves, he rejects knowledge."[136]

The act of the intellect precedes the will as supplying knowledge about a prospective goal. Since intellect is also a power of the soul, the will may also command the intellect to know or to ignore some possible kind of knowledge either positively or simply by neglecting to investigate before acting. If the ignorance precedes the act of the will in such a way that the will can do nothing to alter it, then one experiences either antecedent or concomitant ignorance. Antecedent ignorance would precede the act of the will and causes involuntariness because "the will is opposed to what is done."[137] On the other hand, ignorance which merely accompanies the act of the will is non-voluntary because it is "the mere privation of the act of the will."[138] The difference between the involuntary and the non-voluntary practically speaking can be seen by the sorrow which the act causes when the ignorance is resolved. Since the involuntary act is contrary to the will, once the person realizes what he has done, he is sad and easily repents. Not so with the non-voluntary.

St. Thomas uses the example of a man hunting in the forest who hears a noise and shoots thinking he is killing a deer. Instead, he discovers he has killed a man. If he has taken all the necessary precautions hunters should take, once he sees he has killed a man this will cause him great remorse. His deed is involuntary. On the other hand, if he discovers he has killed his enemy whom he would have killed anyway, he has no remorse, but is glad. Antecedent ignorance is an example of what is traditionally called invincible ignorance. A person cannot resolve this by will and so he is not responsible for actions which result from it, either good or ill.

On the other hand, the act of the will may precede the act of the intellect. The person may will to be ignorant. This is called consequent ignorance. An example of this would be the man who is hunting in the forest and hears a noise. He does not bother to take any precautions to discover if he is killing a deer or a man, not even the most basic precautions all hunters take to discover such a thing. He shoots and kills a man.

He would be morally responsible for such a deed because he could have resolved his ignorance easily if he had wanted to. He just did not want to. In this, he showed a callous indifference to human life though he may not have actively intended the death of a man. In fact, ignorance of this kind increases sin because it shows precisely this callous indifference to the truth which is necessary to will the good. "When then a person directly wills to be ignorant so that he not be restrained from sin by knowledge, such ignorance does not excuse sin either wholly or in part, but rather increases it, for the person seems to be afflicted with a great love of sinning that he would will to suffer the loss of knowledge for the sake of freely engaging in sin."[139] This is classically called vincible ignorance because it can be overcome by the will.

So we can formulate the general principle that like passion, antecedent or invincible ignorance causes involuntariness and thus lack of responsibility. Consequent or vincible ignorance makes an act more voluntary. Concomitant ignorance does not actually relate to willing because it cannot be known and the knowledge of it would not have affected the will one way or the other. It is outside the evaluation of responsibility in the actual deed.

The post-Vatican II church clearly recognizes both these divisions and evaluations of sin in the *Catechism of the Catholic Church*: "Feigned (cf. vincible) ignorance and hardness of heart (consequent passions) do not diminish, but rather increase, the voluntary character of a sin." (*CCC*, 1859) "Unintentional (cf. invincible) ignorance can diminish or even remove the imputability of a grave offense. [...] The promptings of feelings and passion (antecedent passions) can also diminish the voluntary and free character of the offense, as can external pressures or pathological disorders." (*CCC*, 1860)

Note that, in this analysis of moral responsibility, all three of the powers of the soul which participate in the formation of human freedom are involved: the will, the intellect and the passions. If any are diminished or absent, the act does not share fully in the voluntary. So, for example, all three powers must be represented for a sin to be mortal and truly deform the order of the human soul. "For a sin to be mortal, three conditions must together be met: 'Mortal sin is sin whose object is grave matter (objective principle) and which is also committed with full knowledge (intellect) and deliberate consent (will without antecedent passion)." (*CCC,* 1857)

EMOTIONAL PROBLEM VS. MORAL PROBLEM

It is incumbent on the confessor to realize that just because an act is conscious does not mean it is voluntary. Though a confessor is not a psychiatrist, it is often important for him to know the difference between an emotional problem and a moral problem. The one demands treatment and understanding and the individual should be encouraged to seek a competent professional; the latter demands conversion. The former is, of course, a recommendation the confessor can make within the context of confession, but cannot act on outside the confessional. A confessor cannot act on knowledge gained in the confessional. He can encourage the penitent with the idea that his problem is not a moral problem and perhaps he could benefit from a counselor.

One very interesting attempt to deal with this problem is found in the works of Dr. Conrad Baars.[140] For example, in the case of obsessive-compulsive neurosis, a penitent may have a conflict within his passions in which his moral life has been formed merely by the emotion of fear. In the case of sexuality, either because of positive teaching or because of the manner he was taught about sexuality, he may have gotten the idea that all sexual feelings were evil. When these began to arise in puberty, his first response was not based on a reasonable development of these feelings but simply to try to blot them out of his soul by fear. If this is intensified, the person may begin to govern his actions merely from the emotions of fear or energy (courage). If this is deep-seated enough the desire for the original good can be completely blocked from the consciousness which occurs when a neurosis develops. A person may be so afraid of the passions connected with sexuality that he blocks the existence of the sexual urge out of his consciousness.

CHAPTER FOUR MORAL RESPONSIBILITY: THE VOLUNTARY

The trouble is that the passions have a natural tendency to be guided by reason, not by other passions. If the passion of fear or energy is strong enough and there are no images connected with the good allowed into the conscious mind, then the passions of pleasure connected with sexuality cannot be guided by reason and so there can be no integration. A person may be aware of what he is doing but, because reason cannot enter to control the passions which are buried alive by other ones, there can be no virtue. The person's whole life may be dominated by fear and the fear can spread to other things. He hates the whole experience of sexuality but has a compulsive desire to look at pornography. This person needs psychological counseling, not confession, because there is no freedom in what he does.

Dr. Conrad Baars calls the therapy which he believes is most indicated for someone who has blocked pleasure only by the passion of fear "mortification therapy".[141] Most Catholics know that they must mortify their passions when it comes to pleasure because these can lead to sin. They are less certain that they must also mortify the passions which have to do with the useful or harmful, the difficult good or evil. There are positive ones like energy (courage) or negative ones like fear. Many people try to govern their moral life merely by their feelings of avoiding fear or satisfaction at accomplishing. This again does not lead to a virtuous integration of the passions with the intellect and will.

So a person may be successful at avoiding sexual sin but easily act out on pornography even when they hate the fact that they do this. What the therapist tries to do is get them to change a mistaken idea of the moral law where "ought" is judged merely on the feelings or will power and substitute a correct idea of the moral law. This requires changing the condition in which the moral law is simply seen from the perspective of utilitarianism as a useful good instead of the good as such. When an obsessive-compulsive neurotic hears "must" he only interprets this from fear or energy. The repressing passions of fear or energy must be allowed to naturally lessen so that the real good involved, like sexuality, can emerge and then be rationally guided.

One must slowly mortify fear or energy, but not in a forced manner. The moral difficulty is that sometimes the initial emergence of these passions long buried alive can be quite strong. They may even cause sexual sin. This cannot be with another person, because this is against the order of justice. But if another is not involved this may have to be tolerated by both the confessor and the therapist. The therapist substitutes "you may" for "you must". The confessor may think this is laxism and recommending sin. The therapist can never order a person to experience sexual sin since he speaks with the voice of reason. He merely tolerates this and so must the confessor because neither the will nor moral responsibility enter here and the only way the penitent can resolve the issue is to return to the repression. He may say that he can control himself by will power, but he is just returning to the neurotic condition. Slowly as the passion is allowed to emerge, the person is then encouraged to freely choose not to participate in this because he understands the good involved. The tolerated action remains objectively an evil but it is not subjectively experienced as such because of the lack of reason guiding will. Only passions guide the will in this condition, not the truth.

Pius XII offers some guidance here:

> From this a conclusion follows for psychotherapy. In the presence of material sin it cannot remain neutral. It can, for the moment, tolerate what remains inevitable. But one must know that God cannot justify such an action. With still less reason can psychotherapy counsel a patient to commit material sin on the ground that it will be without subjective guilt. Such a counsel would also be erroneous if this action were regarded as necessary for psychic easing of the patient and thus as being a part of the treatment. One must never counsel a conscious act which would be a deformation and not an image of divine perfection.[142]

Though this is an interesting attempt to separate moral responsibility in neurotics from actions caused by emotional illness, it is by no means without its critics. Many point out that objective sin is still involved in the person doing the mortification. These critics point out, for example, that psychology has progressed much since Dr. Baars' time in the ability to treat obsession with medication like antidepressants rather than process oriented therapy. In addition, though the therapist may wish to limit the sorts of actions which are objectively sinful, the very toleration of some leads this to be easier said than done. The removal of a good bit of the moral life of a person from the moral sphere seems very naïve at best and shocking at worst. Some experts claim that people rarely act out on their obsessions and the attempt to analyze the obsession just makes the individual more hopeless in seeking to avoid it.

So though there is much merit in the analysis of Dr. Baars' approach, new developments would suggest that approaches which do not tolerate objective sin are certainly more helpful and in keeping with Catholic morals. The important thing to emphasize here is that what is conscious is not necessarily willed, that one may have an emotional problem which leads to behavior which is not deeply willed and that authentic Catholic moral teaching never leads to emotional illness but to emotional wholeness.

CIRCUMSTANCE

Since ignorance can affect the voluntary, the question naturally arises if this is true of all ignorance. Thomas Aquinas thinks that the primary ignorance which affects the voluntary in such a way that it makes a subject not responsible for an action is ignorance of a circumstance, not a principle.

Circumstances are treated two times in morals. They are treated in the issue of responsibility and they are also treated when the issue of objective moral truth is concerned. Though the two are related, in this section circumstances will be treated as they bear on ignorance affecting moral freedom.

The word "circumstance" used in the context of morals refers to a condition which "stands around" [Latin: *circum* (around), *stans* (stands)] an action. Circumstances are external conditions which affect the evaluation of an action in some way. Moral theologians must consider circumstances because these conditions relate to the suitability of an action for obtaining a goal and also because "human acts are judged to be voluntary or involuntary according to the knowledge or ignorance of circumstances."[143]

Circumstances are accidents (in the philosophical sense) to determining how an action relates to reason. In philosophy, an accident is not an unforeseen event but rather a being which must exist in another being. A substance is a being which exists in its own right. A dog is a substance; a cat is a substance; a rose is a substance. Man, for example, is traditionally defined as a "rational animal" because this includes both the body and the spiritual soul. The fact that a man has a white or black or brown body is incidental to understanding what a man is. Color is an accident and normally has nothing to do with the nature of a thing in itself. This is an accident pure and simple because one can understand a man fully without taking color into consideration.

However, there are some accidents which are not purely incidental. Though they form no part of the being as such, they always and everywhere accompany this being in such a way that one cannot understand the being without taking these accidents into consideration. In philosophy, these are called "properties". One cannot fully understand a thing's nature unless one also understands the properties though these are not the substance. Examples of classic properties when it comes to human nature are: "risibility" (a sense of humor) and "society" (living in society). These two conditions are not the substance of man, yet they are always and everywhere found where man exists and man cannot be fully understood without them.

Like accidents, circumstances are either completely incidental or they can truly affect how a given action relates to attaining the goal which is willed. For example, when it comes to theft, normally the circumstance of quantity does affect the ability of an act of theft to be either completely contrary to arriving at heaven or not. To steal a very small sum amounts to almost nothing in one's journey toward heaven and so would be a venial sin. One would not deny the possibility of arriving at the end, but the journey would not be as urgent. To steal a large amount would be a mortal sin and completely preclude the presence in the soul of the love of God and so be a denial of the goal of heaven.

Normally the circumstance of place would make no difference in the nature of theft. To steal in one room or another would not alter one's journey to heaven. To steal from a church on the other hand, changes the nature of the lack of love and respect for others and for the deed. Sacrilegious theft is more against God than neighbor and so directly affects how one loves God and tends to heaven in a different way than mere theft would. Knowledge of circumstances is very important because it does affect freedom.

Circumstances must be treated in all sciences related to human conduct but under different aspects. Moralists consider them because they affect "finding or losing the mean of virtue in human actions and passion."[144] The orator is interested in them to persuade people to practice virtues and avoid vices. The politician should be interested in them to judge whether given actions are worthy of reward or punishment in a state.

The traditional circumstances are taken from the *Nicomachean Ethics* of Aristotle. They are: "who, what and where, what were the means, why, how and at what time, and what about."[145] The circumstances can be schematized as follows:

Those which affect the act itself:

> A due measure (when and where)—as, for example, an assassination during the consecration of the Mass or theft in a church;
>
> The quality of the deed (how)—as, for example, a cold-blooded murder rather than a crime of passion

Those which affect the cause of the act

> The final cause or purpose (why)—as in a hidden motive like alms for vainglory
>
> The material cause or subject matter of the deed (about what)—a matter of money, the right to life, the other's wife
>
> The efficient cause (who) did the deed—murder by a priest, murder by a lay person
>
> The instrumental cause (by what aids)—as, for example, murder with a gun, with one's hands or with a terrorist bomb
>
> Those which affect outcome of the action (what)—as, for example, a large or small amount of a theft.

The known circumstances can affect the morality of an act in three ways: 1) they can change the kind of act it is objectively, as in robbery in a church or in a supermarket. 2) They can change the gravity of a deed, as in making it a great or small act of virtue or a mortal or venial sin. This would be the case with the amount of a gift or theft. 3) They can affect the subject's involvement in the deed and thus increase or diminish the depth of his choice for good or evil. In other words, they can make an act more praiseworthy or blameworthy because the will is more or less involved in the deed. In the former two senses, moral science considers them as they affect the actual nature of the deed. It is in the last sense that moral science considers circumstances as they affect freedom.

Several moral cases may be useful to illustrate how circumstances affect the nature of the deed. The fact that a murderer uses a terrorist bomb as opposed to a knife or his hands usually shows that his action is more voluntary because he is more callous in his disregard for the life of innocent bystanders. This depth of freedom in the deed would increase depending on how many bystanders one is willing to destroy to make the point, as in the case of the destruction of the World Trade Center. Those terrorists were willing to have thousands of innocent people perish to make their point which shows a depth of involvement in their deed much greater than ordinary murder. The same would be true of seeking to murder the president or the sovereign of any nation because of the assault on the order of the society involved. Though objectively this is a worse crime than ordinary murder it would also betray a strength of will in the assault on society which would make the assassin callous in his evil.

By the same token, circumstances can show a deeper involvement in good. This is the case of the widow's mite, praised by Our Lord. Though the poor widow objectively gave a very small amount compared to others, in her circumstances it was a lot, all she had to live on, and showed a great depth of will for good, a magnanimous spirit.

OTHER CONSIDERATIONS

There are several other important points which must be made about the contribution of the will to a human act. The distinctions of each are important for determining moral responsibility and goodness and evil.

First, the will is always drawn to being as desirable. Being is desirable because it completes and perfects a power of the soul. However, in both animals and men, this completion includes perception either of the senses or of the intelligence. So the will is both attracted to what seems good and repelled by what seems bad. Though all movement is caused by the good, because appearances make something seem good, "the will does not have to be attracted to the true good, but to what appears good."[146] A sexual action which one knows in his reason to be bad for the soul can be performed and desired in the moment because it appears good because it is pleasurable. By the same token, going to church, which one knows in his reason to be good for the soul, can in the moment become undesirable because one has to get up in the morning after a night of drunken carousing.

Thomists are accustomed to distinguishing three ways in which the will is attracted to the good. The first is the goal or end itself also called the righteous good (*bonum honestum*). The second is the means, which are desired in order to attain the good also known as the useful good (*bonum utile*). The third is the pleasurable good, which consists in resting in the end attained by the means (*bonum delectabile*). "The most basic act of willing is the desiring of what is in itself desirable."[147] One can desire a goal without desiring the means but one cannot desire the means without desiring the goal. Utilitarianism is a philosophy of ethics which states that the ends justify the means because there is nothing which is objectively good. Sometimes man desires means only because of the end and would never desire a given means it were not for the end, for example, a painful operation for the sake of health. Sometimes one desires the end but with desire for the means as a pleasant tasting food which is also healthy.

Since the end can be desired without the means but not vice versa, for someone to attain the end both must be considered. As stated above in the order of intention the mind is primary, the end comes first and the means come last. One must decide on the goal of the journey before one decides how to get there. In the order of execution, the will is primary, the means come first and the end is the last realized. To arrive at the goal of the journey one must get up off the chair and move oneself there. Because of the relation of ends and means, "interrupting execution of an action can leave us with the means accomplished but no goal; interrupting willing can leave us with a willed goal but no means."[148]

Sometimes people are very confused about the fact that one can do evil at all. In the case of Adam and Eve, people think that they had such marvelous gifts on the part of the God that they were in a certain sense forced to do good. Some think God should have forced them to do good. Others think that one can be confirmed in grace in this life in such a way that one could not sin.

Since the intellect moves the will by presenting goods, but the will can be born to the apparent good, and since there are several different levels of good, righteous, useful and pleasurable, the will always remains free. In fact, there are two basic causes of free action. There is the cause which moves the subject or the will to act. The will once it moves, moves the other powers to act too. This freedom is called freedom of exercise or to act or not to act. The will is never forced to will anything. "Moving a subject into action requires an agent attracted by a goal, and since what attracts the will is goodness as such (by definition the province of the will) it is our will that brings our other powers into action."[149] The other cause of freedom regards the kind of action which is done. This relates good to truth. This is called freedom of specification. "But the type of action is determined by conformation to some object, and since conformation to being and truth as such is by definition the province of the mind, it is the mind that determines the will by presenting to it its object."[150]

There are then two different exercises of freedom of will. There is first the freedom of exercise, determined by the will which is the subject where freedom resides, also called the material cause. The second is the freedom of specification, which is determined by the intellect, also called the root cause of freedom or the formal cause in traditional terms. "Freedom is the power, rooted in reason and will, to act or not to act [freedom of exercise], to do this or that, [freedom of specification] and so to perform deliberate actions on one's own responsibility."[151] Though both powers go together in freedom and cannot be separated, the formal cause of real freedom is based on the conformity of the will to reality which is caused by the mind. "Will moves mind to perform, since the truth mind seeks is one good among others and an instance of what the will seeks: goodness as such; but mind determines what it is we will, since we know the good we will as one truth among others, an instance of what mind grasps: truth as such."[152]

According to Pope John Paul II, the present malaise in moral theology is caused by a denial of this dependence for the kind of goods sought on the truth of the intellect. "The human issues most frequently debated and differently resolved in contemporary moral reflection are all closely related, albeit in various ways, to a crucial issue: human freedom."[153]

The dependence of the will on the intellect for the freedom of specification is what gives the form to freedom. Pope Benedict XVI has expressed distress at the "dictatorship of relativism" and this is especially seen in the modern attempt to destroy the fact that it is the intellect which gives the form to freedom. The conscience will be treated in a later chapter, but suffice it to say here that conscience has become not only the immediate norm by which the law of God is applied, but also the ultimate norm for determining truth. "Certain currents of modern thought have gone so far as to exalt freedom to such an extent that it becomes an absolute, which would then be the source of values."[154] The great crisis in metaphysics which was initiated by Descartes has born full fruit in contemporary morals by the questioning of all absolute truth in human action except the freedom of the will. "[T]here is a tendency to grant to the individual conscience the prerogative of independently determining the criteria of good and evil and then acting accordingly."[155]

Many post-Vatican II thinkers have questioned whether there is such a thing as an objective human nature on which to base the direction of the human will. Rahner, for instance, thinks that once one has abstracted the orientation to grace from human nature which he calls the supernatural existential, human nature itself becomes impossible to define.

> 'Nature' in the theological sense (as opposed to nature as the substantial content of an entity always to be encountered in contingent fact), i.e. as the concept contraposed to the supernatural, is consequently a remainder concept (*Restbegriff*) [...]. Thus there is no way of telling exactly how his [man's] nature left to itself would react, what precisely it would be for itself alone.[156]

Even the followers of Rahner admit that perhaps unwittingly he cannot save himself from philosophical relativism because he has no clear idea of real objective universals. Though Rahner tried to defend the truth of absolute universal statements against theologians whom he thought were relativists, his idea of essences is sadly unequal to this task.

> Rahner took issue with Küng and attempted to refute Küng's thesis that the Church could not define infallibly because no human statement could be absolutely true, arguing instead that the judgment does take the mind to reality. While we have seen how Rahner argued to this conclusion, we have also seen that there is an inherent weakness within his thought. [...] [I]t is not transparently clear how conceptual thought in Rahner's own epistemological system can be preserved from relativisation."[157]

If this difficulty in knowing universal statements is true generally, it is very disastrous when applied to human nature. Coupled with the fact that conscience creates the truth of the action, this leads to a complete relativism in morals. Freedom becomes exalted against any law. There is nothing to direct the will or to judge ends proposed to it because there is no nature of the powers of the soul, for example, on which to base such a judgment. "Taken to its extreme consequences, this individualism leads to a denial of the very idea of human nature."[158]

Human freedom then is founded on the presence of truth. In fact, it is the ability of the intellect to understand universal ideas which allows the power of the will to see several sides to each thing as perfecting or not. The intellect can be mistaken in this. So the will is drawn to the good as it appears, not necessarily as it actually is. This is the reason that one must take counsel often to be sure that one is not willing the apparent good which would be really evil or shunning the apparent evil which would be really good. "The rightful autonomy of practical reason means that man possesses in himself his own law, received from the Creator. Nevertheless, the autonomy of reason cannot mean that reason itself creates values and moral norms."[159] Human freedom is not a freedom from the moral law, but a freedom for the moral law.

Since the will desires the good as it appears to the person acting, the passions can also influence the will. When a person is in a certain passionate state, for example, fear, anger or pleasure, the exterior objects appear in a different light than they would without this state. This is not because of the condition of the object, but because of the condition of the subject. Something which may appear desirable while in one state, for example, a steak when one is hungry, may not appear desirable when this state changes, the same steak when one is full. A delicious meal may attract when well, but repel when ill. The exterior objects can move the will but not in a deterministic way and their attractiveness may be determined not by them, but by the condition of the subject. "Because what seems good to us must seem congenial, and that depends on our constitution as well as the object presented, it is obvious that emotions can so affect our composure that things appear congenial which would not otherwise do so. In that way emotions can affect the will through the object."[160] This idea is expressed in a principle from Aristotle's Ethics: "As a person is, so does the end seem to him."[161]

The will also can move itself to action. It cannot be forced or determined to any particular good. Modern explanations of evil have a tendency to reduce evil to things like environment. If everyone were rich, there would be no sin. The problem of evil can be solved by better social structures. If a government could just find the right bureaucracy and education system, there would be no evil. Social engineering, with its sad consequences, can ultimately be reduced to this opinion. People have no real freedom and need to be saved from the unfortunate consequences of their birth, which if left to them, would determine them to act in a certain kind of way. Coupled with this opinion is the astonishment some express that Adam and Eve could have sinned given the fact that they enjoyed an almost continuous state of infused contemplation.

These opinions ignore the ultimate freedom of the will which is based on the presence of the intellect. The will is always free to consent or not unless in the presence of an object of knowledge which cannot be considered evil in any respect. This can only occur in the vision of God in heaven. "The will, as mistress of its own actions, works in a way which transcends the way nature works, following one determined pattern."[162]

Instead, there are two extremes regarding the determinism of the will. These extremes correspond to theories concerning knowledge. The first kind of the determinism is based on limiting knowledge to material, sensible experience. This leads to complete denial of freedom. Democritus in the ancient world and Freud in the modern world follow this idea of freedom. Acts of will in this theory are reduced to instincts or exterior influences. For this theory, the only sources of human action are our feelings or exterior influences like the environment.

> Side by side with its exaltation of freedom, yet oddly in contrast with it, modern culture radically questions the very existence of this freedom. A number of disciplines, grouped under the name of the 'behavioral sciences', have rightly drawn attention to the many kinds of psychological and social conditioning which influence the exercise of human freedom. [...] But some people, going beyond the conclusions which can be legitimately drawn from these observations, have come to question or even the deny the very reality of human freedom.[163]

The other sort of determinism has its origin in the idea that knowledge is purely spiritual and interior with no relation to sense knowledge. Plato is the origin of this and basically held that ideas would always bind people to act according to them. This relates to the above mentioned opinion that all Adam and Eve had to know was what is right and they would have done it. This is mental determinism. The mind forces the will to choose something by the knowledge it presents as its motive.

Like all truths, the truth about willing shares something in both these opinions. The sense and environment can influence willing as can ideas. But the will cannot be forced to choose any particular good. Nevertheless, the will remains radically free not to be moved or not to move to this or that good. This is because freedom of will has to do with means and not ends. Though the will is naturally drawn to happiness in general, the only good which can naturally draw the will is one in which the intellect can see nothing negative. Because of this, neither the passions, nor any exterior force nor any limited good can force the will because it is a spiritual power. Finally, the intellect can present the will with a motive for the desirability of something, but the will can only be drawn according to the free nature of the will. "Being free, then, is not opposed to being determined. It all depends on how the determination takes place. In the case of the will, it must be moved in such a way that its freedom remains intact."[164]

The will always remains free then, even in the face of passion. "The will cannot always stop desire arising, as Paul says: 'I do' (read, "desire") 'the evil I hate'; but it can always refuse to desire it or it can refuse to consent to the desire."[165] Passions can sometimes bind man completely and so make a man lose all reason and thus no will is present. This would be the case in someone mad from passion. But if any ability to reason remains, the person can always resist the passion.

God is the primary mover of all things which move on earth. But he moves nothing contrary to its nature. "God irresistibly moves causes to effects in ways suited to the nature of the cause: so he moves the will freely."[166] This is the case even with the act of sin. God causes the act as an act because he causes everything that exists. But man supplies the defect in the act because he freely issues into an act of his will knowing it is contrary to the truth of human nature. "God causes the action of sin, but he is not the cause of sin, because he is not the cause of the defect in the act."[167]

An important corollary of these considerations about the will is that the will in itself exists to pursue goodness. This is true even for the sinner. No one willingly does evil. One pursues evil for the sake of good. The trouble is that this good may be only an apparent good. For example, one is tempted to an evil sexual act. One is presented with at least two goods: the higher good of reason and the lower good of pleasure. In a truly good act, these should reside together. In an evil act, one chooses the good of the pleasure which precludes the presence of the good of reason. One has done evil, but for the sake of a good. "In the same way, to be able to choose more than one course of action leading to a goal is a fulfillment of freedom; but to choose a course departing from the goal and to sin is a defect of freedom."[168] "Man's genuine autonomy in no way means the rejection but rather the acceptance of the moral law, of God's command. [...] Human freedom and God's law meet and are called to intersect, in the sense of man's free obedience to God and God's completely gratuitous benevolence towards man."[169]

Finally, no treatment of responsibility would be complete without briefly enumerating the various actions which are involved in every elicited act of the will and then the various influences of the powers of the soul on responsible human action.

Every elicited act in which the will acts at the very center of the human person is characterized by twelve different steps which involve both the intellect and the will. They are: 1) Knowing the end in the intellect, 2) willing the end in the will, 3) judging the end in the intellect, 4) intending the end in the will, 5) deliberating about the means in the intellect, 6) consent to the means in the will, 7) judging the means in the intellect, 8) choosing the means in the will, 9) commanding the execution of the choice of the means in the intellect, 10) using the various powers of the soul necessary to arrive at the end, 11) judging that one has indeed attained the end in the intellect, 12) enjoying the end attained in the will. These actions of course generally occur all in an instant in the actual choice, yet this interplay is involved in each human choice. One can at once note how complicated it is to examine a given human choice and also how difficult it can be to judge the accomplishment of all these steps.

Responsibility for the commanded act is no less important.[170] There are those who believe when it comes to sexual acts, for instance, that actions done with the body are neutral regarding the will. In other words, they are pure tools to the action of the soul. The use of human seed as given or received then would be governed by reason in the same way as animal sexuality is governed by reason.

This is an impossible position unless one thinks that the soul and the body are in an accidental or worse an inimical relationship. If this were true, then material experience would have no relation to knowledge and actions done with the body would have only a tenuous relationship to the will. However, if one accepts the traditional position of the Church taking the philosophical position that the soul is the "form" of the body, then anything done in the body has some relationship to the perfection of the soul and especially regarding material things which are completely related to the existence of the soul, namely human seed and the womb.

> But more closely ordained to man's life than any external possessions whatsoever is human semen, wherein man potentially exists; hence the Philosopher says in the *Politics* that in man's semen there is something divine, namely inasmuch as it is man potentially; and therefore lack of order in regard to the discharge of semen is a lack of order in regard to the life of man in proximate potency.[171]

This is the answer to the charge of physicalism.

> A doctrine which dissociates the moral act from the bodily dimensions of its exercise is contrary to the

teaching of Scripture and Tradition. [...] In fact, body and soul are inseparable: in the person, in the willing agent and in the deliberate act they stand and fall together. At this point the true meaning of the natural law can be understood: it refers to man's proper and primordial nature, the 'nature of the human person,' which is the person himself in the unity of his spiritual and biological inclinations and of all the other specific characteristics necessary for the pursuit of his end."[172]

After reason moves the will, then will moves the reason and reason commands the other powers of the soul much like a general commanding an army. So the moral evaluation of any given power of the soul depends on the possibility of its being moved by reason. Reason then is the origin of the moral good and the will is merely the principle were reason is applied. "The root subject of freedom is will, but the root cause of freedom is reason."[173] So the formal cause of freedom is the intellect; the material cause is the will.

There has been a long tradition in morals which emphasizes only the will in the commanded action. For example, in religious obedience the will is emphasized often to the expense of the intellect. This is the voluntaristic point of view. Authority and obedience are a competition of wills. "If the voluntaristic viewpoint prevails, the will of the authority is the determining factor, the compelling force. The authority is the master. [...] If authority's law is unreasonable, it is a poor law, but his or her will must be obeyed."[174] Notice however that since the formal cause of freedom is the intellect, this must be emphasized even in the law.

> St. Thomas Aquinas viewed the law as an ordination of reason (*ordinatio rationis*) and the obligation to obey it as stemming from the human person's natural inclination toward the good, namely, that which corresponds to the person's rational nature. [...] It is the task of the person in authority to point out what these objects are. [...] Authority, it is true, must exercise its will to make reason issue an actual directive to the rational good. It must often exercise its will to compel obedience to the common good, but this does not change the fact that the reason why

the proposed law or rule should be obeyed lies in the circumstance that the law is rational, in accordance with reason.[175]

The question therefore of the commanded act is not just a tool of the all powerful rule of the will, but the attempt to introduce reason into the use of the various faculties of man using reason. In other words, when it comes to the spiritual powers of man moving his other powers, they form one moral being as it were, like matter and form in natural things. "What is true of naturally existing substances (like men composed of body and soul) is true also of human acts, in which the actions of lower powers are like material activated by the act of a high power in the way an agent activates the tools he uses. So the act commanding and the act commanded are one and the same composite human act."[176]

Reason, for example, commands the bodily organs generally as mere tools. Reason can also command through will the act of the mind so that a person can assent to or deny a given proposition as true. Finally, reason also commands the passions. However, this is in a different way than the body and the perception of reason. The passions are naturally drawn to two goods. They share with animal passions an orientation to individual goods alone and so have a relationship to the present state of the body. They are also naturally born to be obedient to reason. Since they have a knowing life of their own, they can resist the direction of reason. So the traditional way this is put is that the intellect guides the passions as wise governor to free citizen but the body as master to slave: "As Aristotle says, 'reason controls the passions not like a slave master but like a ruler of free men.'"[177] When reason governs these various powers, the moral law is introduced into them and they participate in moral responsibility. But this can only be the case for as long as they can be directed by reason.

When this direction occurs, the formation of a virtue begins. Regarding the passions, this is not sublimation in the traditional sense of Freud. "Virtue does not consist in sublimation taking the word in the ordinary sense of the expression of the lower through the higher. Rather does virtue consist in assumption, a process in which the higher agency takes up and transforms from within the lower powers, giving them a new and intrinsic form and determination, moderating and changing them in a real physical way, and giving them a [...] proportion to a higher end."[178]

SUMMATION

So, it is the power of the will in all its forms which places an act in the genus of morals. The responsibility of the subject is determined by the presence of the will even directing the material appendages of the body. The real issue in all moral acts then is how much and how strongly they flow from the soul as directed by the moving power of reason. Moral praise or blame, and therefore formation and deformation, are determined first by the presence of the consent of the will.

MAN IS A SERVANT: THE SPECIES OF MORALS

CHAPTER FIVE
FREEDOM AND TRUTH: GOODNESS AND EVIL

THE INTELLECT: OBJECTIVE NORM FOR HUMAN FREEDOM

Man is both a servant and free. Once an action is determined to be in the genus of morals because it is free, then the next consideration is to determine if it is good or evil. This determination is based not in the will, but in the intellect. This is the servant character of human choice. This is because human choice does not create the truth of a human action, but responds to it. The truth of a human act is determined by reason. Reason is an objective servant of the nature on which it is based. In a similar manner, freedom is subjective with its origin in the individual who exercises it. "Therefore good and evil in human acts is considered according as the act is in agreement with reason, informed by divine law, either naturally or by teaching or by infusion: hence Dionysius says it is evil for the soul to be contrary to reason, for the body it is evil to be contrary to nature."[179]

Reason is an action of the intellect. In man, reason is the means by which he first participates within his soul in the whole panoply of the world outside of him. The mind is the place where man participates in the specific being of all the natures of all the things he experiences in the world, including his own powers and his own person. If the will is the feet by which man undertakes his journey towards heaven, the intellect is his eyes. Swift movement by those who are blind can lead them over a cliff to their own destruction. Just as the mind experiences and checks the nature of the things in the world in order to know the truth and properties of their natures, so the mind also experiences the true place of all the possible goods which a person can enjoy and evaluates their contribution to the perfection of human nature. The criteria for this judgment is not the subject as an individual but the manner in which a given thing can realize, deny or frustrate man's journey to heaven. This is founded on the common nature of all human beings and human actions in relation to the powers of the human soul.

This is not a physicalism (reducing freedom to just what the body does by nature) but a recognition that both physical and spiritual actions implement the potentials present in the powers of the human soul. What was potential is realized in action and these actions themselves either lead to a further integration or disintegration of human freedom journeying toward heaven.

In a being such as man, physical actions can never be considered merely in their physical dimensions. Physical acts always have some moral meaning because of the union of the powers of the human soul. This is in contradiction to those who view human freedom as the ability to make use of the physical members of the body as mere tools which have no moral meaning in themselves.

> A freedom which claims to be absolute ends up treating the human body as a raw datum, devoid of any meaning and moral values until freedom has shaped it in accordance with its design. Consequently, human nature and the body appear as presupposition or preambles, materially necessary, for freedom to make its choice, yet extrinsic to the person, the subject and the human act. Their function would not be able to constitute reference points for moral decisions, because the finalities of these inclinations would be merely 'physical' goods, called by some 'pre-moral.' To refer to them, in order to find in them rational indications with regard to the order of morality, would be to expose oneself to the accusation of physicalism or biologism. In this way of thinking, the tension between freedom and a nature conceived of in a reductive way is resolved by a division within man himself.[180]

Morals, however, is based on an objective nature. However, there is a difference in the way physical evil and moral evil relate to nature. To understand this difference, one must remember the distinction between being and action or first act and second act. The various powers of the human soul and the human soul itself exist, but they exist in potential to further participation in the being of natures outside themselves, including the nature of God. This requires an action beyond mere existence.

This distinction between being and act is the source of the distinction between physical evil and moral evil. In natures which are not free, their evil in action is caused by an evil in being. In free natures, their evil in being is caused by an evil in action.

> Now good designates a certain perfection. And perfection is twofold: namely the first, which is form or habit, and the second, which is operation. But everything we use in operating can be referred to the first perfection, the use of which is operation. Consequently, and conversely, a twofold evil is found: one in the agent himself, according as he is deprived either of form or of habit or of whatever else is necessary for operation, thus blindness or crookedness of leg is an evil; but the other evil is in the defective act itself, for instance if we should say that limping is an evil. In natures which are free it is the opposite. Evil in action which results from freedom of will, causes evil in being.[181]

In other words, a deformed leg causes someone to walk lame. Willful adulterous action, however, precludes the soul from participating in divine nature because to act against the nature God created is to act against God.

> But these two evils are ordered differently in natural operations and in voluntary operations. For in natural operations the evil of the action follows from the evil of the effective cause, for example, limping follows from a crippled leg; but in voluntary operations the reverse is true, the evil of the agent, i.e. punishment, divine providence regulating fault by punishment, follows from the evil of the action, i.e. the fault.[182]

A fortiori, the same would be true in good things. Goodness of agent causes goodness of action in natural things. Goodness of action causes goodness of agent in moral matters. The intellect and the conscience apply moral reasoning which determines how the various actions relate to the agent who is man and the basis for this are the objects of all the powers of the soul and their relationship to one another.

Without this objective basis, morals degenerates into a freedom which is license. "Certain tendencies in contemporary moral theology under the influence of ...subjectivism and individualism ... involve novel interpretations of the relationship of freedom to the moral law, human nature and conscience, and propose novel criteria for the moral evaluation of acts. Despite their variety, these tendencies are at one in lessening or even denying the dependence of freedom on truth."[183]

PHILOSOPHICAL DIFFICULTIES WITH MORALS

If it is true that reason is the measure of the difference between the human good and evil which guides human choice, it should be obvious that truth and objectivity in morals depend on one's idea of truth in things in general. The question of objective truth is a problem in all science and this is also true of morals where the universal objective truths are the laws which define human conduct. In the Catholic Church, there has been a great malaise since the 1960s in the whole idea that there is an objective human nature on which to base moral judgments. Many of those who both support and oppose the magisterium of the pope in morals have accepted a theory of truth which seems at odds with not only the Catholic tradition but also sound philosophy. This theory has its origin in the Enlightenment in the difficulties in epistemology[184] which attended the great rejection of the ability of man to know real things through universal ideas.

As is well known, Descartes, who is normally considered to be the father of the Enlightenment, was so struck with the lack of certainty in both reason and faith which characterized his age that he rejected knowledge through the senses as the origin of objective truths. He wished a mathematical certitude of the sort found in optics in all areas of human life. This led him from the world of objects to his own subjective experience as the source of truth. In this, he divided sense knowledge from intelligence. Breaking the link between sense knowledge and intelligence led to various philosophies which either emphasized sense experience alone (Hume) or ideas alone (Kant), at least where what had formerly been considered metaphysical realities like God and the moral law were concerned. The long and the short of this was either (1) an unbounded confidence in the ability of human reason to arrive at absolute truth by empirical explanation or (2) a projection of the feelings of human need which created the truths of God, man and morals. The bottom line of this melting pot of ideas was the rejection of the possibility of arriving through sense experience at an objective experience of human nature which would be true for all. The universal idea became devalued and was an impoverished sense experience.

Applied to morals, this leads to a radical distinction between individual happiness and the moral laws as perceived by both reason and faith. If the universal is an impoverished sense experience, then universal ideas like the law are impoverished expressions of the feelings of value an individual has in his conscience. The conscience becomes not just the last and most immediate norm of moral life but the only norm. Conscience then becomes an oracle. The Church has always denied this absolute authority of conscience. "As Cardinal John Henry Newman, that outstanding defender of the rights of conscience, forcefully put it: 'Conscience has rights because it has duties.'"[185] This is due to a difficulty in relating universal ideas to particular, concrete things in both nature and morals.

> In a new European philosophical atmosphere of change and spontaneity which reacted against fixed essences and natures and complete moral predictability, man's moral conscience came to be seen as 'no longer a function applying a general principle to a particular case by an automatic syllogism,' but more as a faculty which under the guidance of the Spirit of God is endowed with a certain power of intuition and discovery which allows it to find the original solution appropriate to each case.[186]

THE PROBLEMATIC MORAL SCHOOL OF KARL RAHNER

Karl Rahner provides an important application of this distinction which forms the foundation for much of the disillusion of post-Vatican II Catholic theologians with moral absolutes and has led to a practical desertion of the confessional. In his important article "On the Question of a Formal Existential Ethics" reproduced in Volume II of his *Theological Investigations*,[187] Karl Rahner introduced a distinction into the moral evaluation of the goodness or evil of actions. This is the distinction between "formal existential ethics" and "material essentialist ethics." According to him, "formal existential ethics" must take account not only of universal norms (laws) but also of the individual historical situation before any true moral analysis of either the good or evil of an action can be considered. This is because each moral act must be something truly personal and unique; this individuality cannot be expressed in a universal norm. "The concrete moral act is more than just the realization of a universal idea happening here and now in the form of a case. The act is a reality which has a positive and substantial property which is basically and absolutely unique."[188] Universal statements like laws can never arrive at expressing personal actions. The basic problem is between the expression of the universal idea and its application to life. "Man is destined to eternal life as an individual and someone in the concrete. His acts are, therefore, not merely of a spatio-temporal kind as is the case with material things; his acts have a meaning for eternity, not only morally but also ontologically."[189]

One must remember that the traditional Thomist solution to the problem of universals is that, in every kind of knowledge, though universals are in the mind and not the things, the concept is a true participation in the being of the concrete individual thing. When one knows a real universal idea (in this case, the laws), one is truly reflecting what is common in the powers of the human soul in action. The concept or idea is found in the mind. So, it is spiritual. At the same time, it is a real participation in the being of the thing which it represents and so is an intimate expression of the concrete things, whether material or spiritual. One who has a true concept of a tree participates in the being of all trees, past, present and future.

The same truth can be applied to man. As in all nature, one understands the powers of a thing by understanding the actions of that thing. When one has a true idea of man because one understands all the powers of the soul and body and their interaction with one another through reason, one truly participates in the being of every man who has existed, does exist or will exist on earth. This foundational idea is at the root of the formation of human choices in the will because in understanding the universal, one can then guide the further participation in goods in particular. Good adds to truth and being the idea of desirability. Conclusions about human conduct must result from laws which are universal formulations of those goods which are desirable in various contexts for man based on the nature and relation of his various powers. It is precisely this idea which gives Rahner pause. The reason is because it seems to limit the personal encounter of God with each soul.

CHAPTER FIVE FREEDOM AND TRUTH: GOODNESS AND EVIL   101

> It would be absurd for a God-regulated, theological morality to think that God's binding will could only be directed to human action in so far as the latter is simply a realization of the universal norm and universal nature. If the creative will of God is directly and unambiguously directed to the concrete and individual, then surely this is not merely true in so far as this individual reality is the realization of a case of the universal—rather it is directed to the concrete as such, as it really is—to the concrete in its positive, and particularly its substantial, material uniqueness.[190]

For Rahner, God's will is discovered by man in each unique event of his life, in each unique historical situation. No universal idea or norm can adequately deal with the situational complexity of the human person. Yet, if this situation is so unique that no universal laws can be formed about it at all, then this makes all morality merely a fulfillment of the needs of the individual. Morality would be truly the greatest good for the greatest number with no objective basis. Rahner's solution to this dilemma is to posit two ethical systems which must be observed in every human choice. The first would be the traditional abstract system formed by universal statements in the laws which is the "material essentialist ethics" already referred to. The second is based on "individual norms"[191] which will complement this traditional system based on abstraction and essences with the existential uniqueness of the individual and is the "formal existential ethics." "The notion of this 'existential' ethics ... shows itself unequivocally as the counter—and complementary notion of an abstractly universal 'essentialist' ethics."[192] Each human act has a "non-derivable qualitative property"[193] which cannot be reduced to a norm.

For Rahner, the development of the second science of ethics, formal existential ethics, is necessary for the development of the full complexity of Catholic thought.

> In so far as there is a moral reality in an existential-ethic sense and of a binding kind which nevertheless cannot (in the very nature of things) be translated into universal propositions of material content there must be an existential ethics of a formal kind, i.e. an

ethics which treats of the basic elements, the formal structures and the basic manner of perceiving such an existential-ethic reality. Just as, on the one hand, there cannot be any science of the individual considered as a really individual singular as such, and yet, on the other hand, there is a universal formal ontology of individual reality, so (and in this sense) there can and must be a formal doctrine of existential concretion, a formal existential ethics.[194]

Rahner roots this second science in the conscience enlightened by the Holy Spirit using the principles for discernment of spirits found in the Spiritual Exercises of St. Ignatius. Until the individual conscience confronts the will of God for the individual manifested by the Holy Spirit personally to him, the laws are merely recommendations. The universal laws are partly binding because they are a part of the discernment process. But because of a kind of "supernatural instinct,"[195] the person could always discern that the Holy Spirit was leading them to preserve the basic value taught by the law but by breaking its letter.

While one can agree with Rahner that the law cannot foresee every situation and that there is lack of mathematical certainty in human actions, still one must disagree with him that the negative laws, the "Thou shalt nots," are mere approximations of the good. It is also true that in the Christian past, there have been some examples of God himself inspiring people to act contrary to the second table of the Ten Commandments, commandments 4-10, as God the creator can dispense from the natural law. There are few instances of this. The examples usually given are Hosea being told to marry a harlot, the Jews being told to despoil the Egyptians before leaving Egypt and Abraham being told to sacrifice his son.

Rahner, however, carries this principle so far as to suggest that the law is never a true indicator of evil actions because of its very universality. Applying his principles, one could agree, for example, that contraception was generally wrong, but discern that in the individual circumstances, it was more life serving to practice it.

An excellent example of this moral reasoning is seen in the celebrated moral difficulty of an abortion which involves crushing the babies' skull also known as craniotomy. Richard McCormick, S.J., presents a case of a mother with many children who is presented with the issue of allowing her child to live and dying herself, or killing the child in the womb. Given this choice, McCormick reasons, the mother should ask herself which outcome is more life serving. If she allows herself to die, she will not serve the life of raising her children. If she kills the child, this is regrettable, but he reasons that it would be morally the correct decision as she has discerned she must sacrifice the letter of the law to preserve its value.

> I have said that 'that alternative should be chosen which is *in the circumstances* the best service of life.' What does that mean? The italicized words are meant to point up in a general way the causal relationship between achieving an urgent good (or preventing an urgent evil) and the causing of evil as the means. *In the circumstances* the relationship between the evil done (abortion) and the good achieved (saving the mother, the only one who can be saved) is a necessary one. That is, abortion of the child is the only way thinkable, given our medical tools, of saving the one who can be saved.[196]

> In other words, in the abortion case one chooses to save the life which can be saved because in such circumstances that is the lesser evil, is proportionately grounded. In other circumstances, it would not be the lesser evil, would not be proportionate.[197]

One can recognize here the mistake of Rahner that the traditional teaching of the laws would be material essentialist ethics. These are recommendations and must always be considered in a moral choice. But discerning the will of the Holy Spirit in formal existential ethics could always lead a person to break the law and is the final court of appeal. The evident error in this way of looking at things is that no law would ever bind absolutely, even the natural law. Though there are unique and rare examples of God inspiring someone to act contrary to the last seven commandments, to maintain that this is possible in every moral decision basically supports the denial of objective ethics.

THE SCHOOL OF MODERATE TELEOLOGY

Some contemporary Catholic moralists have accepted the challenge of Rahner in their various attempts to reconcile moral teaching condemning acts in themselves with a more existential view of morals. The most successful and interesting current of thought in this attempt is the school in Europe and America which reigned supreme in many Catholic academic institutions in the 1970s known under the various names of "moderate teleology", "consequentialism", or "proportionalism". Though all the members of this school do not speak about the same questions, they do have a general similarity in two aspects: a) moral truths cannot be derived from a metaphysical examination of the powers of the human soul common to all men and hence b) there is no action which can be morally judged apart from the morally relevant circumstances.

Richard McCormick and others of this position call their school of thought "moderate teleology". They use terminology derived from Emmanuel Kant to define their ideas. Kant had divided morals into two kinds: deontology and teleology. In deontology, actions were right or wrong regardless of the purpose. In teleology, it is the purpose or end which determines the goodness of the means. Charles Curran, a representative of this school, defines the use of these terms.

> When referring to the model of ethical life, teleology refers to an approach which sees the moral life primarily in terms of goals and ends. In this view, Aristotle and the manualists of moral theology are teleologists, as well as all utilitarians. Deontology understands the moral life primarily in terms of duties, obligations and laws.[198]

This interpretation is somewhat problematic. When moralists have used these terms in the past they have tended to use the word "exclusively" instead of "primarily" as Charles Curran does. In this sense, Aristotle and the Catholic manualists can certainly not be seen as teleologists. Certainly St. Alphonsus, the patron of moral theologians, would not think there are exceptions to means which are contrary to the natural law because they may be advantageous to certain situations which accord with it.

In shifting this emphasis, proponents of this theory wish to save the good and true parts of Catholic tradition and yet allow for certain

CHAPTER FIVE FREEDOM AND TRUTH: GOODNESS AND EVIL 105

exceptions which they believe are necessary according to the historical circumstances in which the Church is situated. They are not so crass as to say that the end justifies the means but, like Rahner, they generally hold that universal moral statements can never cover every situation and so must always take account of the consequences of a choice in the circumstances before they can truly oblige the conscience. Their use of the term "deontology" would roughly express Rahner's "material essentialist ethics" and teleology would roughly express situation ethics. Moderate teleology would roughly be equivalent to Rahner's "formal existential ethics" because the morally relevant circumstances would always be necessary to evaluate the goodness or evil of an act. Richard McCormick summarizes this tripartite division well.

> When I first encountered Curran's threefold division of positions within modern philosophy, I was pleasantly surprised. I had arrived independently at a similar division. Specifically, I had concluded to the usefulness of the following divisions: 1) absolute deontologists (Kant, Catholic tradition on certain points — [for example, contraception], Grisez, Anscombe); 2) absolute consequentialists (J. Fletcher, some utilitarians); and 3) moderate teleologists (Ross, McClosky, Frankena, Fuchs, Schüler, Knauer, and McCormick, among others).[199]

There have been many famous moralists who identify themselves with this school. Whatever terminology they may use, the Rahnerian division which denies that morals is based on metaphysics is presumed.

> They are Curran's mixed consequentialists or my moderate teleologists. Why? Because these theologians, in their explanation of *materia apta* (Janssens), commensurate reason (Knauer), proportionate reason (Schüller), insist that other elements than consequences function in moral rightness and wrongness. I would include myself among them.[200]

These "other considerations" would be Rahner's material essentialist ethics. The difficulty in this division immediately becomes apparent because the conscience becomes the ultimate determiner of good and the servant role of reason is limited to that of vague, general principles which have no obligatory character. There can be no such thing as an individual norm because this would only be normative for one person and for no other. The standard which makes this norm individual is the proportionality of the good achieved by means of the evil done. In the case evoked above of partial birth abortion, there is no nod even given to the question of the right to life of the child. The abortion of this child is simply considered to be a physical evil.

One of the errors condemned in the encyclical *Veritatis Splendor*[201] is consequentialism. There is it defined thus:

> The opinion must be rejected as erroneous which maintains that it is impossible to qualify as morally evil according to its species the deliberate choice of certain kinds of behavior or specific acts, without taking into account the intention for which the choice was made or the totality of the foreseeable consequences of the act for all persons concerned.[202]

In responding to this encyclical, Richard McCormick maintains that this is not the position of consequentialism and then goes on to define it.

> When contemporary theologians say that certain disvalues in our actions can be justified by a proportionate reason, they are not saying that morally wrong actions (*ex objecto*) can be justified by the end. They are saying that an action cannot be judged morally wrong simply by looking at the material happening, or at its object in a very narrow and restricted sense.[203]

Presumably in the example given above of the partial birth abortion, the material happening referred to is the killing of the baby. McCormick gives the example later of theft which is always defined as "taking another's property against the reasonable will of the owner." For him, "taking another's property" is the material object. "Against the reasonable will of the owner" the proportionate circumstance needed to define it. It is true that in formulating moral laws the object must be defined by more than a material happening. Thus murder is not defined as "killing a man" but rather as "killing an innocent man." The latter phrase clearly places this universal act in the order of reason as the phrase "reasonable will of the owner" allows someone to distinguish between theft, borrowing, and using another's property in an emergency situation for legitimate need. Each of these definitions of reason is based on the nature of man in relation to the good involved. In the first, life, the good is life and in the second, property.

McCormick continues:

> In conclusion, proportionalists are not justifying 'deliberate choices of kinds of behavior contrary to the commands of the divine and natural law.' They are saying that we must look at all dimensions (morally relevant circumstances) before we know what the action is and whether it should be said to be 'contrary to the commands of divine and natural law'.[204]

This school denies that it is important to see how physical human nature relates to human actions. They also fail to do justice to the idea that for morals one must understand how the intellect relates to judging goods and presenting them to the will to be desired.

THE SCHOOL OF FUNDAMENTAL OPTION

There is another school of contemporary Catholic morals which results from the general rejection of an objective idea of human nature which includes an assessment of the various actions of the powers of man and how they relate to each other. This is the school of the Fundamental Option. This theory has been very prevalent since the 1970s and is based on the existential rejection of the real idea of essences.

The most popular presentation of this theory is found in the article "The Sins of the Little One" published by Ladislas Orsy in *America*.[205] This article summarizes a shift in moral theology which was caused by a strange use of the classic definition of sin as *aversio a Deo, conversio ad creaturam* (the aversion from God and conversion to the creature). According to this theory, no one human choice can fully express the fundamental option of a man in relationship to God. Instead, this fundamental option has to be the result of a life long tendency or, if it is a grave sin, has to be the result of a conscious denial of God. This again reflects an opinion of Karl Rahner who maintained that the only truly personal choice a man made was in the moment of death between clinical and metaphysical death. Ladislas Boros sums up this idea. "Death is man's first completely personal act, and is, therefore, by reason of its very being, the centre above all others for the awakening of consciousness, for freedom, for the encounter with God, for the final decision about one's eternal destiny."[206]

The implications of this theory are that there is no single act of man which could be so against reason that as an act it would deny the possibility of union with God, except perhaps the final decision at the moment of death which is between clinical death and metaphysical death. Thus there would be no single act which is a mortal sin except perhaps apostasy because it entails the intention to deny God as such. Murder, adultery and missing Mass would not be considered mortal sins as single acts and so need not be confessed in confession because they do not entail the aversion from God as such.

Ladislas Orsy gives a new threefold variation on the former distinction between mortal and venial sin which Msgr. William Smith[207] maintains is also held by people like "J. Fuchs, J. Keenan, T. Kopfensteier, T. O'Connell, B. Häring, et al."[208] His new definitions are as follows: mortal sin—"is a free and permanent option by man to remain alone and to exclude God from his life;"[209] serious sin—"many acts that betray evil trends in the heart but do not necessarily bring about a radical break with God;"[210] venial sin—"is a refusal to grow ... a kind of tardiness in our pilgrimage with God."[211]

Msgr. Smith notes that the definition of mortal sin "is a fair description of 'impenitence,' which if it occurs at the end of life is called 'final impenitence.' What is newly called serious sin is an acceptable definition of venial sin—acts of trends that bring no radical break with God. Although vague and open-ended, the 'venial' sin description can stand, if it says anything at all."[212] The greatest difficulty with this redefinition is that the whole tradition that there are objective material deeds which in themselves involve a denial of a relationship with God is overturned and morals is again reduced to a vague subjective basis which in this case resides mostly in the human intention. This is contrary to the teaching of the Church represented in statements like that of John Paul II in *Reconciliatio et Paenitentia*:

> With the whole tradition of the Church, we call mortal sin the act by which man freely and consciously rejects God, his law, the covenant of love God offers, preferring to turn in on himself or to some created and finite reality, something contrary to the divine

will (*conversio ad creaturam*). This occurs in a direct and formal way, in the sins of idolatry, apostasy and atheism; or in an equivalent way, as in every act of disobedience to God's commandments in grave matter.[213]

The Pope teaches here that fundamental option theory is an error in which the evil of an individual deed can never deny one's relationship with God unless it is directly contrary to God. No individual deed regarding others or things like missing Mass could ever so express the existential stance of the person as to be a mortal sin.

THE SCHOOL OF NEW NATURAL LAW THEORY

The final school of thought which has great difficulty with the derivation of moral laws is one whose proponents wholeheartedly support the traditional moral teachings of the Church on the intrinsic evil of acts like contraception and abortion. This school is the great opponent of consequentialism. The difficulty is that this school accepts the philosophical presuppositions of the other two schools that real universals cannot be derived from the sense experience of man which could be applied to specific human actions. This school holds that there are certain actions which are always good and certain actions which are always evil, but these actions are self-evident and do not depend on knowledge of the actions which follow the powers of man to determine them, especially the powers of the body. Thus, one cannot determine the morality of the free use of human seed by an examination of the purpose God had in making human seed as a material thing.

Proponents of this theory are principally Germain Grisez, Joseph Boyle and John Finnis. According to Grisez, for example, there are eight basic human goods all of which must be experienced for a man to be perfect. "Grisez et al. ... argue that the first principles of natural law (including the basic human goods) are underived, that is, they are self-evident (*per se nota*). Thus, according to Grisez, et al., they do not rest on conclusions of anthropology or metaphysics."[214] "In his early work, Grisez articulated a number of theses that have been developed by the New Natural Lawyers in the subsequent decades. ... First, the New Natural Law view holds that practical reason, that is reason oriented towards action, grasps as self-evidently desirable a number of basic goods."[215]

It seems that this theory was developed to preclude any possibility of moderate teleology with the end justifying the means. These theorists also seem to accept the premise of the moderate teleologists that one cannot derive moral truths from examining physical actions like the sharing of seed in human intercourse. For them, this would be physicalism which would reduce the freedom in morals to a kind of determinism which would not be fitting to human actions. The New Natural Law Theorists have no reasonable basis from faculty analysis to maintain that contraception is always evil. For them, the argument proceeds primarily on the basis of the authority of the magisterium, whether Paul VI's teaching on contraception in *Humanae Vitae* is infallible teaching or not.

All three of these theories claim as their mentor Thomas Aquinas. Whatever else may be said of the merit of these theories, they certainly do not correspond to the teachings of St. Thomas. One text will suffice to show that faculty analysis about a physical action can lead to a judgment that a certain kind of physical action is always incompatible with arriving at the ultimate end of man.

> But more closely ordained to man's life than any external possessions whatsoever is human semen, wherein man is potentially; hence the Philosopher says in the *Politics* that in man's semen there is something divine, namely inasmuch as it is man potentially; and therefore deordination in regard to the discharge of semen is a deordination in regard to the life of man in proximate potency. Hence it is evident that every such act of lust is a mortal sin by reason of its genus. And since the interior appetite or desire derives its goodness or badness from that which is desired, it follows that even the desire of a disordered act of this kind is a mortal sin if it is fully desired, namely deliberately desired; otherwise it is a venial sin.[216]

This text makes the following point: if willed, a physical action does have a moral meaning. This moral meaning may make this action incompatible with the existence of grace in the soul. So it is a mortal sin. Since it is a mortal sin by genus, no consequences can make it good. Finally, at least in the opinion of St. Thomas, this fact is based on an observation by Aristotle which means that it can be known by reason alone through faculty analysis apart from the authority of the Church. This teaching is not self-evident then, but demands faculty analysis through reason since St. Thomas maintains the evil is caused by the fact that the seed is potentially a man.

The same denial of the accusation of physicalism and the affirmation that physical actions do in some cases have a moral meaning in themselves is taught in *Veritatis Splendor*.

> In this context, objections of physicalism and naturalism have been leveled against the traditional conception of the natural law, which is accused of presenting as moral laws what in themselves are merely biological laws. [...] Faced with this theory, one has to consider the correct relationship existing between freedom and human nature, and in particular the place of the human body in questions of natural law. [...] This moral theory does not correspond to the truth about man and his freedom. It contradicts the Church's teachings on the unity of the human person, whose rational soul is *per se et essentialiter* the form of the body. [...] The person, including the body, is completely entrusted to himself, and it is in the unity of the body and soul that the person is subject to his own moral acts. [...] A doctrine which dissociates the moral act from the bodily dimensions of its exercise is contrary to the teaching of Scripture and Tradition.[217]

While the school of the New Natural Law theory has been very beneficial in defending the traditional moral teaching of Church on subjects like birth control, its practitioners seem to fall into the same error of those who deny the Church's teaching on the same subjects. Analysis of the powers of the soul and the body in relation to the will have no place in this theory. Rather, goods are goods because authority has determined them to be so. Such a determination cannot be supported by an analysis of how a given human potential in soul or body relates to reason. These thinkers are essentially nomialists because they think that universal ideas gained from sense knowledge do not completely do justice to the thing known. This is especially true of the moral law.

As a result, moral reflection has its origin merely in discussions of whether a given action has been defined to be good or evil by authority. While this is a worthwhile discussion and arguments from authority are certainly the strongest arguments in theology, this limitation is a real problem when it comes to explaining Catholic morals to those who do not accept such authorities. Legions of important traditional arguments from reason are simply omitted.

SUMMATION

The only true Catholic understanding then is one which corresponds to the teaching in *Veritatis Splendor* and the *Catechism of the Catholic Church* which, following St. Thomas Aquinas, assigns the specification of good from evil to the intellect examining the various powers of the human soul in relationship to God, themselves and each other.

The true teaching is that the intellect which determines whether an action is good or evil truly leads to real moral laws which in many cases what must be done to guide the conscience. At times, these are determined by the use of the physical good in relation to the human soul which the moral subject is making. One can formulate universal moral absolute laws which are always and everywhere true.

CHAPTER SIX
THE INTELLECT: OBJECT, INTENTION AND CIRCUMSTANCES

THE OBJECT OF THE ACT

Moral being is like physical being. In physical being, there is no total evil. If there were, the thing which experienced the evil would not exist because evil is not a thing but the lack of due perfection in a thing. Physical beings are good by nature. To lack a randomly identified perfection of being is not evil either. It would not be evil for a rock to lack eyes, for example. A blind man does not suffer complete physical evil because he still may be able to walk. To lack a due perfection is evil. To have eyes but not to be able to see is a physical evil. To have legs but a curvature of the tibia which leads to walking lame is a physical evil. These things are evil because they are a lack of the fullness of form necessary for the perfect existence of that particular being.

In morally free choices, evil is not caused by a defect of form. Rather, evil in these choices results from the inability of the good chosen to truly arrive at the final fulfillment of man, the vision of God. Choosing something contrary to the order of reason precludes the proper order existing in the soul. Reason determines this order and so to act against the order of reason makes an act specifically evil. This forms the specific difference in human actions. The second great distinction in morals involves the specification of human acts as good or evil. The first great division was determined by the will: human act versus nonhuman act which determined responsibility. The second great division is good human act versus evil human act. This is determined by whether the thing chosen realizes human nature and its powers in an ordered way or not. "Just as a natural thing takes its species from its form; so an action takes its species from its object, like a motion takes it species from its end."[218]

The object of the act is not determined only by physical description or even by the presence of some physical goods. Just as natural being is not evil in every respect but only as lacking a quality necessary for its due perfection of an action, so a moral action is not evil in every respect but only in the sense that this action precludes the existence of the order of reason in the soul both respecting the powers themselves in relation to their end and in relation to each other. "Thus, the first evil in moral actions comes from the object, as to take what belongs to another."[219] Adultery, for example, is good on the level of having children, but is a disordered act because the sharing of seed in human beings demands a certain level of commitment for the perfection of the children brought forth which only the marital relationship can bring. "The truth is that wherever a man lies with a woman, there, whether they like it or not, a transcendental relation is set up between them which must be eternally enjoyed or eternally endured."[220] Homosexual couples may say that they experience love and love children, but the fact is simply that the child is not the fruit of their action because though they could have marital relations with a person of the opposite sex, they choose not to. There is something major lacking in their expression of sexuality from the standpoint of reason because it does not respect the physical difference of the sexes in relation to the sexual act. To maintain then that there are good consequences to an action prescinds from the first question which is: Is something lacking in a serious way in this action respecting the order of reason? "An evil action can have some effect in itself according to which it has goodness and being. Just as adultery can cause human reproduction insofar at it entails the union of man and woman, but not insofar as it lacks the order of reason."[221]

The moral object then cannot be deduced from mere physical description without considering how actions which look the same can relate differently to the order of reason. "By the object of a given moral act, then, one cannot mean a process or an event of the merely physical order, to be assessed on the basis of its ability to bring about a given state of affairs in the outside world. Rather, that object is the proximate end of a deliberate decision which determines the act of willing on the part of the acting person."[222] This order of reason is based on different sources also, each of which is complimentary to the other and ultimately depends on how God orders the universe in creation.

> Hence good and evil in human acts is to be understood according to that which is proper to man as

such; and this is reason. Therefore good and evil in human acts is considered according as the act is in agreement with reason informed by divine law, either naturally or by teaching or by infusion: hence Dionysius says it is evil for the soul to be contrary to reason, for the body it is evil to be contrary to nature.[223]

The *Catechism of the Catholic Church* concurs with this teaching as does *Veritatis Splendor*. The moral object is the first determination of good or evil.

The object chosen is a good toward which the will deliberately directs itself. It is the matter of a human act. The object chosen morally specifies the act of the will, insofar as reason recognizes and judges it to be or not to be inconformity with the true good. Objective norms of morality express the rational order of good and evil, attested to by conscience.[224]

The morality of the human act depends primarily and fundamentally on the 'object' rationally chosen by the deliberate will, as is borne out by the insightful analysis, still valid today, made by St. Thomas. In order to be able to grasp the object of an act which specifies that act morally, it is therefore necessary to place oneself in the perspective of the acting person. The object of the act of willing is in fact a freely chosen kind of behavior. To the extent that it is in conformity with the order of reason, it is the cause of the goodness of will; it perfects us morally, and disposes us to recognize our ultimate end in the perfect good, primordial love.[225]

Moral objects can be good, evil or indifferent depending on their relationship to reason. It is important to emphasize that the order of reason determines these differences. There are certain actions which it is always evil to choose. "Consequently, as the *Catechism of the Catholic Church* teaches, 'there are certain kinds of behavior that are always wrong to choose, because choosing them involves a disorder of the will, that is moral evil.'"[226] Some examples may be helpful here.

The fifth commandment forbids murder. The language of the commandment is "Thou shalt not kill." The killing here refers to human beings, not animals because of the presence of the rational soul. The common translation of the Hebrew text would be that killing here means "murder." The question arises: is every instance of the killing of a man murder? Many people today for various reasons have maintained that to have a consistent ethic of life a Catholic must be equally opposed to abortion, war and capital punishment. They would equate all of these actions as they all involve the death of a man.

Physically this is true, but physical description is not sufficient. The Catholic tradition has always maintained that with the proper distinctions, capital punishment and war are not murder. This is because the determining factor in the judgment of reason is that the affirmation of the right to life which the commandment protects is innocent human life. The key determining condition of the object being in accord or against reason is then provided by the word "innocent." If a person threatens innocent human life then they compromise their own right to life in this particular action. The *Catechism of the Catholic Church* specifies the fifth commandment:

> ...no one can under any circumstance claim for himself the right directly to destroy an innocent human being.[227]

> Scripture specifies the prohibition contained in the fifth commandment: 'Do not slay the innocent and the righteous.' The deliberate murder of an innocent person is gravely contrary to the dignity of the human being, the golden rule, and to the holiness of the Creator. The law forbidding it is universally valid: it obliges each and everyone, always and everywhere.[228]

The right of self defense is not an exception to the fifth commandment and this is true for both the individual and those who are lawfully constituted agents of the common good in society. Those who resist the attack on innocent human life are defending the right to that life. The fact that this is attacked either by an individual or a society allows that individual to defend his right to life and society to defend such a life. If innocent life has been taken, society has a duty to establish a punishment which affirms that right in a social context. In fact,

CHAPTER SIX THE INTELLECT: OBJECT, INTENTION AND CIRCUMSTANCES 117

the state has a right and at least a primordial duty to use even capital punishment if it is the only way to protect the lives of the citizens. This is not an exception to the fifth commandment caused by the greatest good to the greatest number which allows the state to violate an individual's right to life.

The state has the right and duty to invoke the death penalty for two reasons. This is the fitting punishment for one who has violated the right to life of the innocent citizens by capital murder and to defend the right of the innocent by rending the offender incapable of causing further harm.

> Moreover, 'legitimate defense can not only be a right but also a grave duty for someone responsible for another's life, the common good of the family or of the State.' Unfortunately it happens that the need to render the aggressor incapable of causing harm sometimes involves taking his life. In this case, the fatal outcome is attributable to the aggressor whose action brought it about, even though he may not be morally responsible because of a lack of the use of reason[229] [230].

Pope John Paul II in *Evangelium* Vitae makes an important distinction which seeks to limit the application of the death penalty to make it "very rare, if not practically non-existent."[231] This is not however because of the object of the act. One will notice that the object of killing in war, the policeman killing in the face of lethal force and the death penalty are affirmations of the right to innocent life of the citizens of a state who themselves who have a right to defend their personal lives in the face of a lethal threat. These penalties even affirm the right to life of the aggressor in every other context than his aggression. For one inmate on death row to kill another who is condemned to die would not be execution because an individual does not have a right to invoke the death penalty. The one who killed in this context would be a murderer. So, it simply does not serve to say that a consistent ethic of life demands a seamless garment in which all killing of human beings is the same from a physical description of the act. Abortion is always killing an innocent human being and always murder, no matter for what purpose. Capital punishment and wars are in themselves good if prosecuted for defense and with proper means. This is why the then Cardinal Ratzinger distinguished between these two questions in a letter to Theodore Cardinal McCarrick and Bishop Wilton Gregory representing the USCCB in June, 2004 on the subject of communion to dissenting politicians:

> Not all moral issues have the same moral weight as abortion and euthanasia. For example, if a Catholic were at odds with the Holy Father on the application of capital punishment or on a decision to wage war, he would not for that reason be considered unworthy to present himself to receive Holy Communion. While the Church exhorts civil authorities to seek peace, not war, and to exercise discretion and mercy in imposing punishment on criminals, it may still be permissible to take up arms to repel an aggressor or to have recourse to capital punishment. There may be a legitimate diversity of opinion even among Catholics about waging war and applying the death penalty, but not however with regard to abortion and euthanasia.[232]

For all these reasons, capital punishment and killing in self-defense, whether individually or in war, are good in object because they affirm and protect the right of innocent life. Euthanasia and abortion are evil in object because they deny the right of the innocent to live. This is true even though both the good in object and evil in object physically involve the death of a man.

A similar thing is true regarding contraception and natural family planning. A superficial examination of the material act might lead someone to conclude that the moral object of Natural Family Planning (henceforth: NFP) and contraception are the same since they both involve the spacing of birth. But actually the relationship of the two acts is completely different in object.

> In the light of the experience of many couples and of the data provided by different human sciences, theological reflection is able to perceive and is called to study further the difference, both anthropological and moral, between contraception and recourse to the rhythm of the cycle: it is a difference which is

much wider and deeper than is usually thought, one which involves in the final analysis two irreconcilable concepts of the human person and of human sexuality."[233]

The difference in object is demonstrated by many different criteria none of which is based exclusively on authority. "The choice of the natural rhythms involves accepting the cycle of the person, that is the woman, and thereby accepting dialogue, reciprocal respect, shared responsibility and self-control."[234] This is because in NFP the couple seeks to accept the rights of the Creator based on justice in the act. They are also cooperating in the natural infertility which the Creator has placed in the woman's cycle. In his groundbreaking book, *Love and Responsibility*, John Paul II explains at length the traditional teaching of the Church that the two purposes of marriage (the unitive and the procreative) form the background to the proper willing of the sexual act as befits the human person. This is based on the personalistic norm which has a two fold aspect as suggested in *Gaudium et Spes*, 24:3. "The first affirms that man is the only creature in the world that the Creator willed 'for his own sake'; the second consists in saying that this same man, willed in this way by the Creator from the 'beginning,' can only find himself through a disinterested gift of self."[235]

The differences between artificial contraception and NFP are these:

- NFP is person oriented because it recognizes that sexuality must involve life and self-giving to a person; contraception is pleasure oriented because it respects neither of these realities.

- NFP is not a method of birth control because it is not utilitarian since it respects these goods; contraception is merely a method to insure the maximum pleasure to the maximum number.

- NFP affirms both subject and object because it conforms to the order which the Creator himself has placed in the woman's cycle; contraception is subjective only because it respects no other law or order but the desire for pleasure.

- NFP respects divine providence in the act itself as it is open to the order of providence with the possibility of paternity and maternity; contraception simply seeks to deny the role of providence and uses an artificial technique to frustrate its designs.

- NFP is morally good by object when it flows from the personal affirmation of love and so is an exercise demanding self-control and the development of the virtue of chastity through periodic continence; contraception is simply directed against conception and demands not human self-control.

- In NFP, the natural and personal orders unite in intimate communion because in respecting the rights of the Creator, the couple go beyond the mere physical expression of love to a spiritual willing of the person for his own sake and in self-control find themselves in a disinterested gift of the self to the other; in contraception, the couple reduce love to its physical expression which provided it involves pleasure has no necessary personal dimension. Their action is completely self-absorbed and interested.

For all these reasons, though contraception and NFP look the same, they are completely different in moral object. NFP is good in object; contraception is evil.

Another excellent example of difference in object is between occult compensation, loans and theft. First, as always, the judgment has to be based not on some lapidarian value which is self-evident and falls from heaven but on a reasonable objective analysis of the matter involved, in this case the necessity of material possessions for the spiritual progress of man.

Before one can adequately define the object of theft, one must delineate the origin and natural character of private property. To do this, one must distinguish a three-fold basis for the possession of material goods. The first is the fact that such goods are necessary for the human race in this life because man has a body which serves the soul. Further, man has a participated dominion over the material things of the earth because he is the only creature with both a body and a spiritual soul. This dominion is reflected in the command God gave to Adam and Eve: "Br fruitful and multiply, and fill the earth and subdue it; and have dominion over the fish of the sea and over the birds of the air and over every living thing that moves over the earth." (Gen. 1:28)

This primordial dominion is realized in man's case by the necessity of possessing material goods. But this possession before the original sin would not have entailed the rights and sanctions of property. Rather, each person would have been given to according to his need because there was no desire to dominate. Man was spontaneously virtuous and there was no sin. So this dominion would have been realized in society by a perfect possession of material goods and there was no need to guarantee that each would be given according to his need by the institution of property. "In the beginning God entrusted the earth and its resources to the common stewardship of mankind to take care of them, master them by labor, and enjoy their fruits. The goods of creation were destined for the whole human race. [...] The universal destination of goods remains primordial, even if the promotion of the common good requires respect for the right of private property and its exercise."[236]

The necessity of private property enters because of the Original Sin when the desire to dominate enters the human race. The earth resists man's cultivation because man does not do this disinterestedly any more. He does not look upon himself as a steward by participation but as the absolute lord of material goods. This sense of ownership is realized in the competition for material goods which makes profit and personal wealth the only motive for material possessions and not the perfection of the soul. To ensure each one has his thing and what he needs to progress in his spiritual life, society enters by guaranteeing material goods through the institution of private property. "However, the earth is divided up among men to assure the security of their lives, endangered by poverty and threatened by violence. ... The right to property, acquired or received in a just way, does not do away with the original gift of the earth to the whole of mankind."[237]

Since property is a function of society defending the rights of the individual, property is a creation of society. Political society, then, can regulate its use. "Political authority has the right and duty to regulate the legitimate exercise of the right of ownership for the sake of the common good."[238] Regulation does not normally mean state ownership. It is not the purpose of the higher community to rob the lower community of its rights but to ensure that the lower community develops as it should. Thus the Church denies *laissez faire* capitalism which makes profit the only motive for economics. It also denies Marxism where there is no right to private property because the individual is merely a cipher of the State and all property is owned by the State.

When applied to theft, these considerations lead to the normal way of defining theft in moral theology, "the usurping of another's property against the reasonable will of the owner,"[239] precisely because this condition of the reasonable will of the owner is essential to object, given the objective nature and origin of property. A loan would be taking another's property according to his reasonable will. Occult compensation would be taking another's property when his will is not reasonable. "There is no theft if consent can be presumed or if refusal is contrary to reason and the universal destination of goods. This is the case in obvious and urgent necessity when the only way to provide for immediate, essential needs (food, shelter, clothing ...) is to put at one's disposal the property of others."[240] Theft, on the other hand, is an objective deprivation of another's goods when his will to retain them is reasonable because this demonstrates that the action is contrary to the primordial universal destination of material goods which are necessary for a person to progress in his soul.

In his defense of consequentialists on the occasion of the publication of *Veritatis Splendor*, Richard McCormick wonders why if the condition "against the reasonable will of the owner" serves to define theft, the same is not true in the sexual act. He takes this condition rightly to be an addition to the mere material act of taking another's thing. It does define the object. "Yet, when the same tradition deals with, for example, masturbation or sterilization, it adds little or nothing to the material happening and regards such a materially described act alone as constituting the object. If it were consistent, it would describe the object as 'sterilization against the good of marriage.'"[241] In fact, the tradition does make such a distinction. A hysterectomy preformed to excise a cancerous uterus as a cure for the cancer would not be evil but good as it has no contraceptive purpose morally. One performed simply for contraceptive purposes would certainly always be against one of the goods of marriage. It is impossible to conceive of a masturbatory act in which the goods of marriage could be realized.

What determines the difference in object in the two cases above? The difference is between the purpose of the generative power and the purpose of exterior material goods.

Those who argue against some material objects always being evil use the example of standing on the hands or chewing sugarless gum and compare it to contraception. The difference which founds the moral objects in these cases is the various natures of these powers. The hands are purely useful goods and though it may be difficult and unusual to stand on one's hands, this is not against their nature. The nutritive power does not really have a universal object. The health of each person's body is as diverse as the bodies themselves. For some, some foods may destroy this health; for others, the same foods may be necessary for this health and this has some individual determination. But the generative power is oriented to the good of the human race because of children and so has a universal meaning. As a result, there are some universal laws which govern the use of human seed.

> The act of procreation is ordered to the good of the species, which is a common good; and a common good can be prescribed by law but a private good is subject to the ordination of each individual: and therefore although in respect to the act of the nutritive power which is ordered to the preservation of the individual, each one may determine for himself the food appropriate to himself, nevertheless to determine how the act of procreation ought to be ordered does not pertain to the individual but to the lawgiver to whom it belongs to see to the proper ordering in regard to the propagation of children, as the Philosopher says in Book II of the *Politics*.[242]

The constant tradition of the Catholic Church affirms that the object of the act is the first basis for determining the good or evil of an action, that this is determined by reason, and this determination can occur regardless of the consequences or the greatest good for the greatest number. Also, there is a hierarchy in the goodness or evil of moral objects which is based on the hierarchy of human powers and their objects. It is in fact the hierarchy of goods which determines the "lowerarchy" of sins.

> The gravity that a sin has from its species is considered on the part of the object or matter, and according to this consideration a sin is called graver in accord with its genus, which is contrary to the greater good of virtue. Hence since the good of virtue consists in rightly ordered love, as Augustine says, and God ought to be loved above all else, the sins that are against God, idolatry, blasphemy, and other such sins, are considered the gravest according to their genus. But among the sins against our neighbor some are graver than others inasmuch as they are opposed to a greater good of our neighbor. And the greatest good of our neighbor is the person himself, to which is opposed the sin of homicide, which takes away the actual life of man, and the sin of lust which is opposed to the potential life of man, since it is a de-ordination in the action of human generation. Hence among all the sins against our neighbor the graver according to genus is homicide, but adultery and fornication and carnal sins of this kind hold second place, and theft and robbery and the like by which the neighbor suffers injustice in regard to external goods hold third place."[243]

This primary basis for the judgment of the moral object is the first but not the only means for moral determination. "Therefore in general it is said that some acts are good or evil generically, and that an act good generically is one bearing on a due matter, for instance, feeding the hungry, but an act evil generically is one bearing on an undue matter, for instance, taking what belongs to another, for the matter of an act is called its object."[244]

CIRCUMSTANCES

Though there are moral objects which are good or evil in themselves, there are actions which cannot be so judged by these universal considerations. Almsgiving is always good in object; murder is always evil. But one cannot determine whether walking is according to nature or not until one determines the context. Also, man's moral actions occur in the concrete not the abstract. So there may be further individual conditions which render an act in accord with or contrary to reason. Knowledge of these conditions is also necessary to make a complete moral judgment. The reason is that as is the case in nature, knowing the substance of something is not sufficient to have a complete knowledge of the being. A substance is a being which exists in its own right. But for a complete knowledge of some things, some further conditions which stand around and express the substance are necessary. These are called accidents. They do not exist in their own right, but must always exist in something else. Place is an accident, time is an accident, color is an accident. Normally these conditions are merely incidental to a knowledge of the nature of a thing. But sometimes they are vital information needed to have a complete understanding. The former kinds of accidents (the unimportant ones) are called separable accidents; the latter (the important ones) are called properties. A sense of humor and the social character are examples of properties in human beings.

In morals, accidents are called circumstances. "Circumstances are related to moral acts as accidents which are outside the definition of the species pertaining to natural things. But a moral act ... receives its species from its object as it is compared to reason."[245] This was demonstrated in the previous section. But in addition to this species of the object relating to reason, there is another determination which may add a further constituting condition to reason and this may affect how the action relates to attaining the end. This is the circumstance. "But to this goodness or badness can be added another goodness or badness from something extrinsic called a circumstance, such as the place, the time or the condition of the agent and so on, for example, if someone takes what does not belong to him from a sacred place or apart from need and the like."[246] Theft in a sacred place, for instance, is more sacrilege than theft and is more against the second commandment than the seventh.

Two points must be made about circumstances. As circumstances, they are truly exterior to the object of the act and so they do not constitute a moral species in themselves. However, the morally relevant circumstances do add a character of good or evil to an action insofar as they are according to or against reason. The circumstance of place as shown above can change theft into sacrilege. Also, some sins admit of parvity of matter and so would be considered mortal or venial depending on the circumstances. Theft, for instance, is venial if what is stolen is small in value; mortal if it is large in value. Of course, this can vary depending on the circumstances.

Secondly, as is the case with accidents, not all circumstances add further conditions which relate to reason but only those which affect the relation of the act to attaining the ultimate end of man as determined by reason. Normally, the hair color of the victim or the murdered is only a circumstance when it comes to the sin of murder. Place would normally not be a morally relevant circumstance. Whether or not a person were standing in point A or point B would normally not change the moral nature of the deed, unless these points were a church, for instance, which would again add a further constituting condition to the nature of the deed.

Regarding the argument of the consequentialists that an action cannot be fully morally determined until the morally relevant circumstances are known, this could be conceded in general with some distinctions. An action which is good in object could be rendered evil by circumstance. For instance, capital punishment is good in object, but if, as both Pope John Paul II and the *Catechism of the Catholic Church* teach, other means could insure the good which capital punishment protects, then to make use of the death penalty in those circumstances would be contrary to reason. "If, however, non-lethal means are sufficient to defend and protect people's safety from the aggressor, authority will limit itself to such means, as these are more in keeping with the concrete conditions of the common good and more in conformity with the dignity of the human person."[247]

By the same token, if a posse were to prosecute vigilante justice, even on a justly condemned capital criminal, they would be committing murder from circumstance. This is because only a lawfully designated officer of the common good or the state has a right to invoke such a punishment.

In the case of natural family planning and artificial birth control, these formally differ in object. Yet, if a couple were to practice natural family planning for slight reasons (for example, wanting another car or just not wanting children) this would be contraception by circumstance.

An action which may be indifferent from object, like walking or talking, may be determined to be good or evil by circumstance. The consequences of a deed are included in the circumstances. They are not in themselves part of the object. "The circumstances, including the consequences, are secondary elements of a moral act. They contribute to increasing or diminishing the moral goodness or evil of human acts (for example, the amount of a theft). They can also diminish or increase the agent's responsibility (such as acting out of a fear of death). Circumstances of themselves cannot change the moral quality of acts themselves; they can make neither good nor right an action that is in itself evil."[248]

Regarding the difficulties of the consequentialists, one could certainly say as Richard McCormick did in his reaction to *Veritatis Splendor*, that one cannot fully morally analyze an action until the morally relevant circumstances are considered. This is because something good in object can be rendered evil by circumstance. Also if something is evil, a circumstance can make the evil of a different sort or increase the evil of the action. However, the claim that all consequences must be known before an action which is evil from object can be determined to be morally evil is simply false. It does not matter how many people benefit from a direct abortion, the abortion is still contrary to the right to life of the innocent child and cannot be justified for any reason.

A similar thing is true regarding difficulties in accepting papal teaching regarding abortion, euthanasia, capital punishment and war. Abortion and euthanasia are always evil in themselves. No circumstance can justify them. War, capital punishment and a policeman killing in the line of duty are all good in object though circumstances may render them evil. Since circumstances are often difficult to evaluate and depend on extensive practical knowledge of a case, there may be a legitimate disagreement among Catholics about the morality of a given execution or war.

Cardinal Ratzinger reflected this problem in the already cited official communication he made to the USCCB in the persons of Theodore Cardinal McCarrick and Wilton Gregory. This teaching is based on a legitimate disagreement about specific conditions which may lead to a particular war or the specific conditions of a prison system in a given country.

In summary then, moralists must consider circumstances because:

> 1) They can add a further reason to the suitability or unsuitability of a given means to arriving at an end (e.g., to steal from a home or to steal from a church).

2) They can aggravate or diminish a good or evil (e.g., to steal a small amount or a large amount).

3) They can contribute to the praiseworthy or blameworthy character of an act (e.g., the widow's mite or ignorance of a circumstance).

They cannot, however, make an action which is already evil from object good.

INTENTION

Actions which are indifferent from the point of view of object and circumstances nevertheless can still be morally evaluated using a third criterion. This is the individual reason a person has while he is performing the deed. No action which is done from choice can be considered indifferent from this point of view. This is because every action must be done with an accompanying personal motive and this motive must be good for the deed to be wholly good. Merely doing an action absentmindedly or from fear may lead to a good action exteriorly but it will not interiorly form the person doing it regarding love for the ultimate end. "Hence, before a person has the virtue he may perform a virtuous act, yet in a different way than after he has the virtue. [...] So accordingly, it is evident that there is a threefold grade of goodness and badness in moral acts: first according to their genus or species as determined by comparison to the object or matter, secondly from the circumstances, and thirdly from the informing habit."[249] This reflects T.S. Eliot's remark in Murder in the Cathedral: "The last temptation is the final treason: to do the right thing, for the wrong reason."

This principle is also reflected by St. Thomas: "Actions which are by definition neutral are turned into good or bad actions in individual cases by attendant circumstances, by the intended goal if by nothing else."[250] This is because in addition to the objective order which is present in the action, there is the personal use the person makes of it in relation to the proximate or remote goal they are pursuing and since this results from choice, it has its own relation to reason.

This is not to justify an evil action from a good intention. Intention may add a further goodness to the good of an action which already exists, as to give a cup of water to someone for the love of God adds

CHAPTER SIX THE INTELLECT: OBJECT, INTENTION AND CIRCUMSTANCES

a further goodness to merely giving them the cup of water because of respect for the dignity of the human person. Intention may also change a good action into an evil action. For example, one who gives alms blowing the trumpet before him for the sake of vainglory. The receiver of the alms certainly benefits from this act of generosity, but because the intention was pride and not generosity, the donor experiences an interior deformation in this good action. This is because there are two ends in each exterior deed: the end it has in itself and the end which the doer intended. "Voluntary action is made up of the external activity the will is controlling (defined by the object of that activity), and an interior act of will controlling it (defined by the will's object, namely the goal of the activity). [...] Human activity is defined formally by its goal and materially by its external object."[251]

Since the purpose or intention for which the doer acts is the final interior implementation of his pursuit of his goal, the goal of the doer is the formal reason why an exterior act is performed. The exterior act is like matter to this form of interior life. However, St. Thomas is clear that the matter in this case is used in an extended sense as the subject which receives the action of the person performing the action. It is the matter about which a deed is done and not just a kind of inert matter out of which something is constructed which is indifferent to the purpose of the builder. But since the interior reason of the doer is more important than the matter about which the deed is done, judgment about the reason of this interior person takes precedence over the action which is the means or matter performed to accomplish it. "Human activity therefore is defined formally by its goal and materially by its external object."[252] A person who commits adultery in order to obtain entrance into a house so they may more easily steal something from the house is morally more a thief than an adulterer.

Since this is the case, could a person claim that a good intention gives form to the action which involves an evil matter which is premoral because it is not intended? To maintain this is to forget that for St. Thomas form and matter form two principles of the same being. They are used in a very general sense here. Since good comes from an integral cause, if the exterior act and the interior act are to be good, they both must be good. The goodness of the formal intention does not trump the evil of the exterior action but makes the exterior action an unfit means to carry out that good intention, for example, a contraceptive act while staying in the state of grace. This is not possible.

If the object of the external act is intrinsically related to the intention of the interior act then the two form one species. The example St. Thomas uses is fighting to achieve victory. There is one species of act and the interior act truly uses the exterior act in one flow of will towards the good.

If on the contrary, the object of the exterior act is not intrinsically related to the interior act, then the end of the internal act of the will cannot give the species to the object of the external act. The example St. Thomas uses is stealing to give alms. The interior intention of doing good cannot satisfy for the prior existing defect in relationship to human nature of stealing. The species of the intention would be good and the species of the exterior act would be evil. Since the exterior act is still willed, it falls under moral responsibility and so there are two moral species.

St. Thomas states the principle well: "If the object of an external activity is not intrinsically related to its goal (stealing in order to give alms), then the action belongs morally to two disparate species; otherwise (fighting to achieve victory) one species must be subsumed under the other."[253]

This is the answer to McCormick's statement already quoted that killing a child in the womb to save the life of the mother in the case of partial birth abortion is more life affirming and in the circumstances is the only way to affirm life. One may have the intention of affirming the value of life, but it is not possible to see even in these circumstances how the prior existing defect of directly attacking the life of an innocent human child can be cured by simply using it for the purpose saving the mother's life.

MORAL WHOLENESS

The objective judgment on the goodness or evil of human acts is based, then, on all three moral determinants. Just as a natural thing experiences evil of being when it lacks something necessary for its characteristic act, so a moral person experiences evil of action when the person does a free human act which is not in accord with reason from all three points of view. No action in the final analysis can fail to be evaluated unless it is done without freedom which falls under the area of the presence of the will. From the standpoint of the intellect, once one arrives at the intention, any given free act must be evaluated as either in accord with nature or not. Since a person becomes what he wills under the aspect of the thing itself which is willed, when a person wills an action which is contrary to reason, they forge a union with reality which is actually contrary to the reasonable order of the world as willed by God, especially the order in man.

This attachment precludes the order of reason being present in the soul of the person who wills it. If the attachment is about something truly serious in expressing man as he is created as an image of God, then there is a serious lack which results in the soul. Any given action which is contrary to the order of the world as created by God cannot be referred to God as an act of love. This is what is traditionally known as a mortal sin. This is because grace is the form of the soul as the soul is the form of the body. If this disorder is already present in the soul from some aspect of the object, the circumstances and intention cannot change that. In the example invoked from Richard McCormick, regardless of the benefit to the woman and the family which are clearly good things, the direct attack on an innocent human child is already contrary to justice and cannot be reconciled with love of God.

All three moral determinants must be in accord with nature for the action to be good.

> Four elements therefore contribute to a good action: first, its generic existence as activity to all; secondly, definition by an appropriate object; thirdly, the circumstances surrounding the act; and fourthly, its relation to a goal. Actions are good in the straightforward sense of the word only when all these elements are present: as pseudo-Denys says, any defect will make a thing bad; to be good a thing must be wholly good.[254]

ANSWERS TO MODERN PROBLEMS

In light of this teaching of the Church, it is important to identify the errors of all three of the moral schools mentioned already. Regarding consequentialism, this system is based on an error which comes from Nominalism. The nominalists of the Middle Ages basically held that the intellect only knew the concept, which was universal and expressed by the name (*nomen* in Latin) of the thing, not the thing itself. Thus, universal ideas were only present in the soul and their relationship to reality outside the soul was tenuous at best, non-existent at worst. When applied to laws which are universal statements of truth about human conduct, this means that there is no moral action which can always be said to be evil. Though there are many variations on this theme following Descartes, whom it will be remembered did not think one could arrive at true ideas through the senses, all the modern schools have in common the theory that no act can be evaluated just by considering it as a universal. It is this which led Rahner to his two-ethical-system theory in which universal statements were completely divorced from the individual conscience. He would say that universal statements may be recommendations, but certainly not commands. The way he put this was that it is absurd to hold that conscience consisted in merely the application of universal laws to particular cases because no universal can ever express every particular case.

Like all errors there is a lot of truth in what Rahner says if one is talking about human law. These cannot express every single case just because of the panoply of situations possible for human justice. However, it is quite a different story for natural law; universal expressions do apply to every case because they express human nature, albeit that this is sometimes difficult to capture in a universal human statement.

Another way of expressing Rahner's position is to maintain that one cannot judge an object of an act without all the morally relevant circumstances. This amounts to saying that all actions are indifferent regarding human nature until circumstances and intention are considered. Again there is something true about that statement because for good actions, all three of the moral determinants must accord with reason. Also, a circumstance can alter the nature of an action into another one if it is in accord with or contrary to reason. However, no circumstance or consequence can change an action which is evil itself into something good. The good desire to raise a child cannot justify artificial insemination.

The *Catechism of the Catholic Church* summarizes the rejection of consequentialism thus:

> A morally good act requires the goodness of the object, of the end, and of the circumstances together. An

evil end corrupts the action, even if the object is good in itself (such as praying and fasting 'in order to be seen by men'). The object of the choice can by itself vitiate an act in its entirety. There are some concrete acts—such as fornication—that it is always evil to choose, because choosing them entails a disorder of the will, that is, a moral evil. It is therefore an error to judge the morality of human acts by considering only the intention that inspires them or the circumstances (environment, social pressure, duress or emergency, etc.) which supply their context. There are acts which, in and of themselves, independently of circumstances and intentions, are always gravely illicit by reason of their object; such as blasphemy and perjury, murder and adultery. One may not do evil so that good may result from it.[255]

Regarding the fundamental option theory, this is based on a complete redefinition of the whole idea of sin. According to this redefinition, sin seems to be reduced to no more than a vague general intention throughout one's whole life which is generally directed towards God and is not implemented in any particular action. Using the traditional definition of sin from St. Augustine, conversion to creatures and aversion from God, adherents of fundamental option teach that one can convert to creatures by loving them in a way contrary to the order placed in them by God and NOT avert oneself from God. Msgr. Smith puts is well; "[...] the agent could claim that no matter what his activity, he or she is fundamentally opting toward God."[256]

Clearly, fundamental option would say that any objective evaluation of a single act from the standpoint of reason is precluded. This is especially true of any single mortal sin. Sin no longer involves serious matter which could be morally evaluated in one act. Whatever evil resides in an act is always pre-moral and a series of actions is required to judge one's life choice.

Veritatis Splendor rejects this reasoning because it is certainly possible to deny one's relationship to the ultimate purpose of life or indeed affirm it so as to merit heaven in one act which is sufficiently in accord with love for God or contrary to it. "To separate the fundamental option from concrete kinds of behavior means to contradict the substantial integrity or personal unity of the moral agent in his body and soul. A fundamental option understood without explicit consideration of the potentialities that puts it into effect and the determinations which express it does not do justice to the rational finality immanent in man's acting and in each of his deliberate decisions."[257]

Veritatis Splendor teaches that the traditional teaching on mortal sin is to be preserved. The fundamental option theory directly teaches that the only mortal sins are sins like apostasy or idolatry which are sins directed against God himself because presumably they would entail an intention which is an aversion from God. The traditional teaching of the Church has always maintained that there are material acts directed against human beings which are so contrary to the nature which God has created that, as is taught in the Ten Commandments, they *ipso facto* entail an option against the Creator. A serious attack on the order always involves contempt of the one who created the order. "This can occur in a direct and formal way, in the sins of idolatry, apostasy and atheism; or in an equivalent way, as in every act of disobedience to God's commandments in a grave matter."[258]

Finally, the New Natural Law Theory seems also contrary to this when it comes to material acts which involve the body. This theory seems to agree with the consequentialists in that those who propose it maintain that faculty analysis or anthropology derived from philosophy cannot be used to determine truth and falsity in moral conduct. Much of the admitted orthodoxy of this school seems to turn on the authority of the teachings involved. Though the argument from authority is the strongest argument in theology since it is a science based on faith, many of the teachings of the Church on the evil of contraception and masturbation can be derived from the natural law in faculty analysis.

Common everyday experience is sufficient to know the truths entailed here. After all, this is the normal way that all thinkers following Aristotle arrived at a realistic and objective metaphysics. To deny this also leads to some strange conclusions. For one thing, none of the basic human goods established by authority as simply good can be listed in a hierarchy so that one can surrender one for the sake of anther. Some of these thinkers even go so far as to maintain that Christ is not a perfect human being because he was not married. Or that priests and religious are truncated human beings because they are not married. One could also wonder if martyrdom is a good as to sacrifice one's life for the truth about God would seem to place truth before life as to important goods.

Traditionally, all human goods have been rated in a hierarchy based on the most noble powers of the soul. For instance, the virtues were rated by St. Thomas as to which were more noble. Charity has always been considered the highest of the virtues which gives form to the soul because it involves direct union with God. The Church has affirmed that the concept of the natural law embraced by this school cannot stand. "The Church has often made reference to the Thomistic doctrine of natural law including it in her own teaching on morality."[259] The traditional theory of a law which derives primarily from both Aristotle and the Scriptures is a necessary foundation for determining truth in moral theology.

CHAPTER SEVEN
THE PASSIONS

THE PLACE OF THE PASSIONS IN MORALS

The third power which is central to free choice is the passions which are variously divided between the concupiscible and irascible appetites. The participation of the passions in the moral act is necessary because man is an animal and also because they form, as we have said, a kind of "no man's land" between the spirit and the body. As such they participate in both realms. While not the central issue, they are present in every choice because a movement in the higher part of the soul must be accompanied by a movement in the lower part. Well-formed passions support spontaneity in good choices; ill-formed passions support spontaneity in evil choices.

There are eleven passions according to Aristotle most, of which are enumerated directly by the *Catechism*. Stoicism had a substantial influence on early Christianity; because of this, there was a long debate from early Christian times regarding the place of the passions in morals. This has been compounded today by the rediscovery of the passions in the 1960's as important human experiences. Basically, the moral problem of the passions can be summarized in two contrary and extreme schools of thought.

STOICISM

The school influenced by Stoicism[260] maintained that the passions were sicknesses of the soul. The passions were viewed as interfering with human freedom and were the principle cause of human beings acting contrary to their nature. They were, therefore, seen as evil in themselves. The best way to become virtuous, then, would be to become completely dispassionate. A perfect human being would be one who was cold, aloof and had no passions.

When applied to things like the pleasure in sexuality, this attitude led to the puritanical teaching that the pleasure a couple experienced in the sexual act was a tolerated evil for the sake of the goods of procreation and unity. Pope John Paul II discussed this when he was a philosophy professor:

> Another such is the rigorist or puritanical interpretation [...] This view [...] holds that in using man and woman and their sexual intercourse to assure the existence of the species *Homo* the Creator Himself uses persons as the means to an end. [...] seeking pleasure and enjoyment in intercourse—is wrong. [...] it is an intrinsically evil element, a sort of necessary evil. That evil, however, must be tolerated since there is no way of eliminating it.[261]

This understanding of virtues holds the passions in suspicion, as though they were evil in themselves. It also maintains that the virtues do not involve the passions at all. On the other hand, the classical idea of virtue which has been accepted by the Church would maintain that virtue should create a certain peace in the character. That includes the passions. For example, to exercise self-control based only on the passion of fear of sin and not on the choice of the good according to the truth of man is not really the virtue of temperance or fortitude. "The obsessive-compulsive patient's success in leading the moral life gives him a satisfaction that he may believe to be happiness. However, unless a person's satisfaction derived from willing and doing good is accompanied by the feeling of joy, his happiness as a person is incomplete."[262] If there is no joy and peace, there is no real virtue.

THE HEDONIST IDEA OF THE PASSIONS

The opposite extreme is the Hedonist interpretation of the passions and is equally problematic. In this approach, one should always indulge one's passions and any attempt to control them would produce a psychological complex. This is the contemporary idea of morals. Again, there is no need to control and direct one's passions. If it feels good, do it! Though this is the opposite extreme to the rigorist interpretation, extremes touch each other in this case. The passions should not be controlled and virtue involves merely using them for pleasure. "The transmission of life, procreation, is in this conception only a secondary end, an end *per accidens*. ... In this conception the person is reduced to a subject 'externally' sensitized to enjoyable sensory stimuli of a sexual nature."[263]

CHAPTER SEVEN THE PASSIONS 139

This hedonistic cultural climate led even Catholic theologians to a soft attitude on the nature of sexual sin. Indeed, for many Catholic moralists in the decades immediately following the 60s, the solution to modern problems with obsession about sexuality was to remove the stigma from sexual sin by suggesting that perhaps there are no sexual sins. In 1979, for example, the Catholic Theological Society of America produced a study concerning the morality of the passions connected with human sexuality called *Human Sexuality*.[264] According to this book:

    a) no physical expression of sexuality is in itself 'morally wrong or perverse' (*H.S.*, p. 110); consequently:

    b) even those sexual practices which people have up to now considered deviant do not clearly produce evil consequences either for the individual or for society (*H.S.*, p. 77);

    c) the use of contraceptives is 'wholesome and moral' whenever it helps couples to build 'a community of love' for one another (*H.S.*, p. 127);

    d) deliberate masturbation (even after unresisted indulgence in erotic imagery) is never a serious sin and can be an act of virtue (*H.S.*, pp. 220, 227);

    e) fornication and adultery are in themselves morally good experiences (*H.S.*, pp. 154-158, 178-179);

    f) 'living together', 'swinging', and communal sex are not morally unacceptable (*H.S.*, pp. 151-152);

    g) Jesus was indeed opposed to the exploitation of women by men, but He did not prohibit self-liberating, other-enriching forms of prostitution, fornication, or adultery, joyously performed, as long as there was genuine concern for possible third parties involved (*H.S.*, pp. 20-22, 30-31, 96);

    h) homosexuals have a moral right to homosexual activity and to homosexual self-expression in the eyes of civil society (*H.S.*, pp. 198, 214);

i) it is both harmful and unprofessional to 'moralize' with children who have the habit of sexual intercourse with animals (*H.S.*, pp. 229-230);

j) fetishism and transvestism are a physiological and therefore not a moral problem (*H.S.*, pp. 230-231);

k) the only presently effective treatment for transsexualism is a sex-change operation coupled with hormone treatments and supportive counselling (*H.S.*, p. 233);

l) even hard-core pornography is not immoral for adults except to the extent that it may exploit persons by reducing them to objects to be used (*H.S.*, pp. 235-237);

m) obscene words formerly not used in decent conversation are now just part of the common vocabulary (*H.S.*, p. 235).[265]

THE CORRECT IDEA OF THE PASSIONS

The two extreme positions regarding the passion simply fail to take account of the fact that the passions are natural components of the human psyche. The pursuit of virtue cannot involve the suppression of all the passions because in themselves the passions were created by God as a natural part of the human soul and they must be allowed to fulfill their God-given role. The rigorist thesis treats the passions as though they have no right to exist and the hedonist thesis that their satisfaction is the only human good to the expense of the intellect and the will. Virtue involves a middle course between these two extremes.

The life of virtue in fact involves the passions. The passions must be guided in self-restraining love by the intellect and will. This does not mean killed or indulged in with complete abandon. "It belongs to the perfection of the moral or human good that the passions be governed by reason."[266] This leads to a real difference in the way the intellect and will govern the members of the body and the passions. The members of the body have no knowing or desiring power and so they cannot resist the command of the intellect and will. But the passions have sense knowledge to guide them and sense desire and so they can resist the command of reason.

> Hence, Aristotle says in the *Politics* that the soul rules the body as a despot would, as a master rules a slave who does not have the capacity to resist the master's command. But reason rules the interior parts of the soul by a royal and political governance, that is, as kings and princes rule free men who have the right and capacity to resist to some degree the commands of the king or prince.[267]

The passions are not moral as such, but they are always present in the human psyche. Since they have an affective life of their own, they are taken up into the virtues and can make virtuous acts more spontaneous. On the other hand, they can also pervert the vices more and make them more freely desired.

After the Original Sin, the passions tend to arise in us before reason can be brought to bear and color our judgment. It is precisely for this reason that the formation of the passions in a good way is so essential to morals. When the appetites are not suppressed, but participate in the reasonable good, there is a peace in the character and the person truly enjoys doing the good more freely.

FORMATION OF THE PASSIONS AND FREEDOM

The correct and reasonable formation of the passions is the basis for an important distinction made in Aristotle and further enunciated by St. Thomas between the temperate and the continent man. A person who is continent avoids sin, but without the passions being integrated. He may in fact avoid sexual sin, but without enjoying it. He does so without peace. It is therefore easy for him to fall into sin. The temperate man also avoids sin, but because there is a quality introduced into his passions which makes them easily amenable to reason, it is very hard for him to sin and he really enjoys being virtuous. He is not weak.

The opposite is true for the intemperate and incontinent man. The incontinent man does evil actions motivated by the passions but is always torn in their regard. He does not really like them. He is weak. The intemperate man really enjoys sins against temperance and they are deeply rooted in his character. He can convert but it is much more difficult and he must live with a certain resistance in his character for a long time to his conversion.

Many people influenced by Stoicism and the common experience of the human race thought that the passions themselves should not be involved in human freedom. Although they are not found in those powers which control human freedom as such, the intellect and the will, in themselves any actions in the higher part of the soul must take them into account.

Their bad reputation is due not to them, since they were created by God, but to the weakness of will man has after the Original Sin regarding them. This weakness is the cause of some people thinking that virtuous life means not having passions at all. After the Council of Trent, the passions were held in especially bad repute by those who were very interested in the reform of the Church. Unfortunately, their zeal was sometimes misplaced and they tended to suggest that those who had virtues would have no objects in their passions. This is contrary to common sense, since they are natural motivating factors in man and also to traditional teaching like that of St. Thomas. "It does not pertain to virtue to deprive the powers subject to reason of their own proper actions, but to make them carry out the commands of reason in their own characteristic acts."[268]

St. Thomas maintains with Aristotle that the virtues do not destroy the passions. "Virtue overcomes inordinate passion; it produces ordinate passion."[269] By ordinate, one must emphasize that St. Thomas does not mean small passions or passions which are not intense. Ordinate in this case means those which fit the case according to reason. If one is strongly drawn to a true good or to reject a true evil, the passions which accompany that in a virtuous person should be equally strong. In reaction to all Stoical distrust of the passions in themselves, St. Thomas concludes, "By reason of a kind of overflow (from the intellect moving the will), the more perfect a virtue is, the more it causes passion."[270]

Though it is true one must deny inordinate passions which lead one to only be concerned for satisfying the ego at the expense of the truth, a person who is really virtuous should enjoy the good and experience real sadness at evil. The case is clear in Job. St. Thomas was the first person in the history of the Church to write a commentary on the literal sense of the book of Job. There is a famous patristic commentary on the allegorical sense, the *Moralia* of St. Gregory the Great. The reason is that the Church was influenced by Stoicism and it was difficult for theologians and spiritual writers to understand how Job could be considered a just man and curse the day of his birth. It seemed too passionate.

St. Thomas is clear that the intense emotional outpouring of Job is most moral and virtuous and corresponds to ordinate passions.

> The Stoics said that there was no place in the wise man for sorrow. The Peripatetics said that the wise man is indeed sad, but in sad things he conducts himself with a moderation in accord with reason. This opinion accords with the truth. For reason does not take away the condition of nature. It is natural to sensible nature to rejoice and be pleased about fitting things and grieve and feel pain about harmful things. So reason does not take away this natural disposition, but so moderates it that reason is not deflected from its right course because of sorrow. This opinion also accords with Holy Scripture which places sorrow in Christ, in whom there is every fullness of virtue and wisdom.
>
> So, Job then indeed feels sad as a result of those adversities which he suffered described above, otherwise the virtue of patience would have no place in him. But his reason did not desert the right path because of sorrow but rather ruled the sorrow. This is proved when the text says, 'After this, Job opened his mouth.' 'After this' means after he had passed seven days in silence. This clearly shows that what he is going to say is said in accord with a reason which is not confused by sorrow. In fact, if they had been spoken from a mind confused by sorrow, he would have said them sooner, when the force of sorrow was more acute.[271]

So the passions are like tools of the will, albeit tools with a knowing and desiring life of their own. If one were an expert carpenter but tried to make a bench with a bent saw, it would be impossible. In a similar way if the intellect and will are to sufficiently guide free human choices, the passions must be well formed to support this guidance. So they must be respected and habits must be introduced into them which make them easily amenable to the movement of reason and will.

Dr. Conrad Baars compares this moral formation of the passions to a horse and rider. Through long training and education, the horse and rider establish a rapport which allows the horse to do most of the work in getting the rider where he is going. If the rider just lets the horse go where he wills, the horse can lead the rider to his death. On the other hand, if one seeks from fear or energy to beat the horse into submission, then the horse may become weak or die. The rider is left to go it alone by sheer will power which can never be truly integrating in man.

> In the end, the rider, having become an expert horseman, was free to go where he wanted because the horse had become a willing servant instead of a slave subdued by force.
>
> The neurotic person is represented by a big, strong, muscular rider mounted on a partially crippled, half-starved, nearly exhausted, pony-size horse. It requires much kicking, shouting, and pulling of the reins by the rider to make the horse go where he wants it to go. Every ride exhausts both the rider and the horse.
>
> The psychopathic personality is represented by a big, spirited, but untamed horse by a seemingly experienced rider. On almost every ride the horse throws the rider and runs off aimlessly. The rider's efforts to train the horse are in vain—he never learns to control him properly. Only when the horse has grown old does the rider seem to attain a measure of control over him.[272]

The passions must also be taken seriously in morals because in addition to the natural tendency in them as such to obey reason, each person has an individual natural orientation of his passions to some virtue. This is because of the union of the soul with the body. Each person's body is different and so each person has a natural inclination to some virtues but not to others. This is insufficient for moral formation because one must have all the virtues and if one merely indulges his inclinations to one or two virtues, he will fail to develop the other virtues and perhaps even develop vices as a result. Human integrity demands all four of the cardinal virtues for example. One may be courageous, but not just. One may be just but not temperate, and so forth. The unity of the powers of the soul is the origin of this. These cardinal virtues form the one unity of action of all the powers which participate in human freedom. Prudence forms the intellect to judge correctly. Justice forms the will to love correctly. Fortitude forms the irascible passions to pursue good and resist evil despite risk. Temperance forms the concupiscible passions to enjoy pleasure and feel pain without detracting from spontaneously embracing the true good in the will.

The natural tendency of the individual person to one virtue and not to others is traditionally called the temperaments: the choleric (anger), melancholic (sadness), sanguine (superficial joy) and phlegmatic (fear). Whereas the doctrine of the temperaments is based somewhat on outdated physical science, the fact remains that pastorally people are brought to virtue by many different routes depending on their emotional tendencies. One size does not fit all.

Anyone doing spiritual direction, confession, or simply moral education must be aware that there is a definite subjective element in morals. Not that the standard of good and evil is subjective. This is determined by reason. But the manner in which people live up to this standard differs for different people and different sexes. All have the same reason, but since knowledge comes through the senses, and willing is expressed in the passions, one who does direction must take account of the emotional orientation of the person he is directing. The consideration of the contribution of the passions to human spontaneity in doing good for each individual is essential for this judgment.

So, the formation of the passions is as important as the formation of the will by reason. Reason is not the enemy of the passions, but the friend of passionate formation. Because of concupiscence, reason must deny certain experiences of the passions, but also form others which lead to a true joy and pleasure experienced in a human way. Only then can man experience integration in the human act. The words of Scripture are then fulfilled which the *Catechism* quotes in this context: "My heart and my flesh sing for joy in the living God." (Ps. 84:2; quoted in *CCC* 1770)

CHAPTER EIGHT
LAW

LAW AND MORALS

In his encyclical on the consequentialists, *Veritatis Splendor*, John Paul II laments the fact that almost every teaching in moral theology is questioned in the post-Vatican II Church:

> Today, however, it seems necessary to reflect on the whole of the Church's moral teaching, with the precise goal of recalling certain fundamental truths of Catholic doctrine which, in the present circumstances, risk being distorted or denied. ... It is no longer a matter of limited and occasional dissent, but of an overall and systematic calling into question of traditional moral doctrine, on the basis of certain anthropological and ethical presuppositions.[273]

He summarizes the core of the problem: "At the root of these presuppositions is the more or less obvious influence of currents of thought which end by detaching human freedom from its essential and constitutive relationship to truth."[274]

The truth spoken of here is what is traditionally understood to be human reason. The real issue in determining the object according to reason is the ultimate origin of this reason. Catholicism has traditionally held with Aristotelian philosophy that the origin cannot merely be human reason itself. Instead, since man can only discover the truth by examining the objective world, his reason is determined by that and the truth of the external world is in turn the result of the higher truth which is its origin, the truth in God's mind. "Man's reason can lay down standards by which the goodness of men's wills must be measured, because it is a reflection of God's reason, the eternal law."[275]

The source for the three moral determinants already discussed is the law. An understanding of the nature of law and its kinds is central to fundamental morals. Before embarking on this, some analysis must be made of the crisis of truth which has led Pope Benedict XVI to say that there is a "dictatorship of relativism" and Pope John Paul II to state that there is a crisis in the exaltation of freedom over truth. Human freedom would create the truth. There would be no other standard for the moral determinants than our freedom. "Certain currents of modern thought have gone so far as to exalt freedom to such an extent that it becomes an absolute which is the source of values."[276] There would be no objective prior nature which our freedom must express, but man would create his being as he went along. "Taken to its extreme consequences, this individualism leads to a denial of the very idea of human nature."[277]

The relativism of truth is very much related to all the errors examined already in this book. They all result from a nominalism or existentialism which is based on a denial of a real objective human nature which is the standard for truth. Those who think this may reduce freedom either to a statistical study (e.g., most Catholics disagree with papal teaching on contraception, so it must be changed), a complete autonomy from physical or biological nature (thus, removing the body from a consideration of human freedom), or the "untrammeled advancement of man's power"[278] In this view, cultural need would, thus, create man, who would be ever-changing depending on which culture or environment he was in. "Indeed, when all is said and done man would not even have a nature; he would be his own personal life-project. Man would be nothing more than his own freedom!"[279]

Instead, both reason and faith teach that: "What the law requires is written on their own hearts." (Rom. 2:15) There is an objective standard for the truth of human reason to which human reason is servant because man did not create himself. This objective standard is God's reason, the source of which is the eternal law.

A complete explanation of that law which is the source of man's moral determinants is found in Thomas Aquinas. For St. Thomas, the source of all reason is the idea present in God's mind when he creates the world, a creation which not only occurred in a time but which must be continuous. God's thought is the source of the distinction in created things and the ultimate blueprint or model on which all the things in the cosmos are based. "The Council refers to the classic teaching on God's eternal law. St. Augustine defined this as 'the reason or the will of God, who commands us to respect the natural order and forbids us to disturb it.' St. Thomas identifies it with 'the type of the divine wisdom as moving all things to their due end.'"[280]

To understand the original conception of St. Augustine and St. Thomas about eternal law, one must have reference to Plato. As is well known, Plato basically held there were three levels of reality in knowledge: the Good, the material things and the Divine Ideas which were neither the Good, nor the material things. When St. Augustine began to explain the nature of truth as the source of the world, he used these ideas of Plato, but modified them to fit a Christian context. He preserved the Good which would be God and the material beings, but did not consider them illusions as did Plato. They are real. It is true the ideas are spiritual, universal and real but they do not enjoy a middle existence between the Good and the things. Instead, they are seeds truly present in the mind of God, the *logikoi spermatikoi*, the *rationes seminales*, the reasonable seeds which are perfectly expressed in each individual existing material being. The idea or concept of a tree is spiritual as God conceives it, but material as each created tree reflects this original plan in God's ideas.

In the same way, when man understands the tree the concept shares in both the being of the tree and his own being. It is material as expressing the nature of the individual material tree and spiritual and universal as expressed in a spiritual intellect. This can only be the case in human knowledge because God gives the human intellect a participation in his divine light called reason which allows man to experience singular, material beings in universal spiritual ways. "The eternal law is indeed nothing else than God's wise plan for directing every movement and action in creation."[281]

In his use of this concept, St. Thomas is at his synthesizing best. He adapts a definition and idea taken from ordinary human law in everyday life and expands it analogously to express the eternal plan present in God's mind as the source for all the actions in the universe. To fully understand eternal law and its application to morals, one must understand this definition.

Thomas Aquinas' classic definition of law is: "An ordinance of reason made for the common good by the one who has care of the community and promulgated."[282] Some explanation is in order so that one may apply this definition to the conscience and the moral determinants.

First, it is important to point out that this definition includes all four of the famous four causes of Aristotle and so this is a complete explanation and proper definition of law. As a result, one must examine each one of the causes in this definition.

LAW: AN ORDINANCE OF REASON

The law is an ordinance of reason. For St. Thomas, this is the formal cause. The formal cause is what makes a thing to be what it is. The law must be an expression of reason or the truth about the objective order. There has long been a philosophical dispute as to what forms the essential nature of law, both the natural and the positive. One school of thought emphasizes the will as the power which is the primary basis for law. This is the voluntarist school. The other emphasizes the intellect. This would be the intellectual school. Though both of these philosophies agree each law is a product of a combined action of the intellect and will of the legislator and directed at the same powers in the subject, they disagree as to which one of these elements would be primary. This disagreement has important ramifications regarding the nature and location of the moral obligation to obey the law. Is law just a question of competing wills with the more powerful will obliging obedience? Should explanation and reason be a part of a command for it to oblige?

The intellectual school is generally represented by Thomas Aquinas. Since the place of reason in the law is of a formal nature for him, the primary task of the legislator is to direct the subject concerning the various objects which comprise the good of reason in a proposed or accomplished kind of conduct. Once the subject understands these objects, then moral obligation begins. Though the will is the place where this conduct is implemented because it involves a moral act, it is the intellect which constitutes the informing good.

The voluntarist school is represented by Duns Scotus and Francisco Suarez. According to this school, only the power of the will of the one making the law is the source of its obliging nature. Though the law must be reasonable, this is not the determining factor in its obligation. The will of the lawmaker would be arbitrary and this is born out above all in the will of God. God's will does not have to accord with his truth. Though there is something true in this analysis, Ockham drew the extreme conclusion that God has no restriction on his will, not even contradicting himself. Suarez, who was the great

Jesuit synthesizer after the Protestant Reformation, drew a further conclusion that even the natural law was only arbitrary in nature.

> In one of his works, Suarez asks whether the law is an act of the intellect or of the will. After presenting different opinions, he supports the voluntaristic view that law is an act of the will of a person in authority by which he wills the subject to be bound. Suarez applied this conclusion first to positive law, and later also to the natural law, even though he did not deny that what the natural law requires or forbids is intrinsically good or evil. In order to solve this apparent contradiction, he arrived at the following compromise: 'Although there is a kind of moral value independent of God's commandments, the natural law derives its character of law and legal obligation, in the fullest sense of the word, only through the will of the divine authority.'"[283]

The voluntaristic school became even more predominant in the contemporary world because of the influence of Immanuel Kant. For Kant there were two kinds of moral norms: utilitarian and deontological ones. The utilitarian laws were laws only because they were useful to some further good. The deontological ones were laws just because they were good. There was no deriving them from human nature by reason because there was no real human nature to derive them from. They fell from heaven in a lapidarian sort of way. There was also no hierarchy of goods. In other words, reason could not investigate or define the true good in law by examining the material world.

The problem with the voluntarist view is that it limits the obligation of the law merely to two competing wills. On the contrary, St. Thomas is clear that though the material cause of law, the subject where it is implemented is the will of both the legislator and the subject, the intellect of both is the formal stimulus for this implementation. The intellect of the one making the laws engages the intellect of the one obeying the laws presenting the good to be done and this forms the basis of the moral obligation which engages the will. As a result, a law which is not reasonable (e.g., a sin) cannot oblige in conscience and is a usurpation of law. It does not matter how powerful the will of the one making the law is.

LAW: THE COMMON GOOD

The purpose of the law must be a good which the subject cannot attain on his own. Otherwise, he would not need a law. This is called the common good. The common good can be defined as both the end and the order of the community. The order is the means which exists for the sake of the end and every end entails its own fitting order. To determine a given order then, one must determine the end of a given society and analogously this includes the end of the universe and the whole human race as in the case of the eternal and natural laws. Since law is an ordinance of reason, every end and every order must be morally good, must be a true common good of more than one, not just some self-interest group which has more power than another and this law must respect the proper hierarchy of other values. The common good is not just the sum total of the material goods of the "greatest good for the greatest number."

> Thus the priority of the common good, its superiority over the partial or individual goods does not result solely from the quantitative aspect of the society; it does not follow from the fact that the common good concerns a great number of the majority while the individual good concerns only individuals or a minority. It is not the number or even the generality in the quantitative sense but the intrinsicalness (*sic*) that determines the proper nature of the common good.[284]

This means that the truth must govern both the end and the order of the community and the law must respect this truth. Both the means and the end must respect the truth of human nature. The "intrinsicalness" spoken of above refers to a realization of human powers which one cannot experience simply left to himself. For example, in the virtue of justice one does not need a further habit in the will to will one's own good. But one does need a further habit in the will to will the good of another (justice) or the good of God (charity). One cannot sacrifice the truth of a prior existing human nature to either the end or the order of the community, nor can they be sacrificed to each other. Order without end is totalitarianism or an exaggerated social bureaucracy; end without order is chaos. Plato thought the difference between a tyranny and a democracy, oligarchy or monarchy rested on the fact of whether the authority in either of these governments preferred their private good to the common good or vice versa.

The Church has set the standards for the common good determined according to the truth:

> First, the common good presupposes respect for the person as such. In the name of the common good public authorities are bound to respect the fundamental and inalienable rights of the human person. [...] Second, the common good requires the social well-being and development of the group itself. Development is the epitome of all social duties. [...] Finally, the common good requires peace, that is, the stability and security of a just order. It presupposes that authority should ensure by morally acceptable means the security of society and its members.[285]

LAW: AUTHORITY

Finally, the law must be made by a competent authority. One who has not been constitutionally established in a human community cannot make laws. He can correct as a private citizen, but his laws have no binding force on the conscience. This is the efficient cause or how something becomes a law. If one seeks to impose laws without the proper authority, this is unjust usurpation and such laws cannot bind the conscience to action. Rather they are examples of institutionalized violence.

Included in the efficient cause is the tool which the effective authority must use in order to inform the person who is bound by the law of what the law is. The law must be promulgated. One cannot obey a law unless he has the possibility of knowing it is the law. The word "obedience" comes from the Latin word *obaudire* which means literally "on account of listening" but by extension means "to obey." Human laws are normally promulgated orally or in writing as in the saying: "So let it be written, so let it be done."

St. Thomas uses this definition to explain all the various kinds of law though in an analogous way. The primary model for all law is eternal law which is the paradigm in God's mind of all the things he has made in creation. As stated already, this paradigm relates to all creation and is present in God's mind as an efficient cause. It is promulgated by creation.

THE NATURAL LAW

The primary source of this truth present in God's mind for human conduct is the natural law. This differs from eternal law in that it is present in man's mind and promulgated by his very reason. When man begins to think about all the various goods to which the powers of his soul are oriented, their order and hierarchy and how they relate to the ultimate end by means of his God-given reason, he is participating in the eternal law for man. When he applies this to human conduct, he is expressing the natural law. "The natural law enters as the human expression of God's eternal law."[286]

Since human nature is unchanging, the natural law is basically unchanging as well. Only those who do not think that universal ideas can express real things and moral reasoning involves logical application of universal principles which are real to individual human actions think that the natural law is completely culturally conditioned. One example of this sort of reasoning is found in the works of John T. Noonan.[287] In an article he wrote in *Theological Studies*, called "Development in Moral Doctrine," he first asserts: "That the moral teachings of the Catholic Church have changed over time will, I suppose, be denied by no one today."[288] Noonan gives some examples of these changes. "In the course of the displacement of one set of principles, what was forbidden became lawful (the cases of usury and marriage); what was permissible became lawful (the case of slavery); and what was required became forbidden (the persecution of heretics)."[289]

There are several possible reasons for these changes but Noonan summarizes what he thinks is the proper explanation which corresponds to moral theology after Vatican II. As a basic principle, he quotes Bernard Häring: "Christ does not become greater through ongoing history, but our knowledge of the plan of salvation which is revealed in this world in Christ does become more complete and close to life in our heart through the working of the Spirit in the history of the Church and above all in the saints."[290] Though this principle is generally true, the truth of it depends on the basis for the origin of the change.

For Noonan, this explanation must be sought in the changing social structures of the Western word and perhaps other cultures. He summarizes the work of the moralist Louis Vereecke: "Moral theology is where the unchanged gospel encounters changing cultures."[291]

CHAPTER EIGHT LAW

It would seem on this basis that the understanding the Church has of human reason based on human nature can only be truly discovered in a historical evolution which includes continuous dialogues with the culture in which the Church finds herself. This would mean that cultural influence could lead the Church to constantly modify her understanding of moral truth and that there would be no unchanging objective human nature underlying this understanding. In fact, Noonan thinks this is what has happened with certain Church teachings on morals. "The gospel as interpreted by Protestants and as mediated by Rousseau and the revolutionaries of 1789 achieved much. [...] All these factors, plus re-evaluation of the words of Christ, created the new moral doctrine."[292] Ultimately, "All will be judged by the demands of the day in which we live. [...] Must not the traditional motto *semper idem*[293] be modified, however unsettling it might be, in the direction of *plus ça change, plus c'est la meme chose?*"[294],[295]

This way of looking at morals can very easily be reconciled with consequentialism. Though it may be true that certain objective expressions of the actions befitting human nature may admit of cultural variation (for example, the manner in which property is determined), to suggest that a continuous dialogue with the culture is necessary for the Church to discover the full truth of the Gospel about human reason is to reject an objective human nature. There really would be no natural law then, but merely a continuous re-evaluation of human conduct which would not be the same over time or in every place and culture. Of course, this could easily lead a moralist to claim that what the Church considered evil in one culture or epoch (for example, polygamous marriage or contraception) could become a good with the further development of culture or times. If contraception and polygamy are truly contrary to human nature, this must be for every culture and in every time. There may be an evolution in Church teaching, but this must be homogenous and not heterogeneous. It must include and approve the former teaching as an adult does a child and not disagree with it.

Pope John Paul II comes down succinctly on the side of the unchanging human nature which is the source of the natural law which each man may discover in his reasoning by examining the powers of his soul in *Veritatis Splendor*: "The Church has often made reference to the Thomistic doctrine of natural law including it in her own teaching on morality."[296] He quotes Leo XIII approvingly: "It follows that the natural law is itself the eternal law, implanted in beings endowed with reason, and inclining them towards their right action and end; it is none other than the eternal reason of the Creator and Ruler of the universe."[297]

So, the Church has made a part of her own teaching the explanation of St. Thomas that the truth of human nature is something which is objective and immutable. Human beings can know this because they have an intellect and can penetrate to the mind of the Creator who guides man by examining the various powers of the human soul, the goods to which they are ordered and their relationship to each other in a hierarchy. This analysis leads to the general prescriptions of the natural law and are the same for everyone. Pope Benedict expressed this well in a Wednesday Audience conference he gave on John of Salisbury: "… what John of Salisbury calls the 'tyranny of the sovereign' or, what we would call 'the dictatorship of relativism,' ends up taking over—a relativism that … 'recognizes nothing as definitive and that has as its measure only the self and its desires.'" (*Misa pro eligendo Romano Pontifice*, homily, April 19, 2005)[298]

Though this is true, it is also true that it is not always easy to know the truth of the natural law in practice. This is true both because of the nature of practical reason and also of the darkness of the human intellect after the Original Sin. "But in practical matters though the general starting points are true and right for you as for me, particular courses of action are not; and even when they are, not everyone knows it. Usually deposits ought to be refunded, but cases occur when it would be dangerous and therefore unreasonable to do so: when, for example, what is refunded would be used against one's country."[299]

The natural law is a reflection of the eternal law and is objective, but it is not sufficient to guide all human action. However, the natural law is something which is not externally enunciated as such and takes place in the inner understanding of each man.

HUMAN LAW

In addition to the natural law, there is need for practical judgments in the ordinary arena of human society. This law is human law and it is not sufficient to have it merely determined by individuals who exercise judgment. It should be enunciated by the group and preserved orally or in writing by more that one man.

Aristotle thought it 'better to regulate issues by law than to leave them for judges to decide.' It is easier to find the few wise men needed to frame good laws than the many needed to judge every case aright. Laws can also be formulated at leisure from accumulated experience, whereas particular cases have to be judged under pressure as they crop up. And finally lawmakers making general judgments for the future are likely to be less prejudiced than those sitting in judgement over immediate issues.[300]

Man is by nature a social animal. There have been several contradictory currents of thought about the origin of society in the last several hundred years. One extreme is the theories of the social contractualists who are usually taken to be Hobbes and Rousseau. According to this theory, society is an accident to human nature. It is completely formed by the free consent of man. The human will, therefore, creates not only society but also the truth of law. According to Hobbes, in the primitive state of men there was no society, no other measure of human good than utility, the innate instinct of self-preservation, the war of all in all. *Homo homini lupus* (man to man is a wolf). To Hobbes, man is naturally anti-social. To put an end to this condition, man created society and erected the great social institutions, whose mind and soul was the ruler informing all the governing members. Nothing was just by nature before the creation of these institutions. This was called the social contract. The contract created justice and authority. What is called theft, homicide, adultery or any injustice in the civil order is not evil by nature but only by civil institution.

This same opinion that the social character is an accident is shared by Rousseau but for different reasons. For him, man by nature is asocial but not because a state of war exists, but a state of friendship. Man in the beginning led a life of contentment with no desires, envies or struggles. He little by little developed art, agriculture, class, property and riches and these led to discord and usurpation. To do away with the evil caused by these things, man was driven to make a pact. This was the origin of society which is a creation of the people as opposed to the sovereign and to which every man must cling like a plank in the shipwreck. Like Hobbes, the will of the people creates justice, law and authority.

Extremes touch each other. The opposite error to saying that society is an accident is to say it is the substance of man in such a way that man has no action apart from society. This is Marxist and Totalitarian theory. The state or civil order is like a person. Order is exalted at the expense of the individuality of the members. The law is a creation of this order and the members are like appendages of one giant person usually embodied in the Leader. Again there is no prior law to the will of the Leader who creates rights.

Each of these theories is mistaken. Society is neither a pure accident nor a substance. In Scholastic terms it is a property which is an accident, but one which must be found wherever the substance is found and the substance cannot exist perfectly or be perfectly understood without this accident. Society could thus be defined as follows: *Adunatio hominum ad unum aliquid communiter agendum.* Society is the unity of order of men united in origin and purpose and acting in common.

Society is an order because it is not merely a conceptual union but a real moral and virtual union of intellects and wills which is based in the nature of the being, man. This union of acts perfects the interior level of man and the kind of society is determined by the human goal which it seeks to implement. The origin of society is human nature but its perfection in execution demands the willed participation of all the members and an attitude of solidarity.

Society is a real union of relationship of willed action among individuals. It is also a unity of order, not merely a plurality or union of the mind. Society is not an absolute unity either, like the unity of one person, so there is no collective will or intellect. In society a part can have an operation different from the whole. But the operation proper to the whole must be carried out as such. Society is then a union of composition or operation. John Paul II says it well:

> Participation thus represents a property of the person himself, that inner and homogeneous property which determines that the person existing and acting together with others still exists and acts as a person.[301]

The law which governs this society is called human law and comprises all those practical laws which govern both the civil order and the ecclesiastical order though canon law. This law is made by men and can change. It must however not contradict the natural law. "Reason's ultimate standard is the law we have in us by nature, and law framed by men is law only to the extent that it derives from that law."[302] As a participation in the order of truth about human nature, albeit of a changeable and sometimes superficial nature, human law binds the conscience with the same obligation as natural law. The definition already given of law is actually a definition of human law gleaned from all the characteristics of every day experience of law.

Authority is essential to the implementation of any law. There is a theory of society today which holds that society can exist without any authority except the collective will. Obedience is made to the group and not to an individual. Though it is true that obedience is to the common good of the society as transcending the individual, one cannot obey a committee. The common good of the society is invested in the properly constituted authority. This authority always acts in the name of God and with the sanction of the natural law, but the people decide who will constitute this authority according to the constitution of the state.

The Church does not canonize one particular kind of government. The important thing is that the person who exercises authority does so according to the true good, a good which must reflect the truth of human nature as determined by the natural law. So, the difference between a just or an unjust government (likewise, between a just or an unjust law) is not that it is made by a monarch, an oligarchy or a congress and president, but is determined by whether the authority acts according to the true common good or his own private good.

Since this is true, no matter how powerful the human authority may be who makes the law, if it does not accord with the natural law it is not a law but a usurpation of law. "If it runs counter in any way to the law in us by nature, it is no longer law but a breakdown of law." [303] So, though authority is necessary to society and speaks with the sanction of God through the natural order, it can still be mistaken. Thus, the command which results from this mistake is not a real law and so cannot bind the conscience. "The only reason which men have for not obeying is when anything is demanded of them which is openly repugnant to the natural or the divine law, for it is equally unlawful to command and to do anything in which the law of nature or the will of God is violated."[304]

DIVINE POSITIVE LAW

Natural and human law are insufficient to govern the moral life of man for two reasons. First, man is called to a supernatural end. Second, even if man was very intelligent about human conduct, in the state of Original Sin there are still things about which he could be mistaken because of the darkness of the intellect. For these reasons, there is one more kind of law necessary to form the intellect in guiding the will towards the ultimate end: the divine positive law or the revealed law.

This law is directly given by God to direct us to a supernatural end, the Beatific Vision, and to specifically instruct men as to the objective good and evil of their particular actions. This law is revealed in two progressive moments: the Old Law and the New Law of Christ. The Old Law is not a different law from the New Law but the preparatory stage for the New Law. It was a grace given on Mount Sinai to Moses and interpreted by him and Aaron in the various books of the Pentateuch in the Old Testament. It had as its purpose the preparation of the community of Israel to be the community from which the Messiah would come.

The Old Law was a definitive step in the preparation of the community for the coming of the Messiah. God founded the community of Israel which is not a civil community in the Old Testament, but a "people of God," a *populus Dei*.[305] Moses and Aaron aided God in the establishment of this community. The kingdom of Israel is the Church in shadow. There are three principal authorities in this kingdom: the priest, the prophet and the king. Each expresses some aspect of the Old Law to the people. The kingdom of Israel is not really a theocracy, but a hierarchical community with God Himself as the rector.

The divine positive law on which this community is founded is far superior to the human laws, which govern ordinary human states. This is well expressed in the verses of Psalm 19: "The law of the Lord is perfect," i.e. it allows no filth of sin unlike human law. "It revives the soul," i.e. it is directed to both interior and exterior acts as opposed to human law. "The rule of the Lord is to be trusted," i.e. it is completely truthful and reliable as opposed to human law. "It gives wisdom to the simple," i.e. it lifts humanity to a divine and supernatural end. Deuteronomy expresses this well: "I call heaven and earth to witness against you this day, that I have set before you life and death, blessing and curse; therefore choose life, that you and your descendants may live." (Dt. 30:19)

The precepts of the Natural and Human law are not enough because man is destined for a higher end that this world. Therefore the divine positive law or revealed law is necessary. This law exists in two stages: the priesthood of Levi (the Old Law) and the priesthood of Christ (the New Law). These two laws are not different species of law. The Old Law is the same species of Law as the New Law, i.e. Divine Positive Law. The purpose of both laws is the same: charity and grace in the life of the Holy Spirit. These two types are distinguished as imperfect to perfect in relationship to this goal. The Old Law instructed people like children. The New law instructs people like adults.

THE OLD LAW

The people of Israel have analogously been compared to children. Every analogy limps. They were compared to children spiritually because of the progressive revelation of the Old Testament. Children need many commandments because they have not interiorized the values of the laws. They are encouraged to the practice of good by material punishments and rewards. According to the people at the time of Christ there were 613 precepts, 248 positive and 365 negative precepts of the Old Law. This was because the people were like children with respect to the life of grace. The common good of the Old Law is reflected in material and earthly promises. For instance, when Job is finally vindicated at the end of the book of Job, he receives back two fold from God the material goods he had lost. This is because the men of the Old Law could not have understood him receiving only spiritual promises even though the meaning of the book is that one can lose all material goods and as long as one has not lost God, one has not lost his humanity.

The promises of the New Law are spiritual. They are heaven and the Vision of God together with the grace, virtues and gifts necessary to arrive there.

The relationship of the Old Law, the New Law and the Vision of God could thus be schematized in this way:

THE OLD LAW	THE NEW LAW	THE VISION OF GOD
UMBRA	IMAGO	VERITAS
(SHADOW)	IMAGE (CHRIST)	TRUTH OR REALITY

Human Law is only sufficient for guiding man to certain ends in this world, but not to the Ultimate End which is heaven. The Old Law goes beyond both the Natural and Human law and prepares man for his ultimate destiny, the Vision of God. God Himself founds a community of divine election by means of the Old Law from those who have common descent from Abraham. Angels promulgate the Old Law (cf. Gal. 3:19). This shows that in itself it is gift from God. The Old Law establishes a new community, which has heaven itself as its end. The Old Law unifies two aspects of God, which are necessary for the coming redemption in which Christ will open the gates of heaven: God as author of nature and as Father of Jesus Christ. For this reason the primary precept of the Old Law is monotheism.

The Natural Law gives us the inclinations by which we are generally morally obliged to do good and avoid evil. The Old Law presupposes these principles and restates them as a specific preparation for the holy people of God from which the Messiah will come. This restatement and application is the Ten Commandments or the Decalogue.

For this purpose the Old Law had three sorts of precepts. The first were the general moral precepts, which this law shared with the natural law. These are the Ten Commandments considered in general. The second was the application of these precepts to the worship of the one God of monotheism, which God himself demanded to consecrate the community to himself, to make them a holy people. These are called the ceremonial precepts and they are contained in the first three commandments which respect the correct attitude of man toward God. These are usually called the First Table of the Law because the Law was by Tradition given on two tablets to Moses. The third kind of commandments respects those actions which befit a holy people toward human beings. These are called the Juridical Precepts and are usually referred to as the Second Table of the Law. They comprise the last seven commandments. So there are three sorts of precepts in the Old Law: moral, ceremonial and juridical.

In both tables the moral precepts are identical with the natural law. When Jesus says, "Do not think I have come to abolish the Law and the Prophets," (Matt. 5:17) he is referring to the moral precepts. The moral aspect is implemented in Israel with very special ceremonial and juridical precepts which are characteristic of their society alone and now have been superseded by Christ in the society of the Church.

The Israelite community formed by God himself has a special relationship to him. The whole people was consecrated, the laity by circumcision, the priests by ordination. The ceremonial law as found in Exodus and Leviticus especially had to be punctiliously observed. This ceremonial law included everything from the observance of feasts in the Temple to laws governing the purification of foods and vessels in everyday life. The people showed their consecration by living these everyday rituals. God shows in this that he is not only the Creator of each person, but also the founder and ruler of the community. The Israelites acknowledge God as the rector by these practices.

The external practices are ordered to an interior formation. Charity as the love of the Holy Spirit and faith as embraced in the Holy Spirit are the first principles of the Old Law. The founder of the community demanded that the exterior rituals reflect these interior states of mind. Because Israel is a commonwealth of God, the prophets must constantly remind Israel of this. The ceremonial precepts have both a literal and a figurative meaning. The figurative meaning is more important than the literal. God founds civil society indirectly through nature. God founds Israel and her successor, the Church, directly. Jesus reproves the Jews of his time repeatedly for emphasizing the literal meaning of the ceremonial precepts over the figurative. The cleansing and purification of the vessels and the Sabbath rest, for example, merely prepare the people for the moral purification and rest in God which the Messiah will bring with grace.

The ceremonial precepts are applied in the juridical precepts. The juridical precepts are basically found in the book of Deuteronomy. These laws are very unusual in their constant emphasis on mercy towards others while applying justice as well.

> Beginning with the Old Testament, all kinds of juridical measures (the jubilee year of forgiveness of debts, prohibition of loans at interest and the keeping of collateral, the obligation to tithe, the daily payment of the day-laborer, the right to glean vines and fields) answer the exhortation of Deuteronomy: "For the poor will never cease out of the land; therefore I command you, 'You shall open wide your hand to your brother, to the needy and to the poor in the land.'"(*CCC*, 2449)

The meaning of the juridical precepts is, therefore, just the opposite of the ceremonial precepts. In them the literal meaning is more important than the figurative. Jesus often reproves the Jews of his time for trying to reduce the mercy towards others demanded by the Law of God to mere human casuistry, thus excusing them from any real practical charity. The juridical precepts present a symbol of the kindness of the future eschatological kingdom. The literal expression of this figure is much less important and urgent than the present demands of virtue in the practical actions which the Israelites each day.

> God, our Creator and Redeemer chose Israel for himself to be his people and revealed his law to them, thus preparing for the coming of Christ. The Law of Moses expresses many truths naturally accessible to reason. These are stated and authenticated within the covenant of salvation.[306]

The Old Law is the first stage of revealed law. Its moral prescriptions are summed up in the Ten Commandments. The precepts of the Decalogue lay the foundations for the vocation of man fashioned in the image of God. They prohibit what is contrary to the love of God and neighbor and prescribe what is essential to it. The Decalogue is a light offered to the conscience of every man to make God's call and ways known to him and to protect him against evil: "God wrote on the tables of the Law what men did not read in their heart."[307]

The Old Law was a necessary stage in the progressive education of Israel by God in the ways of God. This stage remedied for the defect of ignorance in the intellect in the human race, which was one of the two principle punishments for the Original Sin. The other was malice in the will.

Human Law is directed to one end and Divine Law to another. Human Law is directed to peace in temporal affairs. This law accomplishes this by forbidding certain acts harmful to the peace of the state in external affairs. Divine Law is meant to guide man to eternal happiness through both interior and exterior acts. Human Law restrains the hand. Divine Law restrains both the heart and the hand. The Divine Law is medicine for the wound of the Original Sin. The Old Law is an incomplete and limited remedy because it can only heal certain symptoms of the disease, but cannot arrive at the root cause in itself. The Old Law does this by removing sin and so its purpose is to remove obstacles in both interior and exterior acts to accepting the coming of the Holy Spirit through the Messiah. The Old Law, therefore, has as its purpose union with God in heaven by means of the reception of grace here. The problem is that the Old Law does not in itself confer grace. It was good and perfect for its time, but not in relation to the final consummation of the world.

The Old Law was imperfect. "For the law made nothing perfect." (Hebrews 7:19) It could only remove obstacles but could not bring man to his end because the law did not in itself confer grace. In this sense, the Old Law kills. It is not the efficient cause of death and sin because it is good. It is only the occasional cause. The Latin way of putting this is that the Old Law did not cause death *efficialiter*, but *occasionaliter* (not as an efficient cause, but as an occasion). One can live the fullness of even the Old Law only by grace. One might keep the letter of the commandments but not their spirit without the Holy Spirit conferring grace. Man after the giving of the Law was more guilty of sin because he knew how all the sins were connected with God the Creator. He could not plead ignorance. Also, forbidden fruits are the more attractive. Man understood very well why all the sins against the Natural Law were forbidden.

It was not that God tempted man to sin. The people under the Old Law could experience grace if by faith they looked forward to the future redeemer. The yoke of the Law could only be born with grace, a grace that it did not in itself give. What is first in intention is last in execution. Christ was first in the intention of God. The purpose of this creation was the glorification of God in Christ. One could be justified under the dispensation of the Old Law and receive grace by prayerful faith in the coming of Christ as the future Messiah. "The Spirit who gives a law which none can obey without grace is also the Spirit who grants the grace of observing it by first inspiring a prayer of petition to this effect."[308] One could receive grace under the dispensation of the Original Sin. The one who has faith receives grace but not the character of conformity with Christ. So if he sins, he reverts to the Original Sin.

In Hebrews 11, St. Paul enumerates all the people in the Old Testament who were justified by faith. "And without faith it is impossible to please him. For whoever would draw near to God must believe that he exists and that he rewards those who seek him. ... And all these well attested by faith, did not receive what was promised, since God had foreseen something better for us, that apart from us they should not be made perfect." (Hebrews 11: 6 and 39-40)

Those who had cooperated with God under the dispensation of the Old Law should have immediately recognized Christ when he came, as this is the one they were preparing for. The Lord says that the fact that they did not accept him is because they were not true Israelites. In fact, they will be judged more harshly than the pagans will.

Both the Ceremonial and Juridical precepts were oriented to fulfillment in Christ. The Ceremonial precepts of the cult are all fulfilled in Christ's passion. Simeon expresses the fulfillment by Christ of both the Natural and the Old Law when he sees the Child who comes to meet the Temple and begin the completion of the cult. He says, "Now, Lord, you can let your servant go in peace. Your word has been fulfilled. For my eyes have seen your salvation. A light (the means of knowledge in philosophy) of revelation to the Gentiles and the glory (the *shekenah* which covered Mt. Sinai and filled the Temple during the sacrifices) of your people Israel." (Luke 2: 29-32) The veil of the Temple is torn in two at the hour of Christ's sacrifice to show that Jesus completes the cult. The Juridical precepts of the Old Law are brought to completion because Jesus shows us what our relationship with our neighbor is to be like.

The sacraments of the Old Law did not confer grace, but they did look forward to the future Messiah. Luther taught that the sacraments of the New Law of Christ and the sacraments of the Old Law caused grace in exactly the same way, i.e. by faith. Catholics believe that the sacraments of the New Law in themselves cause grace. The sacraments of the Old Law only cause grace by being means to express the faith of the recipient.

> According to Christian tradition, the Law is holy, spiritual, and good, yet still imperfect. Like a tutor it shows what must be done, but does not of itself give the strength, the grace of the Spirit to fulfill it. Because of sin, which it cannot remove, it remains a law of bondage. According to St. Paul, its special function is to denounce and disclose sin, which constitutes a "law of concupiscence' in the human

heart. However, the Law remains the first stage on the way to the kingdom. It prepares and disposes the chosen people and each Christian for conversion and faith in the Savior God. It provides a teaching, which endures forever, like the Word of God.[309]

The Old Law is a preparation for the Gospel. "The Law is a pedagogy and a prophecy of things to come."[310] It prophesies and presages the work of liberation from sin which will be fulfilled in Christ: it provides the New Testament with images, "types," and symbols for expressing the life according to the Spirit. Finally, the Law is completed by the teaching of the sapiential books and prophets which set its course toward the New Covenant and the Kingdom of heaven.

THE NEW LAW OF CHRIST

The Old Law was written on tablets of stone. It was comprised of many commandments, which could be expressed in human speech. It remedied for the punishment of ignorance in the intellect for the Original Sin, but in itself it did not remedy for the defect of malice or weakness in the will. Only Christ could do this in the New Law. This New Law of Christ is taught in the Sermon on the Mount. In this sermon, the interior motivation for the observance of the commandments is stressed as the foundation for the written letter. The New Law of Christ is primarily not a written law. Christ remedies for malice by sending the grace of the Holy Spirit into the soul. The New Law is both an interior law, taught by the Holy Spirit and a written law. It is primarily an interior law. Secondarily and no less essentially it is a written law. The written commandments in the New Law dispose someone to the grace of the Holy Spirit (dispositive) and teach someone how to act according to the grace of the Holy Spirit (executive).

The New Law justifies in itself, something the Old Law could not do. Still, it does not justify because of the written part, but because it contains in itself the grace of the Holy Spirit. If someone under the New Law only follows the letter without the Spirit, then they live as though they were under the Old Law.

> There were ... under the regimen of the Old Covenant, people who possessed the charity and grace of the Holy Spirit and longed above all for the spiritual and eternal promises by which they were associated with

the New law. Conversely, there exist carnal men under the new Covenant, still distanced from the perfection of the New Law: the fear of punishment and certain temporal promises have been necessary, even under the New Covenant, to incite them to virtuous works. In any case, even though the Old Law prescribed charity, it did not give the Holy Spirit, through whom 'God's charity has been poured into our hearts'.[311]

The New Law was not given immediately at the beginning of time because man had to be prepared to receive grace by realizing his dependence on God. This preparation of the human race was progressive. Nothing in nature is immediately brought to perfection and the same is true of the life of grace, which builds on nature. Had God offered grace to men as soon as the sin was committed, they would not have accepted it because they would not have understood their need for grace, their need to surrender to Him. Had God waited longer, the human race might have despaired of ever receiving grace.

This New Law was given in the fullness of time and includes the interior grace of the Holy Spirit. Therefore, it justifies in itself as opposed to the Old Law, which only justified by the faith of the recipient. Since this is the essence of the New Law as given through the complete revelation of God, Jesus Christ, there will be no further revelation of God. No "new revelation" could be more complete than that given in Christ and completed when Christ sent the Holy Spirit on the Apostles at Pentecost.

In the Middle Ages, there was a heretical movement which taught that there were three ages of the world: the age of the Father (The Old Testament), the age of the Son (The New Testament and fleshly Church founded on Pentecost) and the age of the Holy Spirit. This latter age would be on this earth and would entail a more complete revelation of God than the one given in Christ, expressed in the sacraments and the hierarchical Church. The implication was that the hierarchical Church would evolve into a more complete Church of the Spirit which would be without structure and sacraments and entail only the perfect.

St. Thomas answers this heresy by saying that there are indeed three ages of the world: the age of the Father and the Son (the Old Testament which finds completion in the Messiah); the age of the Son and the Holy Spirit (the New Testament which finds its completion in the Sending of the Holy Spirit on the Apostles at Pentecost); the Final Perfect age. This last age is not experienced in this life. It is only experienced in the Vision of God in heaven. There will be no more complete revelation of God on this earth than the one given to the Apostles on Pentecost and which is expressed in the hierarchical and sacramental Catholic Church. The two fonts for this revelation are Scripture and Tradition which fulfill the promise made by the Lord: "But the Councellor, the Holy Spirit, whom the Father will send in my name, he will teach you all things, and bring to your remembrance all that I have said to you." (Jn. 14:26) There Jesus promised the Paraclete who will guide into all truth. The Spirit is given to guide the Church on its way to the Kingdom.

The Old Law and the New Law are not two essentially different laws, but two stages in the same law. They are related like the plant to the rose or child to the adult. As Christ said: "Do not think that I have come to abolish the law and the prophets; I have come not to abolish them but to fulfill them" (Mt. 5:17). The one is an imperfect stage of the other. Both are oriented to charity, but the Old Law could not in itself give this charity, though it was perfect for its time and place. The Old Law instructs us like children; the New Law like adults. For this reason, there were many temporal punishments and promises given under the Old Law. The New Law on the other hand is a Law of Love. It is grace itself and motivates people as spiritual adults.

As stated above, The Old Law contained 613 precepts according to the authorities at the time of Jesus. It contained so many precepts because it instructed people like children who need constant reminders. Those who lived under the Dispensation of the New Law had only those precepts which are in themselves according to or against the living of charity.

Jesus fulfills what is lacking in the Old Law as to both its end and its precepts. As to the end, Jesus truly gives the grace of the Holy Spirit and so the Old Law is brought to perfection. As to the precepts, he fulfills them in both his actions and in His teaching. In His actions, he was born under the Old Law and did all that was required under the Old Law. In the great hymn for Corpus Christi, *Pange Lingua*, Thomas Aquinas writes, "He obeys the law's directions, even as the Old Law ends."

In His teaching, Our Lord shows the proper understanding of the Old Law. The exterior principles of the Old Law were about charity, the interior love of God brought by grace. Jesus interprets the authentic meaning of the law by pointing to its ethical dimension, which implements the intention of charity.

For this reason, the New Law is more difficult to live than the Old Law. Though the Old Law had many precepts, in itself it did not give the grace to live them properly. Since the New Law gives this grace, it demands that what it commands and forbids be done from the right interior intention. The person who acts according to the New Law must perform whatever works he performs from spontaneous joy and free internal love born from the supernatural perspective of life according to the Holy Spirit. The interior hardship which the New Law demands can only be born with the indwelling of the Holy Spirit who supports us with his presence and power.

The New Law is therefore a law of freedom, but not in the sense that there are no works commanded. The external works of the New Law are few when compared with the Old Law, but this is because this is a law fulfilled. The external works commanded are those which lead to grace (the sacraments) and those which are in accord with (positive precepts) or contrary to (negative precepts) the living of the life of faith working through love. There are still, then, absolute moral norms under the dispensation of the New Law against those actions which are incompatible with the living of grace, e.g. murder, theft and adultery.

The Kingdom of God is primarily interior, and so all exterior actions which do not correspond to interior reconciliation with God are forbidden. Those which are indifferent to this interior peace have no relation to this law, e.g. food. All foods are permitted under the New Law and there are no ritual laws of purification or ablution. The New Law is a law of freedom in two senses: 1) it does not constrain us to do or avoid anything except what is necessary to or contrary to salvation and 2) it demands that we fulfill the precepts freely from the inner stirring of grace. The Old Law restrains the hand. The New Law restrains the heart and therefore also the hand.

Finally, Jesus adds to the precepts of the Old Law counsels of perfection in the New Law. These counsels recommend that one gives up even legitimate goods because of the possibility of manipulation under the New Law. They correspond to the legitimate goods which tempt us with the lust of the flesh (sexuality)—chastity; the lust of the eyes (money)—poverty; and the pride of life (perfection)—obedience.

> The New Law is called a law of love because it makes us act out of the love infused by the Holy Spirit, rather than from fear; a law of grace, because it confers the strength of grace to act, by means of faith and the sacraments; a law of freedom, because it sets us free from the ritual and juridical observances of the Old Law, inclines us to act spontaneously by the prompting of charity and, finally, lets us pass from the condition of a servant who 'does not know what his master is doing' to that of a friend of Christ—'For all that I have heard from my Father I have made known to you'—or even to the status of a son and heir. [312]

CHAPTER NINE
CONSCIENCE

THE PROBLEM OF CONSCIENCE

Once all the objective principles of fundamental moral theology have been identified, then it is necessary to apply them in the final problem which is that of the conscience. The problem of conscience is the principle problem of post-Tridentine theology because of the practical need of the Church to train confessors and moral theologians.

Fr. Servais Pinckaers emphasizes in his landmark moral study that the casuistic moralists and the manualists saw conscience and its formation as the principal moral problem because of the difficulty in post-Tridentine theology of relating freedom to law. "The treatise on conscience was a creation of casuist morality, which introduced it into fundamental moral theology and hoisted it to the heights."[313] Whereas the moral tradition emanating from the *Summa* of St. Thomas strongly related conscience to the virtue of prudence, in post-Tridentine theology conscience became "comparable to an intermediate faculty placed between law and freedom."[314] Morals was reduced to case studies to try to determine how much room there was for freedom in the face of the obligations of the law. "The principal task of moralists was to assist conscience in these functions: to inform it of the law and above all to enlighten it in its work of interpreting and applying the law to human acts."[315]

This was the age of Descartes and methodical doubt about all truth was the order of the day. In the moral realm, this doubt was applied to conscience. "Ethicists were constrained, too, to distinguish carefully between different states of conscience in view of the law and freedom: the firm conscience, the doubtful conscience, the broad conscience, the scrupulous conscience, and so forth."[316] This problem of the doubtful conscience resulted from this methodical doubt. Attempts to inform the doubtful conscience characterize all modern European philosophy and, hence, theology gave rise to the whole issue of probabilism. This is a moral system which maintains that when it is a question of the lawfulness or unlawfulness of an action it is permissible to hold the solidly probable opinion which favors freedom even if the opposing view is more probable. This was one way of dealing with the issue of the doubtful conscience. Suffice it to say that the formation of the doubtful conscience occupies a good deal of the moral problems in the Church even today.

As has been seen in the examination of Rahner and the school of moderate teleology above, the problem of the conscience is an important one because it is here that truth is applied to individual conduct. One will recall that Rahner made a distinction between formal existential ethics and material essential ethics which seems to be at the basis for the theories of the consequentialists. According to this theory, there are basically two systems of ethics. One is the material existential ethics which would include all the laws as examined in Chapter Seven of this book. These are seen as important recommendations to take into account when the individual discerns the truth of moral conduct. But in addition to this, there is another system of ethics, formal existential ethics which is where the individual confronts the Holy Spirit in his private conscience using the tools recommended in the *Spiritual Exercises* of St. Ignatius. These tools may lead the person to discern that they would have to break the universal expression of the law in order to preserve the value the law was meant to express to be true to the inspiration of the Holy Spirit.

In this view, formal existential ethics is necessary because no universal statement can cover every individual instance especially in morals and because conscience is never just an application of a universal law to an individual action. The implications would be that no judgment based on the law of moral objects can ever be complete until the circumstances and intention are confronted. Also, once a judgment is made by the conscience that *ipso facto* guarantees that the conscience speaks with the authority of the Holy Spirit and no authority can criticize such a judgment nor should the person ever alter such a conscience because it cannot be mistaken. How can the Holy Spirit lead someone to discern that a given judgment arrived at using the proper tools can be in error?

Rahner's explanation of the private conscience certainly cannot be sustained, however, especially concerning the erroneous conscience. The why and wherefore for this fact demand an examination of conscience in general.

CONSCIENCE IS A PRACTICAL JUDGMENT

Conscience is judgment of reason. It is a syllogism and as such is a statement of the objective truth concerning a moral action which is to be performed or has been performed by an individual. The nature of the syllogism is as follows: the major comes from the general relationship of the moral law to being and is called *synderesis*. For example, as expressed by the natural law it would be: "I must do good and avoid evil" or as expressed by the revealed law it would be: "I must obey the law of God." The minor would be a more specific statement gleaned from something like the Decalogue. For example, "The killing of an innocent human being is evil and proscribed by the law of God." Then this is applied in the conclusion. "Therefore I must not kill this innocent person because it is evil and proscribed by the law of God." Note that this is a simple application of logic.

This description of conscience not only comes from the works of St. Thomas but is also taught by the *Catechism of the Catholic Church*:

> The dignity of the human person implies and requires *uprightness of moral conscience*. Conscience includes the perception of the principles of morality (*synderesis*); their application in given circumstances by practical discernment of reasons and goods; and finally judgment about concrete acts yet to be performed or already performed. The truth about the moral good, stated in the law of reason, is recognized practically and concretely by the *prudent judgment* of conscience.[317]

The theoretical implications of this teaching are important. The conscience is the place where reason taught by the natural, divine or human law is applied and so in some remote or proximate sense it speaks with the authority of God. "Deep within his conscience, man discovers a law which he has not laid upon himself but which he must obey. Its voice, ever calling him to love and do what is good and to avoid evil, tells him inwardly at the right moment: do this, shun that. For man has in his heart a law inscribed by God."[318] However, the fact that conscience speaks with the voice of God does not mean that it is beyond criticism or even error.

The present tendency to place freedom and law in opposition to each other has led to "a *'creative' understanding of moral conscience,* which diverges from the teaching of the Church's tradition and her Magisterium."³¹⁹ This "creative" understanding precisely teaches that no general moral laws can cover all cases. "While such norms might be useful for a correct *assessment* of the situation, they cannot replace the individual personal *decision* on how to act in particular cases."³²⁰ The authors who recommend this "creative" understanding propose a "double status of moral truth,"³²¹ one abstract and the other concrete. This is very reminiscent of the opinion of Rahner. Conscience becomes an oracle which always proclaims the truth.

To view conscience as an application of the divine and natural law or as the place where man in his most personal aspect confronts God on the subject of moral choice, it is necessary to affirm that it is "the application of the law to a particular case ... the proximate norm of the morality of the voluntary act, 'applying the objective law to a particular case.'"³²² It is this fact which makes conscience the "proximate norm of personal morality."³²³

Since conscience is a process of reasoning based on a syllogism, like any process of reasoning carried on by human beings, it can be mistaken either in its premises or in the construction of the syllogism. As a result, "[c]onscience is not an infallible judge; it can make mistakes."³²⁴ Once this fact is admitted, the whole problem of how it binds arises. One must always follow the judgment of one's conscience. But this statement cannot be made without some distinctions.

Conscience is a judgment of practical reason in which an individual applies general principles of the moral law to specific actions here and now. Conscience is much like prudence which is also about right reason applied to action. The difference is that the conscience ends in the intellect with the judgment whereas prudence ends in the will. One is free to will against his conscience in which case he sins. If one wills against prudence however, one is imprudent.

Since conscience is a judgment of reason, such a judgment can occur about a prospective act one wishes to do or about an action one has actually performed. The first is referred to as an antecedent conscience; the second, a consequent conscience.

As it is sometimes difficult to know the truth in moral actions because of all the circumstances involved in practical reason, conscience is also specified as to the possibility of knowing how to apply these principles. So it is variously called a scrupulous conscience when a person for trivial reasons fears that all his actions are evil; a perplexed conscience, in which a person sees equal reasons for choosing or avoiding an action; a lax conscience in which a person easily judges he has no sin (again based on insufficient reason); or a pharisaic conscience, which minimizes grave sins and maximizes trivial sins.

CONSCIENCE AND CERTAINTY

The freedom to act on one's conscience can be compromised by the degree of certainty in one's judgment. This is commonly divided between a certain conscience, in which one has firmly judged that a given course of action should be pursued or avoided because the reasons for such a course are clear; a probable conscience, which involves a reasonable certainty given the problems of certainty in moral acts; or a doubtful conscience, in which one has no certainty. Some of the classic manualists were of the opinion that that expression doubtful conscience was a contradiction in terms because the whole purpose of making a judgment of conscience was to resolve doubt.[325]

Moralists for centuries have engaged in various opinions about how far one must resolve one's doubt in the conscience in relation to the truth. These various opinion include probabilism, equiprobabalism, tutiorism, pure probiliorism, law probabilism, rigorism and on and on. Actually, with the exception of rigorism and laxism, all the other opinions have been permitted by the Church. Another very important point is that one cannot act with a doubtful conscience, but since many moral judgments involve a host of circumstances and these are sometimes difficult for the ordinary person to gauge, an imperfect certainty is sufficient. In other words mathematical certitude (two plus two equals four) or metaphysical certitude (the whole is equal to the sum of its parts) are not required for moral judgments. Rather, moral certitude is required. The *Catholic Encyclopedia* of 1917 defines this as: "Though almost any detail in these events may be made a subject of dispute, especially when we enter the region of motives and try to trace cause and effect, and though almost any one of the witnesses may be shown to have made some mistake or misrepresentation, yet the occurrence of the events, taken in the mass, is certain."[326] This definition is still valid today.

One may never act with a truly doubtful conscience. Using the principles above one can usually resolve one's doubt by education or consulting a confessor. Since morals does not admit of the same certitude as metaphysics or mathematics, the Cartesian problem of certitude should not delay speculation or research too long. In classical Thomistic morals, prudence (which is the virtue concerned with determining and applying the truth to a given action) does not demand absolute certainty before acting.

> Reason first and foremost grasps general truths, but is also applies them in particular cases; from general premises it argues particular conclusions, turning around, so to speak, to consider the matter. Human experience reduces the unmanageable infinity of particular cases to a finite set of usual situations adequate enough for human prudence.[327]

THE MISTAKEN CONSCIENCE

The most difficult problem in contemporary morals is not the doubtful conscience but, given the tendency toward subjectivism of the post-Kantian world, the status and binding force of the mistaken conscience.

In the Middle Ages, there was a debate about whether a mistaken conscience could bind one to act. Many were of the opinion that a right conscience bound but not a mistaken conscience because obviously the mistaken conscience does not correspond to the natural law whereas the right conscience does. St. Thomas maintains that this opinion is untenable. This is because subjectively speaking the person perceives what the false conscience commands as commanded by God. So in acting against such a conscience, he may objectively be following the law of God. Still, since he subjectively perceives this to be against the law of God, he is acting against something which God commands and so sins.

The problem is that a man with such a formed and certain conscience cannot avoid sin. If he acts according to his conscience, he sins against the law of God objectively. If he acts against his conscience, he sins against what he subjectively perceives to be the law of God.

> Moreover, it does not seem possible for a man to avoid sin if his conscience, no matter how mistaken, declares that something which is indifferent or evil

is a command of God and with such a conscience he decides to do the opposite. For, as far as he can, he has by this very fact decided not to observe the law of God. Consequently, he sins mortally.[328]

Does this mean that a person with such a conscience cannot avoid sin? St. Thomas says no because he can always change his conscience. The necessity of changing this conscience and the responsibility for doing so are based on the manner in which the correct conscience binds. The correct conscience binds "absolutely because it binds without qualification and in every circumstance".[329] An erroneous conscience on the other hand binds only by an extrinsic consideration. So it binds "only in a qualified way, since it binds conditionally."[330] What is the condition? If it can be changed, there is a moral obligation to change it. So, a false conscience only binds "accidentally."[331]

The evaluation of responsibility for a sin which results from an erroneous conscience is based on the same principles as vincible and invincible ignorance. If one chose not to know, and for this reason cannot change his conscience, then he is responsible for the sin as he is for the ignorance.

> A false conscience which is mistaken in things which are intrinsically evil commands something which is contrary to the law of God. Nevertheless, it says that what it commands is the law of God. Accordingly, one who acts against such a conscience becomes a kind of transgressor of the law of God, although one who follows such a conscience and acts according to it acts against the law of God and sins mortally. For there was sin in the error itself, since it happened because of ignorance of that which should be known.[332]

So if a person can know that his mistaken conscience is mistaken, then he is obliged to change it. The conscience binds as long as it remains, but it does not bind essentially. The person has a moral obligation to form a right conscience. To change a right conscience is a sin; to change an erroneous conscience is an obligation. "Hence, this does not prove that a false conscience does not bind as long as it remains, but that it does not bind absolutely and in every event."[333]

AN INFORMED CONSCIENCE

Moralists following St. Thomas have generally been of the opinion that ignorance of a circumstance can excuse but not ignorance of the law. "When the error itself is not a sin, the conclusion is true, as when the error is due to ignorance of some fact. But, if it is ignorance of the law, the conclusion is wrong because the ignorance is itself a sin."[334]

For example, much has been made in the last few years concerning the fact that decisions about contraception should be left to the conscience. The implication is that if a couple have consulted their consciences and if they see that artificial contraception is the only way for them to avoid certain physical or material difficulties like poverty then they are morally excused or even justified in choosing it. This opinion corresponds to the idea that conscience is a moral oracle and is almost Gnostic so that even the authority of the Church cannot criticize such a decision. Though a couple may be confused or perplexed as to whether a given act like vasectomy is contraceptive and their perplexity may be increased by theologians who actively promote dissension from papal teaching in this matter, this does not excuse them from the obligation to inform themselves and resolve their perplexity. This would include reference to papal teaching which is now easily accessible on the Internet for most educated people. Of course, if their perplexity is due to the false teaching of their professors or pastors, then these bear an even greater responsibility for error.

What would be the source of this sinful ignorance? Vatican II and the *Catechism* give some possible sources. "Ignorance of Christ and his Gospel, bad example given by others, enslavement to one's passions, assertion of a mistaken notion of the autonomy of conscience, rejection of the Church's authority and her teaching, lack of conversion and of charity: these can be the source of errors of judgment in moral conduct."[335]

St. Thomas also explains how to resolve moral perplexity. "One whose conscience tells him to commit fornication is not completely perplexed, because he can do something by which he can avoid sin, namely, change the false conscience. But he is perplexed to some degree, that is, as long as his false conscience remains."[336] Those who say that one must follow one's conscience and therefore cannot be criticized are only speaking of a right and certain conscience. "The more a correct conscience prevails, the more do persons and groups turn aside from blind choice and try to be guided by the objective standards of moral conduct."[337]

Two more points must be emphasized about the conscience. The fact that one is excused from moral responsibility in an invincibly erroneous conscience does not mean that the action which results from this is a good. Objective sin remains objective sin. Such an action cannot be taken up into the virtues. It remains an alien body in the moral life, neither good nor evil, but an area of the moral life which cannot be a step either toward or away from heaven. This is because the will is not present in it. Resolution of the ignorance is an important obligation on the part of others so that the person may use every means possible to express his love for God and arrive at heaven.

If this is true for invincible ignorance, it is even more true of vincible ignorance. This is often caused by sin and compounded by repeated sin, so that a person changes his value system to look on apparent good (real evil) as real good (apparent evil). "This ignorance can often be imputed to personal responsibility. Such is the case when a man 'takes little trouble to find out what is true and good, or when conscience is by degrees almost blinded through the habit of committing sin.' In such cases, the person is culpable for the evil he commits."[338]

FREEDOM OF CONSCIENCE

Second, there has also been much discussion about the right of a Catholic to dissent from papal teaching with reference to the principle of freedom of conscience regarding religion as taught in Vatican II's document, *Dignitatis Humanae*. From the outset, it is important to keep clear that though there should be a freedom of conscience in embracing the truth, this is not true regarding what constitutes the truth itself and especially the religious truth in relation to the society of the Church.

Some theologians after Vatican II saw the Council's teaching as an assault on the Scholastic idea of an objective nature of man which had been the basis for moral teaching in the Church for centuries. For example, John Mahoney, S.J. in the Clarendon Lectures at Oxford published in 1987 opines:

> It may also be a growing dissatisfaction with the traditional concept of 'nature' which has contributed

in recent years to the focus on moral attention moving from 'human nature' to 'human person' or 'human dignity.' Thus, the Second Vatican Council was certainly not unaware of the whole moral tradition centered on the law of nature when it nevertheless considered basing objective moral standards on 'the dignity of the human person,' and finally decided to propose the need for such standards as based on the 'nature of the [human] person and his act.'[339]

People like Daniel Maguire[340] used the teaching on religious liberty as a touchstone to show that the Church had basically jettisoned the traditional Scholastic idea of an objective human nature.

> Even this brief look at the history of our moral teaching should prompt us to describe our teaching competence in more modern terms. Either we must admit a drastic relativism which would allege that all of that teaching was right in its day or we must admit the presence of error in the history of the pilgrim church [...] To stress the point: [...] the teaching of Gregory XVI and Pius IX that it was 'madness' to allege religious freedom as a right of man and a necessity of society, and the proclamation of Vatican II that such freedom is a right and necessity in society—such teaching are not consistent or mutually irreconcilable. Even full recognition of the historical context that spawned these statements does not establish doctrinal continuity.[341]

Dan Maguire even goes so far as to say, "Still, to assert that in all this there is no [doctrinal] change is to play semantic games."[342]

Though it is true that for many centuries the Church had taught the importance of the confessional state,[343] this was never represented in such a way as to teach that people should be coerced into a particular religion by the state. In fact, before Vatican II, Leo XIII had emphasized a kind of civil right of religion free from coercion in a distinction he made in one of his encyclicals, *Libertas Praestissimum*:

> Another liberty is widely advocated, namely, *liberty of conscience*. If by this is meant that everyone, as he

> chooses, worship God or not, it is sufficiently refuted by the arguments adduced. But it may also be taken to mean that every man in the State may follow the will of God and, from a consciousness of duty and free from every obstacle, obey his commands. This indeed, is true liberty, a liberty worthy of the sons of God.[344]

Vatican II makes clear that the religious freedom referred to is that freedom from coercion invoked by Leo XIII, which is based on the nature of the will embracing any moral act. "But men cannot satisfy their obligation in a way in keeping *with their own nature* unless they enjoy both psychological freedom and immunity from external coercion. Therefore the right to religious freedom has its foundation not in the subjective attitude of the individual, but in his very nature."[345] Thomas Aquinas teaches this same freedom from coercion which is taught by Vatican II.

> Among the unbelievers there are some who have never received the faith, such as heathens and Jews: and these are by no means to be compelled to the faith, in order that they may believe, because to believe depends on the will. Nevertheless they should be compelled by the faithful, if it be possible to do so, so that they may not hinder the faith either by blasphemies, or by evil persuasions, or even by open persecutions."[346]

In addition, the religious freedom which is invoked in Vatican II is only in the civil order, not the ecclesiastical order.

> So while the religious freedom which men demand in fulfilling their obligation to worship God has to do with freedom from coercion in civil society, it leaves intact the traditional Catholic teaching on the moral duty of individuals and societies towards the true religion and the one Church of Christ.[347]

The *Catechism of the Catholic Church* also makes the teaching on the matter of religious freedom of conscience more precise.

> The right to religious liberty is neither a moral license to adhere to error, nor a supposed right to error,

but rather a natural right of the human person to civil liberty, i.e. immunity, within just limits, from external constraint in religious matters by political authorities.[348]

This is true because this right is not based on positivism which states that the civil law determines the objective truth by the laws. The only source for truth would be the creation of human reason and power. When the *Syllabus of Errors* condemns freedom of religion this is against the error of indifferentism. This is the idea that all religions are equally true and that regarding the truth of the intellect all faiths are indifferent as to man's fulfillment. Error never has rights but must be based on objective truth. However, a person may not be coerced into embracing a certain religion by the state. This latter fact is a reflection of the nature of the will in embracing the truth. Both respect the objective requirements of the relationship between the intellect and will.

So the freedom of conscience cannot certainly be invoked against the authentic teachings of the magisterium to justify moral dissent. In the civil order, there is freedom from coercion but the moral obligation nonetheless remains in both the Church and the State to seek the truth insofar as one can know it. In the Church, the magisterium is a trump card when it comes to issues of moral law and certainty. A Catholic should have freely embraced the faith and so freely accepted the judgment of the magisterium when it comes to both reason and revelation.

THE FREE SERVANT—SPONTANEITY AND HEAVEN

CHAPTER TEN
VIRTUE

VIRTUE AND FREEDOM

One of the exterior sources which guide moral discernment is law. The law was treated in Chapter Eight. There are two interior sources for moral formation and one other exterior one. The internal sources are virtue and sin; the other exterior source is grace. To understand how sin detracts from moral formation and how grace is necessary for the completion of moral formation, one must first understand virtue. One cannot appreciate sickness until one understands health and one cannot understand the need for medicine or aid in general unless one understands the limitations and demands of health.

Catholic moral teaching since the Council of Trent has often been plagued by the serious limitation imposed by the idea that, once the law and freedom in a certain sense were seen in opposition to each other, the primary moral problem became how far one could stretch the law by freedom without breaking the law. In the manuals the whole emphasis shifted from seeking happiness through interior formation to playing it safe within the boundaries of the law. Though St. Thomas has given the virtues pride of place in the *Summa*, the schools of moral theology for the last four hundred years have basically removed them to the periphery of moral analysis. "In specialized moral theory, the *virtues* yielded their place to the commandments, and were given very slight importance. They were viewed merely as good habits, and were studied only in light of the obligations involved—hence the neglect of virtues such as hope and courage, which carried no obligations, but were in daily demand."[349]

When the extraordinary Synod met in 1986 and commissioned the new *Catechism of the Catholic Church*, one of the things the Fathers requested was that the new *Catechism* would show a more evident connection between the commandments and the virtues. The doctrine of the virtues is in fact the central pivot on which the whole treatment of morals rests. So a realistic understanding of them is central to moral formation.

The three principles which must all participate in every human act are the will, the intellect and the passions. These three interior forces must be present in every exterior action which leads one to heaven. The problem is that since human beings enjoy freedom in every action, this very freedom itself must be channeled or, better perhaps, formed in such a way that human nature is not compromised by it. Freedom interpreted as indifference is again the issue here. Pope Benedict addressed this in his Wednesday audience discourse on Duns Scotus: "If freedom is detached from truth, it becomes, tragically, a principle of the destruction of the human person's inner harmony, a source of prevarication of the strongest and the violent and a cause of suffering and sorrow. Freedom, like all the faculties with which the human being is endowed, increases and is perfected."[350]

The intellect and the will can be realized in an almost infinite variety of ways because they are spiritual powers. The passions, though they are realized in very finite ways, must be integrated into the actions of the intellect and will because of the unity of the human soul. Because of the very presence of reason, there must be many factors which converge for these human powers to be integral and produce more than just an obligation in acting, but a happiness and delight.

In the intellect there is a natural tendency to know the truth which cannot be fulfilled just by possessing the capacity. Objective study is necessary. In the will there is a natural tendency to do the good which cannot be fulfilled just by possessing this tendency. Freedom allows one to practice evil. This tendency must be realized by loving the good and committing this love to practice. In the passions, there is both a natural tendency to satisfy one's feelings, but also a natural tendency in man that these passions be obedient to reason. The latter cannot be fulfilled simply by possessing the power but human feelings must be developed by experiencing pleasure in real human goods according to human nature understood by reason. These result from choice once one has reached the age of reason.

Since animals are limited to material goods, instinct suffices for them to act according to their nature. Since God has no potential which needs to be developed as he is pure act, there is no need to realize potential in practice to perfect it. Only man must develop qualities in his powers by practice which makes acting according to reason "second nature." Only in man must habit and spontaneity cooperate in happy combination for him to experience true perfection of soul. The stable development of these qualities is called a *habit* which may be defined in this context as: "a permanent quality which enables us to act in a way that is not only prompt and skillful, but full of zest and pleasure as well."[351] A habit which accords with nature and so is good is called a virtue. A habit which does not accord with nature and so is bad is called a vice.

THE NATURE OF VIRTUE

When Thomas Aquinas treats virtue he uses a classic definition which has its origin in several places in St. Augustine, but is specifically expressed by Peter Lombard.[352] "Virtue is a good quality of mind, by which we live rightly, of which no one make bad use, which God works in us without us."[353] St. Thomas explains that virtue is a good formation of powers in man towards their own characteristic activity. These powers are those spiritual powers involved in free choice, hence the use of the word "mind." Human formation must be stable so that a person generally has a tendency to prefer those acts which develop unity in his powers in acting for a proper goal. Regarding knowledge, for example, no one can truly be said to be a scientific expert who makes mistakes in his field. The clause "by which we live rightly of which no one makes bad use" distinguishes intellectual virtue, for example, science from opinion. Finally, St. Thomas says that if one leaves out the last clause, this definition will suffice for those virtues which man can acquire through his own powers and so are called *acquired* virtues. If the last clause is left in, the definition serves only for those virtues which man can develop in light of grace. These are traditionally called *infused* virtues though some today use the term "*instilled*" for them.

HOW ONE OBTAINS VIRTUE

There are three basic sources of virtues which are necessary to experience complete human integration: nature, free choices and God. If virtue had its source only outside the soul, it would be an imposition on nature. If it had its source only within the soul, it would be innate and study and practice would not be needed which is contrary to common experience. Instead there are *seeds of virtue* present in the intellect, the will and the passions. These are the natural tendencies discussed already. But they must be completed by the practice which results from free choice in order to develop human integrity.

Since man is called to an end by nature he cannot attain by nature because of the exalted character of the end, people must develop further qualities which correspond to acts by which this end is attained. There are no seeds of virtue for these acts. Instead, they must be placed in man by God and are given together with grace.

Virtues play a part in the spontaneous formation of an interior freedom according to the truth. Actions are not enough. In man the good sought in the action must be interiorized. Morals cannot be reduced to mere external conformity to a series of rules which are regarded as exterior impositions on the freedom of the will. Rather, the law is an embodiment of moral truth which must be understood and eventually spontaneously practiced because the subject understands how the actions commanded or forbidden by the law form freedom to spontaneously desire and rejoice in the good and the beautiful. "This results from habit which, since it acts in the manner of a kind of nature, makes the activity proper to it, as it were, natural and, consequently delightful. For fittingness is the cause of delight. Hence, the Philosopher in *Ethics 2* gives as a mark of habit the delight taken in acting."[354]

One action is not sufficient to develop positive or negative habits, virtues or vices. Aristotle says, "One swallow does not a spring make." Nor does a mere repetition of actions form these habits or strengthen them once they have been formed. This is because this interior formation is something spiritual. Interior formation is complete when the intellect, the will and the passions are all poised to cooperate together when presented with a choice for good. This is what happens in the formation of human affection or love for the good. Virtue is increased not by multiplication of acts but by the intensity of interior desire with which these actions are performed.

If the formation is only in the intellect then though there may be a habit of science, for example, this does not participate completely in the idea of a virtue because it is not oriented to right use. Moral virtues, on the other hand, include right willing since they form loving and so presume right use.

KINDS OF VIRTUE

There are many virtues. The most basic are the acquired virtues. The principal ones which form freedom are called the cardinal virtues from the Latin word *cardo* (a hinge) because the moral life hinges on them. They are found in the four powers of the soul which contribute to human freedom: in the intellect, prudence; in the will, justice; and in the passions, fortitude and temperance. The infused virtues necessary for man to arrive at heaven are those respecting God: faith, hope and charity, and those respecting others: infused prudence, justice, temperance and fortitude. All of the cardinal virtues are necessary for human happiness and integrity because all of the powers they form cooperate in every free choice.

PRUDENCE

Prudence is necessary in the intellect because one cannot love what one does not know. Since human action must be according to reason, one must be able first to know what human nature entails in human actions and then how to apply the general principles of human conduct whether they have their origin in the natural law, revealed law or divine inspiration to each particular action. The virtue of prudence begins in the intellect but since it is oriented to practice, it ends in the will. The good of virtue is said to involve a mean of reason between two extremes: defect and excess. The mean of truth in prudence is the truth of the individual action and whether it truly perfects human nature in the here and now. The excess would be when one affirms that a given act perfects or destroys human nature and desires it when it does not; the defect would be when one affirms that an action is not good or is not evil when in fact it is. For prudence to be perfect this knowledge must actually be implemented in an act of the will.

As a result, unlike ordinary human knowledge, prudence is not corrupted by forgetfulness but rather by contented worldliness. Bad loving corrupts moral knowledge. This can also affect conscience so that a person can easily act against his conscience because of his prior formation in wrong loving. This follows the principle: As a person is formed, so does the end seem to him. To one who is sick, healthy food is repulsive. In the same way, to one accustomed to sin, the truly good often appears evil and undesirable.

This knowledge can be present yet reason's judgment concerning the particular act be intercepted with the result that one does not judge correctly. That is why moral science is said to avail little for the acquisition of virtue, because even when it is had a man can still sin again virtue. It is the task of prudence to judge correctly concerning singular things to be done, to be done now, a judgment that is indeed corrupted by any sin.[355]

JUSTICE AND CHARITY

The will must also be the subject of habits, not that a person has to will his own good. Man's will is naturally born to his own good. But that man may will the good of another or of God, another virtue is necessary. The virtue which perfects the will of the good of the other is justice. That which perfects the willing of the good of God is charity.

> Hence, the will is in no need of a habit of virtue in order to be inclined to the good proportioned to it, to which it tends because of what it is, but with respect to a good which transcends what is proportioned to the power, it needs a habit. [...] Thus there are two virtues in the will as in a subject, namely, charity and justice.[356]

The mean of these virtues is determined by an exterior, objective standard which itself is based on the nature of the other and what is willed. The traditional term for what is willed is a right and so justice is based on rights. Rights are determined either by the nature of man himself (*natural right* — as in, for example, the right to life) or by human determination (*positive right*—as in the case with political rights or other rights which depend merely on human promulgation). Justice is not determined then by how one feels when giving rights nor about who the individual is as an individual to whom rights are given, but rather by what the case demands given the various powers of the human soul. Rights determined by men (*positive right*) cannot contradict natural right no matter how powerful the person is making the law. This is because natural right is based on the transcendence of the human soul as a spirit over material considerations. This fact is reflected by Vatican II in the famous personalistic norm: "The truth about man, which the Council's text explains ... has two main emphases. The first affirms that man is the only creature in the world that the Creator willed 'for its own sake'; the second consists in saying that this same man ... can only find himself through a disinterested gift of self (*Gaudium et Spes*, 24:3)."[357]

There is a great difference between ancient and modern ideas of justice and right. The ancient idea of justice reflected by the definition approved by the Church: "the constant and firm will to give their due to God and neighbor" (*CCC*, 1807) places the accent of justice on giving another person his due. Justice therefore is always other centered and is judged *ad alterum*, based on the needs of the other. This is the source of the famous idea of Plato that it is better to suffer than to do injustice. If one suffers injustice, one loses nothing morally. But if one does injustice, one is morally impaired. Instead, the contemporary idea of justice emphasizes the subject receiving rights from others.

The whole weight of character formation is at stake here. The modern world is characterized by the attitude: "I have my rights, so I want justice." The rights of the other do not enter. But the whole consideration of rights is based on the understanding that there is something untouchable about the human person because of the presence of the reasoning soul. Since morals is about the interior formation of the person, whether one gets one's rights is immaterial to this formation. When one does not give the other his due, this leads to a condition in which he is lacking in soul. Coupled with the Christian idea of loving one's neighbor as oneself and blessing enemies, this lack can be catastrophic if it involves mortal sin, for instance.

FORTITUDE AND TEMPERANCE

Moral freedom also includes the passions because the higher power moves the lover ones to action. In another section, this movement was explained as that of a wise governor to a free citizen, a political rule, not master to slave, a tyrannical rule. This political rule of the intellect and will also extends to the passions and so there must be virtues in the passions. This political rule is expressed in the formation of the virtues of temperance and fortitude. Temperance governs the concupiscible appetite and fortitude the irascible appetite.

These virtues differ from the virtue of justice whose mean is determined by an objective, external law. The mean in these virtues includes reference to the subject because people with different temperaments approach these virtues in different ways because the passions are involved. One size does not fit all. Fearful people are brought to the virtuous life in a different way than energetic people. The objective nature of the law regarding justice is the same, but the manner of approach differs.

Because the moral constitution of the person often colors the way a person pursues the truth, formation in these virtues is absolutely necessary to develop prudence and justice. Many have been thwarted in pursuing what they knew to be right because of a weakness in their passions.

GROWTH IN VIRTUE

Some people have the idea that growing in the virtues is just a matter of repeated actions. Since at least for acquired virtue one action does not suffice to form a virtue, many think that just repeated actions create a virtue. Sheer number of actions is the issue. Actually, since virtue is character formation in the mind, the will and the passions, the issue is not the number of acts but their intensity. It is possible to fall away from virtue and begin to prefer vice if one's actions are lukewarm. The point is clear in the intellectual virtues. One hundred hours of distracted study are often not as valuable to developing science as a few hours of intensive study. So the general principle is that it is not number of acts but the intensity of acts which forms and increases virtues.

The same thing is true in developing the will in love. One cannot remain on the same plane in the interior formation of love. One is either growing in the intensity of love or falling out of love. The intensity of the act of love is the basis for this growth or loss. For virtues acquired by human powers, one action is not sufficient to lose the virtue. A great many actions which are less intense must be performed.

Human practice is not the source of the virtues which are necessary to form the intellect in knowing about God or in desiring him. These are called the infused or theological virtues. God is the source of these virtues. Man does not get or keep these virtues by his human practice. Instead, these virtues are directly infused by God into the soul when one receives grace. Since these virtues have the direct action of God as their origin and can only be maintained by his continuous inspiration, human acquired virtues can only be a disposition to receive them. Man does his part, but he cannot cause either grace or these virtues. He merely opens himself to receiving these with God's inspiration. St. Thomas comments on the text in Luke regarding meriting grace, "When you have done all these things that are commanded, say: 'We are unprofitable servants; we have done that which we ought to do'". (Lk. 17:10) He says: "Man merits, inasmuch as he does what he ought, by his free-will; otherwise the act of justice whereby anyone discharges a debt would not be meritorious."[358]

In the case of these virtues, since they are divinely given with grace, one action in accord with or contrary to grace is sufficient to lose them. The sacrament of baptism is sufficient to receive the theological and infused virtues and one mortal sin is sufficient to lose them.

The question arises if one loses grace by mortal sin, how does this loss affect the virtues which one has formed by personal cooperation with grace? For example, if one loses infused justice, does he acquire by that action the vice of injustice. The tendency acquired by human cooperation with grace remains unless it is corrupted by further and more intense acts of injustice. So if one loses an infused virtue by one action, he does not thereby acquire a vice.

THE THEOLOGICAL VIRTUES

In addition to the acquired virtues, a person must be perfected regarding the pursuit of union with God as his ultimate end. No human action can bring this about. Rather, God must infuse virtues into the intellect and will so that the person can actively know and desire God by a union of friendship. Sanctifying grace elevates a person in being to this union. Since by this grace man becomes a participant in divine nature, it is fitting for God to provide inclinations in the intellect and will by which one knowing as God knows and loving as God loves becomes second nature. Divine nature becomes as second nature to the engraced Christian. These virtues are called the theological virtues because by them a person can act motivated by the same knowledge and love which is found within the Trinity. "If a man loves me, he will keep my word, and my Father will love him, and we will come to him and make our home with him." (Jn. 14:23)

Faith is a gift from God given to the intellect by which a person knows as God knows. Faith is the beginning of salvation because one cannot love what one does not know. Faith is a quality present the intellect, by which a person can know and understand the truths of God, especially those which are not open to human proof from knowledge acquired through the senses, like the Trinity and the Incarnation. Faith is the only kind of theoretical intellectual knowledge which depends on the will. The will motivates the person to continuous trust and dependence on the trustworthiness of the person revealing the truth. Human faith ends when the learner fully understands the truth. The virtue of divine faith can never be brought to an end by such understanding because there is always more to know. Investigation in the mind and assent in the will run together continuously because the more one understands the more one can understand. There is no mean for this virtue because the infinity of God is the standard on which faith is judged. Still, there can be extremes in faith as in all science. When one assents to a truth which is false, this is an excess. When one fails to assent to a truth, this is a defect.

The virtue of hope is in the will. It is also communicated together with grace and allows the person to see heaven as possible of attainment. Hope sustains the daily moral life of a Christian by allowing the Christian to keep his gaze fixed on heaven as his final completion in everyday acts of the will. Since God's nature is the standard for this virtue also, one can never hope in God enough while on earth. Though there is no strict mean for this virtue, there can be a kind of excess and defect in hope based not on God's nature which is its measure, but on human nature. One who thinks he will get to heaven no matter what he does is guilty of the excess of presumption. One who has no hope for heaven no matter what he does is guilty of the defect of despair.

The virtue of charity exists in the will and involves union with the infinite God. By this virtue man loves God as he is in himself above all things and his neighbor as himself. This virtue is the proper intention for which one lives the commandments and for that reason the love of God and the love of neighbor form the basis for even the division of the commandments. The first table of the law of God comprising commandments 1-3 preserves the love of God. The second table of the law comprising commandments 4-10 preserves the love of neighbor.

Many people in Christianity emphasize spectacular or unusual experiences. Some others maintain that the only action which can merit heaven is in the final moment of death. Though religion may indeed involve spectacular experiences and though the moment of death is obviously a very important experience in the moral life, the actions done which result from charity are the most important. This is why St. Paul emphasizes that true interior formation must be based on the union with God expressed by charity. "If I ... have not charity," says the Apostle, "I am nothing... Charity is superior to all the virtues. It is the first of the theological virtues."[359] This is the reason St. Thomas and the *Catechism* refer to charity as the "form of the virtues".[360] This also means that one act done from charity, it does not matter what it is, is sufficient to merit heaven, not just the one act done at the moment of death.

In addition to the theological virtues, there are also infused moral virtues which grace brings to the powers of the soul. It would be unfitting for God who provides natural means of obtaining acquired virtues to provide any less for a life based on the supernatural standard of his own inner life. So, in addition to grace and the theological virtues, God also infuses into every baptized person infused moral virtues of prudence, justice, temperance and fortitude and the gifts of the Holy Spirit. A discussion of the gifts is beyond the scope of this book, but the virtues are central to living the life of charity in everyday human life and an essential indicator of progress in the spiritual life.

Though there may be spectacular manifestations in religion, these are of relative unimportance compared to the daily practice of ordinary virtues done from charity. When embraced according to the duties of one's state, this is the foundation of going to heaven. The practice of the ordinary virtues from extraordinary love is essential. Francis de Sales clearly expresses this most necessary truth:

> Opportunities for the practice of fortitude, magnanimity, and magnificence do not often occur; but gentleness, moderation, integrity and humility are virtues with which all the actions of our lives should be colored. There are virtues nobler than these; but the practice of these is more necessary.
>
> Among the virtues we should prefer that which suits our duty best, and not which is most to our taste and, although everyone ought to have all the virtues, yet not everyone is bound to practice them to the same

extent. Each ought to give himself specially to those which are required by the kind of life to which he is called.[361]

These virtues lead to a certain peace of character within. If unhappy saints are lost from the beginning, then the more one develops the virtues of temperance and fortitude the more spontaneous one will become in living the virtues of prudence and justice. One will not only do the good, but rejoice in the good. When this happens habit and spontaneity exist in beautiful integrity with each other.

> Their way to achieve this end, however, is to make the best use of emotive energy and not to suppress it. ... So far as the reference to truth is concerned, the integrating process of developing and improving the psyche gradually produces the result that the will—guided by the light of reason—learns how by spontaneous reference to emotion, by a spontaneous move of attraction or repulsion to choose and to adopt the real good; it also learns to reject the real bad.[362]

In a note on this text, John Paul II clarifies: "This belief appears to also be contained in what Aristotle says of the power of the intellect and will over emotions having a 'political' (or 'diplomatic') rather than an absolute character. (cf. *Politics*, bk. 1, chap. 3: *Nicomachean Ethics*, bk. 4, chaps, 3-5)"[363]

Finally, the emphasis on the development of the virtues, as opposed to the obligation and duty simply to live an external standard, points to two different ideas of freedom on which they are based. According to Fr. Pinkaers, these are freedom of indifference and freedom of excellence. These in turn are the foundation for two entirely different ways of approaching morals which also lead to two different points of view on happiness.

Freedom of indifference comes from William of Ockham and emphasizes the simple lack of external constraint which could be realized in either good or evil. "A freedom such as this is in opposition to the desire for happiness ... it can base itself only on law, which restricts freedom with the sense of obligation or duty."[364] Freedom of excellence on the other hand, "is rooted in a desire for happiness which proceeds principally from a sense of truth and goodness, together with the inclination to life in society."[365] Thomas Aquinas would be the origin for this idea of freedom which emphasizes not only the will but also the intellect and passions as the origin for freedom. In this latter kind of freedom, the pursuit of virtue which *ipso facto* also involves freedom from sin causes human integrity. This brings the powers of man and so the person to an interior harmony with each other which is firmly held because based on choices which induce qualities of union between the truth, love and emotions. The perception of this inner harmony leads to a joy through intellectual understanding, willed experience and emotional delight.

HEAVEN ON EARTH BEGUN

The Catholic tradition in morals is rooted in the freedom of excellence. It is in this freedom that human integrity consists because all the powers of the human soul cooperate together. When the powers of the soul have induced in them a quality which is halfway between simple ability and action, then acting according to reason and nature becomes almost second nature. The potential present in the human soul in man's initial creation is realized. A person really enjoys doing good but even more being good. This happy combination leads to an experience of inner peace and happiness and when blessed by cooperation with the theological and infused moral virtues ensures that the life of the Trinity is already in the heart of man through grace. As the life induced by the virtues becomes more rooted in the character, sin and temptation are more easily avoided because one depends more on an interior perception of God and his merciful desire to aid man to get to heaven. Heaven is in a sense begun on earth and nothing remains but the vision after death.

CHAPTER ELEVEN
SIN

RECOVERING THE IDEA OF SIN

In 1973, a famous minister psychiatrist, Karl Menninger, wrote a book called *Whatever Became of Sin?*[366] In that book he lamented the replacement of a religion of moral responsibility with psychiatry. His lamentation is perhaps even more pressing in contemporary society and astonishingly even more pressing in the Church. For decades people have been persuaded that they need not confess a "laundry list" of sins, cataloguing even venial sins. Many religious educators deny there is a distinction between mortal and venial sin. The whole question of personal sin and responsibility has been in escrow since the Council.

Pope John Paul II characterizes the malaise well. First he quotes Pius XII who said: "The sin of the (20th) century is the loss of a sense of sin."[367] Then he summarizes the contemporary consequences for the Church in a lengthy paragraph.

> Even in the field of the thought and life of the church certain trends inevitably favor the decline of the sense of sin. For example, some are inclined to replace exaggerated attitudes of the past with other exaggerations: From seeing sin everywhere they pass to not recognizing it anywhere; from too much emphasis on the fear of eternal punishment they pass to preaching a love of God that excludes any punishment deserved by sin; from severity in trying to correct erroneous consciences they pass to a kind of respect for conscience which excludes the duty of telling the truth. And should it not be added that the confusion caused in the consciences of many of the faithful by differences of opinions and teachings in theology, preaching, catechesis and spiritual direction on serious and delicate questions of Christian

morals ends by diminishing the true sense of sin almost to the point of eliminating it altogether? Nor can certain deficiencies in the practice of sacramental penance be overlooked. These include the tendency to obscure the ecclesial significance of sin and of conversion and to reduce them to merely personal matters; or vice versa, the tendency to nullify the personal value of good and evil and to consider only their community dimension. There also exists the danger, never totally eliminated, of routine ritualism that deprives the sacrament of its full significance and formative effectiveness.[368]

The more glaring schools of thought which make sin problematic today were discussed in Chapter Five. The importance of emphasizing virtue and joy which are intrinsic principle of moral integrity were discussed in Chapter Ten. Sin is also such an intrinsic principle. Though it is true that there has been an overemphasis on avoiding sin within the strict confines of the law which is interpreted as an external imposition since the time of the Council of Trent, an emphasis on virtue must entail a realistic assessment of just what sin is. This is because sin leads to a condition where virtue is compromised or in some cases even destroyed and so our road to happiness becomes a dead end. Virtue has to be treated first because one should know the nature of health before he can appreciate illness. Sin is moral illness.

SIN, MALICE, AND VICE

Thomas Aquinas distinguishes three conditions regarding sin which underline the interior nature of sin as illness regarding the health of virtue. They are: virtue, goodness and the act of virtue. Virtue makes the possessor and his act good. Good deeds are not enough for virtuous formation. Since the deeds are intimately connected to the formation of freedom, they must flow from free choice if they are to contribute to interior formation which includes union with God and pursuit of man's ultimate end. So, regarding virtue, there is the interior disposition which is virtue properly speaking, the action which results from it and contributes to its formation and the interior wholeness among all the powers of the soul which such an action forms. To have one cardinal virtue one must have them all and they

CHAPTER ELEVEN SIN

each form one of the three powers of the soul which are a necessary component of every moral action: intellect, will and passions.

The term sin "refers" to the deed which is contrary to an act of virtue. Repeated acts of sin like repeated acts of virtue cause a disposition in the powers of the soul in which the subject not only does evil but begins to love and enjoy evil. This colors his judgment concerning the true and authentic good. This is called vice as opposed to virtue. Such dispositions provoke a lack of order among the powers of the soul where they are out of sync with each other so that even if a person were to convert and seek to do good, other powers of his soul would not easily come along and he would be constantly pestered by feelings and thoughts which would war against his good intentions. This is called malice which is opposed to goodness. "So three things oppose virtue: sins (or misdeeds), evil (the opposite of goodness) and vice (disposition unbefitting one's nature)."[369]

These three things all lead to human deformation because they are all contrary to the order of reason which in turn expresses human nature. So they are truly sicknesses of the soul. Though the deepest sickness occurs when the person develops dispositions which are contrary to his nature so that he prefers sinful acts, the deeds themselves are worse than the mere condition because dispositions though they may affect freedom are not deterministic. One can always act contrary to a disposition be it a good one or an evil one. This means that it is better to actually do well than merely have the developed capability of doing well and the same is true of evil.

This distinction also allows one to understand the fact that, in all naturally induced integrity, one evil act does not so form freedom that it makes one a vicious person, just as one act of virtue does not so form freedom that one becomes a virtuous person. One swallow does not a spring make.

On the other hand, there are virtues which are infused or instilled by grace in man. These are the theological and supernaturally formed moral virtues. One act of mortal sin which is contrary to the existence of charity kills grace, the means by which man arrives at heaven, in the soul. So when one act of sin destroys sanctifying grace, all the supernaturally induced virtues except faith and hope end, though these only exist in an inchoate state.

SIN OF OMISSION

Another difference between sin and virtue is that since sin is a negation of freedom, it is possible to commit a sin without a deed. This is called a sin of omission. If the moral law requires someone to do something by a positive command (for example, to worship God on Sunday by attendance at Mass) and they fail to do so, then they are acting contrary to reason in a very important matter and commit a grave sin. This is because the virtue of religion which is a part of the virtue of justice, namely justice towards God, requires that man recognize the rights of the Creator in his actions. There are four actions which man must do in order to have this virtue: two interior and two exterior. The interior acts are devotion in the will and prayer in the intellect. The exterior acts are adoration and sacrifice. Any authentic act of worship in any religion must develop these acts. Christ had all these acts on the Cross. For the Christian, the Mass is the prolongation of the worship of Christ. To be a truly virtuous person, the Christian must devoutly attend Mass each Sunday. Though this is an obligation, it strikes so closely at the interior relationship of man with God that purposely to omit it shows a complete lack of love for God. Thus, it is a mortal sin.

With the fact of omission in mind, the Catholic tradition has defined sin as "(a)ny word, deed, or desire contrary to the Eternal Law."[370] This definition has two parts to it. There is the voluntary action or omission which sin involves in some specific action or deed. Then there is the disorder which this voluntary action or omission produces in the character. As a result of this action, the person loses integrity within, the powers of the soul cannot act together in a cohesive whole and man loses interior union with God if this is a mortal sin.

Two important characteristics of sin follow from this. First, the disorder is outside the sinner's intention, but not the sinner's knowledge. He knows that if he does something (or omits to do it) that such a disorder will follow. But he does not will the disorder as a disorder but rather whatever is the good of the action, albeit an apparent good. For example, in an act of fornication, he wills to enjoy the pleasure, knowing that he experiences this pleasure at the expense of the rights of God and respect for the other person in this act. The other person is only a good for him because they make him feel good. Whereas there is nothing wrong with enjoying sexuality, this must be done respecting both the good of procreation and education and the good of unity. The sinner intends the pleasure but not the disorder. He does know that in loving the pleasure in this disordered way, higher goods which he should love more cannot coexist in his soul, namely the good of charity. Though he may experience satisfaction regarding the good of pleasure, it is at the expense of the good of his spirit.

PHYSICAL AND MORAL EVIL

The difference between physical and moral evil is that, in physical evil, the natural disorder of a being causes a disorder in action. For example, a lame leg causes a lame walk. In moral evil, just the opposite is true. The lack of order in a voluntary action (it is contrary to reason) causes the lack of order in the soul. A mortal sin of fornication causes the loss of grace and the virtue of temperance and perhaps justice.

In the case of physical evil, nature will not be denied. If one abuses nature by drinking to excess, the body rebels against this unnatural condition and one becomes ill or even dies. In the moral universe, the origin of punishment is the reaction of reason to the condition of disorder. A person who dies unrepentant in mortal sin without grace cannot realize his final destiny. Freedom and nature forever disagree and this is hell. Someone murders an innocent person and the civil order reacts with imprisonment or the death penalty. Someone commits masturbation and not only do they lose grace but they experience a lack of freedom in virtuous formation in the sexual urge.

The voluntary nature of the sin is its essence. The punishment for the sin is very real and reasonable but outside the intention of the sinner. Therefore, the kind or species of sin is determined by what the sinner is drawn to, not the punishment. Theft, for example, is "usurping another's property against the reasonable will of the owner."[371] The specific disorder in the character involves the will in justice and is about material goods, not about life, sexuality or the good name. The amount of the theft determines the punishment. To steal a little is a venial sin and outside virtue, not contrary to it. To steal a lot is a mortal sin and completely contrary to the virtue of justice and precludes the existence of grace and charity.

The Church still requires that for the integrity of confession all remembered mortal sins must be confessed species and number. "All mortal sins of which penitents after a diligent self-examination are conscious must be recounted by them in confession ..." (CCC, 1456)

Regarding sin, the exterior action is the most important classification and determines the fault of the action. It is the matter of the sin. The order which is interrupted is the form and determines the punishment for the sin. "Sins then are classified according to the voluntary act involved and the object aimed at, rather than their disorderedness. The goal of an action is its primary source of goodness, the object of the will involved. So to classify sins by objects and by goals amounts to the same."[372]

SIN AND GUILT

The second important consequence is that a part of the punishment for sin is the reaction within the soul to perceived moral disorder. Sin is not like virtue. One must have all the virtues to have one as virtue causes interior integration. This integration when perceived produces a peace of character. The opposite is true of sin and vice. It is impossible for a person to have all the sins and vices because sin causes a disorder. Two vices of excess and defect are contrary to every virtue. They are also contrary to each other, so one cannot possess them all at the same time. Sin creates disorder in the character.

When someone acts contrary to reason, the person himself if he is healthy experiences an emotional uneasiness at this disorder and perhaps even sadness coupled with hatred, fear and perhaps anger. He feels incomplete. His desires have not been formed as they naturally should be according to reason. This feeling causes emotional guilt which corresponds to the intellectual perception of guilt.

> Hence, it is more than an intellectual awareness of the wrong that has been done; it is an actual feeling of incompleteness. This is the way in which well-balanced, mature individuals spontaneously react and it forms the basis of the *feeling of guilt* which results from performing acts that are morally wrong. It is an experience of the psychological incompleteness of the human act.[373]

Guilt then can be healthy. The difference between neurotic and healthy guilt is the difference between the mature and immature perception of a disordered act. Also, there is a distinction between the intellectual perception of the guilt and the emotional reaction to this disorder. "Both are normally present in the well-balanced person, but it is possible for an individual to have only the intellectual awareness of guilt without any sensory feeling, or to have a feeling of guilt which is not substantiated by any rational judgment."[374]

Mature people feel guilt when they should. The abnormal experience of guilt involves either feeling guilty when one has not done anything wrong or what is more pathological and more characteristic of contemporary Western life, not feeling guilty when one has done something wrong. The idea that all guilt is pathological is very mistaken and the result of a Freudian psychology which does not appreciate the place of the intellect in emotional formation.

Indeed, the experience of guilt can be a powerful motive for repentance. It can also be the emotional punishment for a sin committed. Women who have had an abortion often confess this sin over and over again, motivated by the experience of guilt. While the confessor must carefully explain that the continuous confession of the sin is unnecessary and wrong if she thinks her sin was not forgiven, he may also assure her that the guilt she feels is a part of her own satisfaction for the temporal punishment due to sin and should be a motive to pray for her child and an end to abortion.

THE GRAVITY OF SIN

The gravity of the sin is determined not by its punishment but by its object. A progression in gravity is seen in the order of the commandments. Sins against God are the worst (Commandment 1-3). Sins against the self are next in gravity, which includes those very connected to the self like honoring parents (Commandment 4). Sins contrary to the neighbor are next; there is a "lowerarchy" among them depending on how close the good involved is to the person himself (Commandment 5-8). Actions against life are worse than actions against family.

The subjective order is also taken into consideration in determining the kind and gravity of the disorder caused by sin because of the powers of the soul which are principally involved. Catholic theology commonly distinguishes between sins of ignorance, weakness and malice. This division has its source in the powers of the soul principally involved in the particular action of sin. Sins of ignorance are in the intellect; sins of weakness in the passions; and sins of malice are in the will as such.

It is true that the will is involved in some sense in all sins because it is the power of the soul by which a person places acts in morals and determines responsibility. The division of ignorance, weakness and malice express the various ways the powers of the soul relate to the will.

SINS OF WEAKNESS

The first distinction important to evaluate the relation of these powers to human action is that between actions of the will which pass into exterior matter like cutting, burning acts of the will remain in the agent performing them like desiring, knowing, and loving. These are the acts which fall under morals and go to form virtues and vices. The will is the principle. However, because the will moves the other interior powers to act, these powers can also be subjects of sin as they are subjects of virtue. The will moves the intellect to think and the passions to emote.

The passions themselves are good but they are also born to be obedient to reason. Before Original Sin, this was easy. Adam and Eve had an easy virtue. The passions did not arise in them before they could think and did not color their judgment by egotism. After the sin, even for those in the state of grace, the passions arise before reason can be brought to bear and often cause us to sin. Sins which result from this are called sins of weakness.

The *Catechism* refers to sins of weakness in two ways. They can be either the result of the will entertaining and taking up the passion as in "hardness of heart"[375] or of the will being stricken by passion like an "external pressure"[376] which is like an alien force in the will. The difference regarding responsibility for both good and evil is whether the passion arises before the act of the will or results from the cooperation and approval of the will. Approved passions make an act more willing and so more voluntary.

One has only so much spiritual energy and if all the interior spiritual energy is engrossed in the passions the influence of the intellect will be compromised. A person may be so engrossed in realizing his passions that he does not apply the universal judgment of his conscience to a particular action here and now. "Reason is fettered owing to the fact that the attention of the soul is vehemently applied to an act of the sensitive appetite, hence it is diverted from considering in particular what it knows universally and habitually."[377]

In some cases, reason can resist this fettering of the passions and in these cases described as hardness of heart, the person is more responsible depending on the degree his reason approves such passions. In other cases, the passions completely bind him as in the case of psychopathic or neurotic personalities. This frees the subject of responsibility for these particular deeds unless he refuses to use all possible aids to deal with these passions. This is like the alcoholic. Since his reason is bound when drunk, he would not normally be held responsible. However, since he either drank voluntarily or refused to seek a support group if he needs help, in some sense he is responsible for the resulting condition and what results from it. For example, if he killed someone driving drunk, he would not be as responsible as someone who cold bloodedly set out to kill that person, still he would be somewhat responsible as he could have sought help and did not or simply willed not to drink.

> But the will has the power to apply or not to apply its attention to something; hence it is within the power of the will to exclude the fettering of reason. Therefore the act committed, which proceeds from this fettering, is voluntary, hence it is not excused from mortal fault. But if the fettering of reason by passion advanced to such a point that it would not be within the power of the will to exclude this fettering, for example, if from some passion of the soul someone were to become insane, whatever he committed would not be imputed to him [...] except perhaps so far as concerns the beginning of such a passion, that it was voluntary.[378]

Passion then affects the gravity of sin and the goodness of virtue. "The more intense the movement of the will to sin, the graver is the sin; but the more intense the passion impelling to sin, the less grave the sin becomes."[379] So, antecedent passions and external pressures can reduce moral responsibility. "The promptings of feelings and passions can also diminish the voluntary and free character of the offense, as can external pressures or pathological disorders."[380]

A good example occurs regarding masturbation which the *Catechism* maintains is always gravely sinful in object. It then goes on: "To form an equitable judgment about the subject's moral responsibility and to guide pastoral action, one must take into account the affective immaturity, force of acquired habit, conditions of anxiety, or other psychological or social factors that can lessen, if not even reduce to a minimum, moral culpability."[381] This means that though masturbation is always a mortal sin in object, by antecedent passion the subject may only be guilty of a venial sin.

One further point: strictly speaking, sins and goods in which the will increases the passion as a servant are done more freely because a person loves the good or evil more. They are "to be fervent and ardent by reason of choice of good or of evil."[382] In evil things, this is what is meant by hardness of heart. So they are not exactly sins from passion.

> 'The hardness of heart' indicates that which according to the *ethos* of the people of the Old Testament, had given rise to a situation contrary to the original design of God-Yahweh according to Gen. 2: 24. [...] If in the words [...] in the Sermon on the Mount the human heart is 'accused' of concupiscence [...] at the same time and by the same words it is called to discover the full meaning of that which, in the act of concupiscence, constitutes for it 'a value not sufficiently appreciated'.[383]

This increases the voluntary nature of the deed and so moral responsibility. "Hardness of heart [does] not diminish but rather increase[s], the voluntary character of the sin."[384]

SINS OF IGNORANCE

Sins of ignorance occur in the intellect. Every sin can in a certain sense be called a sin of ignorance in the sense that the intellect fails to apply the universal moral law to the particular case. Sins of ignorance involve inability to know something which precedes the act of the will which would have altered the person's judgment or a deliberate refusal to investigate the nature of the moral action either in universal or particular.

Ignorance of the law is no excuse. One is bound to know the laws in conscience before acting. However, since moral actions are carried out in particular circumstances and deeds, there may be many circumstances of which one could not reasonably be expected to have knowledge. The presence of such knowledge might have altered his choice. Ignorance of these is called invincible ignorance because it cannot be conquered by the will. It is unintentional. "Unintentional ignorance can diminish or even remove the imputability of a grave offense. But no one is deemed to be ignorant of the principles of the moral law, which are written in the conscience of every man."[385] This is because the true deformed nature of the deed is not a part of the interior intention since one could or should not have known this circumstance.

On the other hand, ignorance which is caused by the will is called vincible ignorance. A person could and so should have known either the law or a circumstance which would have altered his choice. This ignorance is not real as it is feigned and certainly could be changed by the subject. "Feigned ignorance [...] do[es] not diminish, but rather increase[s] the voluntary character of the sin."[386]

SINS OF MALICE

The worst sin is one of pure will. This is the sin of Adam and Eve who did not experience weakness and ignorance. It is also the sin of the Pharisees in the gospels who could hardly claim weakness and ignorance in their contempt for others and rejection of Christ. Both Aquinas and the Church designate this as a sin of certain malice. "Sin committed through malice, by deliberate choice of evil, is the gravest."[387]

A sin of certain malice is in the will not in the sense that the will directly and principally chooses evil. This is not possible as the will is always drawn principally to some good. Rather, the will is drawn to a good principally which has an evil necessarily attached secondarily. For example, in fornication the will is drawn to the good of pleasure but secondarily attached to this good is the use of the other person and the denial of the truth which God himself placed in masculinity and femininity. "If then a person should wish so much to enjoy some pleasure, say, adultery or some desirable thing of this kind, that he does not shrink from incurring the deformity of sin which he perceives to be conjoined to what he wills [...] Hence, the adulterer both wills principally the pleasure and wills secondarily the deformity."[388]

Sins of certain malice are more grave than sins of weakness for three reasons. First, they are present in the principle which determines moral responsibility, the will. Second, because in sins of passion, the will is only born to the sin while the passion endures. In sins of malice, "the will is inclined to the act of sin from an enduring habit, which does not pass away but persists as a kind of form now become immanent and connatural."[389] This means that the person finds repentance more difficult. He likes to sin. Third, in sins of weakness, the person intends something good but cannot persist in this because of passion. In sins of malice, the will is ordered to an evil end and "has a fixed intention of sinning."[390]

In sins of malice, there is no mitigation. The person who commits a sin of weakness or ignorance easily repents from it. In the case of ignorance, when he can know, he is sorry because the evil itself is not firmly fixed in his character. In the case of weakness, when the passion dies as it must, the person can more soberly consider the situation and also easily repents. But in the case of malice, the person not only does evil but loves it and so he finds repentance much more difficult. "Therefore he who sins from malice sins most gravely and dangerously and cannot easily be induced to refrain from sin as can one who sins from weakness in whom at least a good intention remains."[391] This is the reason the confessor must have a clear and flawless knowledge of the moral law, but at the same time treat the penitent with great mercy because men rarely have such an inner drive to evil that they sin from certain malice.

EXTERNAL CAUSES OF SIN: GOD, MATERIAL THINGS, THE DEVIL

There are three external forces which can influence willing: God, material things and the devil. Three things in turn operate in three ways to influence willing: "the object, appealing to man's will through his external senses, the one who presents the object, and the one who persuades us of the objects goodness (and that could be the devil or some other man)."[392]

Exterior things can move the will to desire but not in a deterministic fashion. Man is only determined to desire the ultimate good. Neither the devil nor another man can force man to sin. They can persuade and suggest, but the will always remains free. "The bad angels [lead] to man's harm either so far as concerns the affect of sin, namely inasmuch as man from the things he apprehends is incited to pride or to some other sin, or to impede the understanding of the truth itself according as man from certain things apprehended by the mind is led into a doubt which he knows not how to solve and thus is drawn into error."[393] In the same way, other men may lead by persuasion and suggestion, though the demons can influence the thought patterns of men directly through the imagination as they can move the body and so those chemical reactions which affect man's sense perceptions, "the demon fills as it were with befogging mists all the paths of understanding though which the mind's ray customarily diffuses the light of reason."[394]

The only sufficient and direct cause for the action of sin is the will itself which though it may be influenced by other people, and sense desires and by the devil always remains free to not be moved. "So, though God is the ultimate cause of all our inward movements, that a man's will makes a bad decision comes directly from the will itself, and indirectly from the devil through persuasion and presentation of desirable objects."[395]

ORIGINAL SIN

Sin is customarily distinguished between Original Sin and Actual sin which regards the cause of sin. Then actual sin is further distinguished regarding punishment into mortal and venial sin.

Original sin and actual sin differ because one is a defect of nature and not an action. The other is an action. Though the Original Sin is caused by an individual action of disobedience on the part of Adam and Eve, the nature of this sin is not a deed. Adam and Eve enjoyed a relationship of contemplative union with God characterized by grace and special gifts in the intellect, will, passions and body. They were "naked and not ashamed." (Gen. 2:25) For them, the body was a means by which they gave themselves as gifts to one another, a gift which was ratified in the sexual act. Since there was no sin, they had no fear that they would be dominated by the other or the gift of self taken from them so that they would be merely objects of pleasure for the other. This condition was one which they could pass on to their descendants. It was a state of being. This condition endured as long as they both demonstrated their loving obedience through respect for God's law. At the suggestion of the tempter, they questioned the gift of God and so showed little love. They lost grace, the source of this condition.

As a result, a new state entered the human race characterized by the loss of grace. That new state has two characteristics. "What defines inherited (original) sin is the loss of the original subjection of will to God, and every other disorder of the powers of man's soul is, so to speak, matter that is now formed by that loss."[396] So the formal cause of original sin is the loss of grace and the state of original justice. The powers of the soul are the subject affected by this loss: ignorance in the intellect, malice in the will, concupiscence in the passions and suffering and death in the body.

Original Sin relates to moral theology in the sense that man's weakness in knowing truth, willing good and spontaneity has its origin here. Man now enters the world with this weakness and though his powers remain in their natural orientation which means man is not totally depraved, they need healing in order to be able to act again in integrity and certainly to desire heaven.

> The whole human race is in Adam 'as one body of one man.' By this 'unity of the human race' all men are implicated in Adam's sin, as all are implicated in Christ's justice. ... It [Original Sin] is a sin which will be transmitted by propagation to all mankind, that is, by the transmission of a human nature deprived of original holiness and justice. And that is why original sin is called 'sin' only in an analogical sense; it is a sin 'contracted' and not 'committed'—a state and not an act. (*CCC*, 404)

ACTUAL SIN: MORTAL AND VENIAL

Actual sin on the other hand is an act.

> Actual sin is found first found in a principle, namely the will, which is the first subject of sin ... and is transmitted from it to the other powers of the soul, and even to the members of the body, according as they are moved by the will. [397]

This has traditionally been divided into mortal and venial sin or sin by which charity and grace are killed because the matter is so central to the journey of the human soul towards heaven, and sin in which grace and charity can still exist.

There has been some debate since Vatican II as to whether the Church still teaches the division of mortal and venial sin. John Paul II clarified the fact that it does.

> Here we have the core of the church's traditional teaching, which was reiterated frequently and vigorously during the recent synod. The synod in fact not only reaffirmed the teaching of the Council of Trent concerning the existence and nature of mortal and venial sins, but it also recalled that mortal sin is sin whose object is grave matter and which is also committed with full knowledge and deliberate consent. It must be added-as was likewise done at the synod-that some sins are intrinsically grave and mortal by reason of their matter. That is, there exist acts which, per se and in themselves, independently of circumstances, are always seriously wrong by reason of their object. These acts, if carried out with sufficient awareness and freedom, are always gravely sinful.[398]

The first point to make about this division is that mortal sin is sin in the strict sense of the word. By it, the soul loses the ability to arrive at heaven because it is an action which is incompatible with the existence of grace in the soul. The requirements for a mortal sin affect all three powers of the soul which divide sins of weakness, ignorance and malice. It must be grave matter so it must objectively be about some serious human good which is not peripheral but central to man arriving at heaven. The will must freely embrace it and so the intellect must move the will without mitigation. The passions must also not be so involved that they compromise the freedom of the will and so deliberate consent is necessary. "For a sin to be mortal, three conditions must together be met: 'Mortal sin is sin whose object is grave matter and which is also committed with full knowledge and deliberate consent'." (*CCC*, 1857 quoting John Paul II, *Reconciliatio et Paenitentia*, 17, 12)

There have been many misunderstandings since Vatican II on the necessity of the confession of mortal sins or whether there can be mortal sins. The Catechism uses these terms[399] and since the Church still recognizes the distinction between mortal and venial sins, confession is still necessary for all remembered mortal sins, species and number. "The first conviction is that for a Christian the sacrament of penance is the primary way of obtaining forgiveness and the remission of serious sin committed after baptism."[400] This is because since mortal sin entails an action which precludes the presence of grace, there is no power in the soul to return to grace. Our Lord established the sacrament of Penance in order to return man to grace after baptism in light of mortal sin. The reason all sins must be confessed species and number is because the mercy of Christ must be applied to each action which has precluded the presence of grace.

In addition, the sacrament of Penance is spiritual medicine from the spiritual doctor who is Christ. In order for the medicine to be applied properly to the individual, the nature of the disease must be identified. If one went to a human physician and refused to express the nature, occurrence and place of the disease, a human physician could not prescribe medicine. In human healing, the physician cannot know the disease without the expression of the patient. God, of course, knows this. The requirement that the penitent accuse himself by expressing his spiritual failings is for the penitent's sake so he can acknowledge where he needs healing. The penitential rite or an act of contrition cannot in themselves heal such a breach of inner life.

Venial sin is not a sin in the strict sense of the word. A person may commit a venial sin and still preserve his inner relationship with God. Venial sin does not involve a disorder regarding the end but only a disorder regarding the means to the end. It can be healed by human actions. Venial sin is not against the law, since the one who commits a venial sin neither acts against or according to the law. He rather acts beside the law by not observing the measure of truth which the law intends. Venial sin is disorder of soul which does not cause a turning away from God either because the action is not grave or the intention is not present. "Venial sin is not turned toward a transitory good as to an end; and therefore it is not turned toward a transitory good as to a terminus other than God to such an extent that on that account it is necessarily turned away from God."[401] Still, people should be concerned about venial sins and confess them because though they do not contradict the heavenly end, they surely cause the need for purification at least in Purgatory, and so are unreasonable in their own way.

Since venial sin does not involve a rupture with the ultimate end, no number of venial sins can cause such a rupture. Venial sin does not involve a stain in the soul. A direct intervention in the soul through the sacrament of Penance is not needed. This does not mean that one should not be concerned about venial sins or not confess them.

This would be to reduce morals again to playing it safe within the extreme demands of the law in relation to freedom. The more man's inner freedom is compromised by willing and performing actions which cannot lead to heaven, even if they are not against it, the more lukewarm the individual is about desiring heaven. This is the reason both concern and frequent confession of venial sins is recommended but not required by the Church. "Without being strictly necessary, confession of everyday faults (venial sins) is nevertheless strongly recommended by the Church. Indeed the regular confession of our venial sins helps us form our conscience, fight against evil tendencies, let ourselves be healed by Christ and progress in the life of the Spirit. By receiving more frequently through this sacrament the gift of the Father's mercy, we are spurred to be merciful as he is merciful."[402]

CHAPTER TWELVE
GRACE

GRACE AND MORAL THEOLOGY

No treatment of fundamental moral theology should be complete without an examination of the doctrine of grace. Strangely, this was usually omitted from moral manuals for many centuries. Reflecting on the omission of the treatise on grace from the moral manuals, Fr. Servais Pinkaers explains:

> Here again, it seems to me, the mechanism of the system of obligation was highly developed. Grace, by definition, could not be reduced to obligation; law and its imperatives had no hold on grace. It could be no part of a law-based morality; strictly speaking, it would be useless there. ... The study of grace would pertain more to dogmatics than to moral theology, would be more speculative than practical.[403]

The importance of grace to the present study should be obvious as it underlies every aspect of the subject matter. First, grace is necessary to arrive at a supernatural ultimate end. This is true regardless of the existence of sin. Grace is necessary for human freedom. One can make free choices without grace between good and evil, but one cannot desire heaven freely without grace. This is the meaning of the statement that man in the state of Original Sin is not free. Grace is necessary to know the truth about God which is open only to faith and to heal the present lack of spontaneity in the moral life.

Grace is not only sanctifying but also healing. Grace is the essence of the law of the New Testament. The reason is that it allows for openness to the guidance of the Holy Spirit. This does not deny the Old Law which was also taught by the Holy Spirit, but allows the person to understand the spirit of the law by living this law with a right intention. This right intention is the road to heaven found in the soul through grace. As the Old Law cured the punishment of ignorance, the New Law cures the punishment of malice. Grace therefore elevates and heals the conscience. Grace is also necessary to form virtues which allow man to arrive at the ultimate end and finally, of course, grace is necessary to heal the wounds of sin, both Original and Actual.

In sum, grace is the necessary means by which man has communion with God and experiences moral growth and healing. This is because communion with God is central to inner righteousness or what traditional Catholic theology has always called justification. Justification is not the virtue of justice. It is rather what Aristotle called metaphorical justice. It is not the constant perpetual will to give to another his due, but inner integrity which allows the intellect, will and passions to act in concert and motivate further actions to arrive at the ultimate end. "More broadly, it means being rightly disposed within ourselves with our lower powers subject to the higher power of reason, and that higher part subject to God and Aristotle calls this disposition in his *Nicomachean Ethics*, V, metaphorical justice."[404] Before the Original Sin justification was the elevation of man's soul to union with God. After the sin, it also involves forgiveness of sins. "Justification is not only the remission of sins, but also the sanctification and renewal of the interior man."(*CCC*, 1989)[405]

GOD'S LOVE AND MAN'S LOVE

Human freedom is formed by grace because of the necessity of willing heaven and also the nature of the soul itself. Because of the supernatural end of the spiritual soul, grace is like the form of the soul. The soul can exist without grace, but it cannot exist well. Man can know truth without grace, but cannot know the whole truth. God loves all the world into continuous existence and the Holy Spirit supports that world in all its natural actions. God loves man with a special love which is love strictly speaking because by grace he makes the human soul like him. "Another is the special love with which he draws reasoning creatures above their natural condition to share in his own good; and this is the way God loves creatures in an unqualified sense, willing them an eternal good which is nothing other than himself."[406] The Scriptures express this well: "His divine power has granted to us all things that pertain to life and godliness, through the knowledge of him who called us to his own glory and excellence, by which he has granted to us his precious and very great promises that through these you may escape from corruption that is in the world because of passion, and become partakers of the divine nature." (2 Peter 1:3-4)

Grace strictly speaking is this participation and must involve a true interior change in the very essence of the soul of man. Luther, however, taught that grace was forensic justification. This was as though man came into a court condemned of a capital crime and God, the judge, chose merely to overlook the crime without any punishment which would resolve for the evil and make the criminal a worthy citizen again. In the traditional Protestant position, sin totally corrupted human nature. The Lutheran position is often characterized as saying that man in the state of grace "a lump of dung covered by snow." St. Thomas is of the opposite idea. He compares the love of God to human love and demonstrates that real human love has to respond to a real good in the being of the other. The same must be true, *mutatis mutandis*, with divine love.

Human love is expressed as grace in three ways: First, the love of someone for someone else as in the phrase, to stay in someone's good graces. Second, the gift given by the lover to the beloved as a sign of his grace as in the phrase, "I confer this grace on you." Third, the gratitude of the Beloved for both the love and gift of the Lover is expressed in thanksgiving as in the words used by Romance languages to express thanks, e.g. *gracias* and *grazie*.

St. Thomas says that each further sense depends on the prior ones. So thanksgiving is a response for a gift received, which in turn is an expression of love. Man's love always responds to a true good in the soul, which he finds already existing there. Were someone to attribute something to a person he loves which that person did not possess, this would not be true love but false love. In the last two senses, the gift and response, love causes something in the soul. When one receives a gift from a lover, the beloved responds with an expression of thanksgiving which is a true recognition in the soul both in the intellect and response of the will of the favor received.

God's love differs from human love in that when God loves someone, he creates the good. His love is not based on a prior good in the person, but God makes the person good in loving him. The first good God causes by his love is existence. Everything, which exists, exists and moves as an expression of divine love. "God saw everything, and it was good." (Gen. 1)

God has a special regard for man. In addition to the primary love by which he loves all things, God by a special love, also creates a special good in man. He loves him strictly speaking (*simpliciter*) because he elevates man to be like him. He allows man to participate in his nature. This is true not only of men, but also of angels. This communication in nature is completely beyond the power of human nature. Man cannot cause grace by his own power. He can only receive it.

> Grace is a participation in the life of God. It introduces us into the intimacy of the Trinitarian life: by Baptism the Christian participates in the grace of Christ, the head of his Body. As an 'adopted son' he can henceforth call God 'Father,' in union with the only Son. He receives the life of the Holy Spirit who breathes charity into him and who forms the Church.[407]

WHAT IS GRACE?

Since God communicates his nature to man, the change is a new quality of existence in the soul itself which must be more than a psychological change. The change is ontological. God must create a new, supernatural quality in the soul. Metaphysically this quality is an accident. An accident here does not mean an unforeseen event. An accident in philosophy is a being which can only exist in another being. Accidents are distinguished from substances, which are beings which exist in their own right. Grace is an accident like health. In fact, it is the health of the soul. The body can exist without health but cannot perform all the actions necessary for a healthy body. In the same way, the soul can exist without grace, but human freedom cannot be wholly formed without grace because without it man cannot performs those choices necessary to arrive at heaven, his natural destiny.

God brings the soul into existence and supports it in this existence. Because man is a spirit, God must be the life of man's soul. Man is not corrupted and changed substantially into God. He still remains man. But, he receives an accidental form. This form is a new quality of life or of being by which he is elevated to partake of divine nature. As the soul is the life of the body, so God is the life of the soul. What is substantially in God is accidentally in the soul.

Grace exists less perfectly in the soul than the soul subsists in itself because it is a supernatural habit. Still, it is more noble than the soul since it is a participation in divine life. Grace is not the same as virtue. Virtues exist in the powers of the soul. Grace exists in the essence of the soul. Just as human virtues which are acquired by human acts perfect human powers of intellect, will and emotions and make them more disposed to free actions according to man's nature, so grace is an interior change in the essence of the soul which enables man to form virtues according to God's nature which are necessary for him to will heaven. There are called supernatural infused virtues and theological virtues. These virtues have a further standard than just human reason. Their standard is the infinite nature of God.

> For the theological virtues the standard is God himself. ... Such a standard is way beyond our powers; never can we love God as much as he deserves or believe and hope in him as much as we ought. So here there is no question of striking a mean, but reaching for a summit.[408]

The summit spoken of here is an extreme (*excessus*).

To summarize grace according to the four causes of Scholasticism may be useful here. This will be the basis for a specific definition. The subject of grace or its material cause is the very essence of the soul itself. The Final Cause or why man has grace is to arrive at the vision of God in heaven through love for God on earth. The efficient cause or how man gets grace is God himself acting in a freely prepared soul. The formal cause or the nature of grace is an accidental quality by which the soul is elevated to know as God knows and love as God loves.

DEFINITION OF THE KINDS OF GRACE

Grace is primarily distinguished by three characteristics which are found with the different graces. The first is that grace which makes a person pleasing to God. The second is that grace is freely given. The third is that since it is freely given it is beyond personal merit. These three characteristics distinguish two principal kinds of grace: *gratia gratum faciens,* grace which makes pleasing and *gratia gratis data,* grace which is freely given. In modern terminology, *gratia gratum faciens* is sanctifying or habitual grace and *gratia gratis data* is charismatic grace. Their difference lies in this. Charismatic grace is freely given by God and not based on prior merit, but it has to do with the sanctification of others. Sanctifying grace is freely given, not based on prior merit and is the sanctification of the person who has it. Charismatic graces can be either ordinary (e.g. power of the priest to consecrate at Mass or the infallibility of the Pope) or extraordinary (e.g. tongues, preaching, healing, etc.). The extraordinary graces are enumerated in 1 Cor. 12. Since these graces do not make the individual pleasing to God, one can exercise both the extraordinary and the ordinary charisms and be in the state of mortal sin. Not so sanctifying grace. This grace makes pleasing because it is the love of the Holy Spirit dwelling in the heart of the holy Christian.

To receive and persevere in sanctifying grace, a third kind of grace is needed which is an interior aid of God. This is called actual grace. Since it is not a quality in the soul, but merely divine aid, it does not in itself make someone pleasing to God, but helps one to convert or live conversion. Sanctifying and actual grace then are defined as follows:

Sanctifying grace: a created supernatural gift, a divine habit of being infused by God, which permanently inheres in the soul by which we participate in the divine nature of God himself.

Actual grace: a temporary supernatural act of God by which he directly and interiorly enlightens the understanding and strengthens the will for the purpose of moving the person to a supernatural act.

The *Catechism* gives a similar definition:

> Sanctifying grace is a habitual gift, a stable and supernatural disposition that perfects the soul itself to enable it to live with God, to act by his love. Habitual grace, the permanent disposition to live and act in keeping with God's call, is distinguished from actual graces which refer to God's interventions, whether at the beginning of conversion or in the course of the work of sanctification.[409]

HOW ONE GETS GRACE

Man can obtain grace only from God. There is no power in man to enter into the inner life of the Trinity. So God then is the only efficient cause of grace. After the coming of Christ, his human nature is the tool *par excellence* by which God gives grace. The sacraments also are tools because they are extensions of Christ's human nature. They operate like the tools in the hand, which acts by the power of the soul. The sacraments are the tools, Christ's human nature is the hand and his divinity is the soul.

Though God is the sufficient cause of God, God never acts contrary to the nature of what he has created. Since man has an intellect and will and so freedom characterizes all his moral actions, the reception of grace also presupposes that man is open to this reception by acts of free will. Sanctifying grace requires some preparation of the free will, at least in someone who has reached the age of reason. God aids the soul in this preparation by actual grace and no prior preparation is required to receive God's help in this.

Man's preparation is the result of God moving and the free will being moved. If preparation is looked at from the point of view of the free will, grace is a sheer gift and God does not have to give it to anyone. But if preparation is looked on from God's point of view, then God necessarily gives grace to one whom he finds prepared. This is not, however, a necessity of coercion as though God was forced by the justice of man or his works to bestow grace on a prepared free will. It is a necessity of infallibility because God has infallibly promised that he will give grace to those whom he finds prepared, and God always keeps his promises. So there is a sense in which God binds himself. "Everyone who has heard the Father and learned from Him, comes to me." (John 6:45) The fact that one does not receive grace is due to lack of preparation then. The first cause of loss of grace is not God, but the fact that man does not prepare his will when he could and should.

The measure of grace received by each soul is due to its measure of preparation. All do not experience grace equally. "But to each one of us is given grace according to the measure of the giving of Christ." (Ephesians 4:7) This does not make God unjust, though, nor does he play favorites. On the part of the object, which is God's own divine nature, God gives himself equally to all. But on the part of the subject's free reception, one who is more freely prepared to receive grace experiences the mercy and love of God more. However, since God is the initiator in preparation, God imparts his love more to one than to another. In fact, the Church possesses a hierarchy of holiness which is analogous to the hierarchy of being in creation. No one, for example, will ever be as loved by God or made as lovable by God's love as the Virgin Mary. She is his bride and, therefore, the most excellent human person (Jesus being a divine person) in the hierarchy of heaven. Her freedom and virtue were most highly imbued with the life of God among both angels and men.

Since grace is a supernatural habit, only God can know who is in the state of grace with absolute certitude. God sometimes reveals to the engraced person by private revelation that he or she is in the state of grace in order to prepare them for some very difficult work like martyrdom. Most Christians though only have a relative certainty that they are in the state of grace. Someone who does what he can to live the Christian life and is not aware of being in serious sin can be relatively sure he is in the state of grace. St. Thomas says that a person has a relative certainty of being in the state of grace if he sees himself "delight in God and despise worldly things and is unconscious of any mortal sin."[410]

This knowledge is imperfect. The *Catechism* invokes the classic example of Joan of Arc to prove this principle. She was asked if she was in the state of grace. This was a trick question. Had she answered "yes", she would have been burned as a heretic because no one can know for sure that they are in the state of grace. Had she answered "no", she would be been burned as a witch because all she did would have possibly been a result of the inspiration of the devil. She answered, "If I am not, may it please God to put me there; and if I am, may it please God to keep me there."[411]

THE EFFECT OF GRACE: JUSTIFICATION

No treatment of man being a servant and free would be complete without an analysis of those effects of grace which have so plagued the Protestant-Catholic division for the last four centuries: justification and merit. To understand these, one must understand operating and cooperating grace. These are not two kinds of grace, but two effects of the same sanctifying grace. They differ in that operating grace has two elements; cooperating grace has three. Grace is a dynamic movement of the soul based on a quality infused in the soul by God to make an authentic pilgrim's progress to heaven. In operating grace, God moves and the soul is moved (freely). In cooperating grace, God moves, the soul is moved and in turn moves all of the other powers of man to those free choices in ordinary moral life to advance toward heaven. Operating grace is also called justification. Cooperating grace is also called merit.

At the outset, St. Thomas makes a distinction between the virtue of justice and justification, which is what Aristotle calls metaphorical justice. The virtue of justice is in the will and has to do with a disposition to give rights to others. Justification refers to a rightness of order within the person himself. It is a disposition which does not just order one power to form a good free act, but is an ordering of the intellect, the will and the emotions in relation to each other to act in concert. In this inner ordering or righteousness, the emotions are subject to the intellect and will and the intellect and will are subject to God. Adam was created in this state before the sin. For everyone after the sin, justification involves a conversion or movement the state of sinfulness being without justice to a state of being in grace. This is righteousness and is caused by the forgiveness of sins. Justification thus includes two conditions now in the time after the Original Sin: the forgiveness of sins and the divine indwelling of the Trinity. The first cannot exist without the second. This is what conversion means.

The first work of the grace of the Holy Spirit is *conversion*, in which, by grace, man turns toward God and away from sin, thus accepting forgiveness and righteousness from on high. Justification cannot just be an overlooking of sin on the part of the offended party, as Luther tended to suggest. It must truly involve a new quality in the soul by which the soul participates in God's inner life. Sin is an offence against God and sin can only truly be forgiven when the mind of the offended party has been reconciled with the offender or when we are at peace with God. God can only be at peace with us because of our natural capacity for Him when his love creates a new form in us. From his point of view, this is his own infinite nature; from man's, it is a created gift by which one participates in the nature of God. This peace with God is sanctifying grace. Forgiveness of sins must be the presence of the divine form of God's own life in us. "[God] gave himself to us though his Spirit. By the participation of the Spirit, we become communicants in the divine nature . . . For this reason, those in whom the Spirit dwells are divinized."[412]

In an adult, there must be a movement of free choice to experience this justification and thus the forgiveness of sins and the divine indwelling of the Trinity. John 6:45 says, "Everyone who hears the Father and has learned from Him comes to Me." Learning entails an act of free choice because in order to learn one must consent to what the teacher is explaining. The movement of free choice cannot occur in someone who does not have the possibility of freely choosing like infants and the insane. They can be justified by baptism. Their catechesis and consent occur after they have reached the age of reason and to a justification already experienced.

Free choice is moved regarding two goods: the renunciation of sin and the movement of faith to God. There are four aspects of this movement of free choice: the infusion of grace from God the mover, the movement of free choice to God from the one moved, the movement of free choice rejecting sin which is also moved by God, and the forgiveness of sins itself which is the termination of the movement of justification. This can be seen in the questions asked at baptism.

The movement of free choice renouncing sin is expressed in the questions: Do you reject Satan? And all his works? And all his empty promises? The positive movement of free choice embracing faith is expressed in the questions: Do you believe in God, the Father Almighty, creator of heaven and earth? Do you believe in Jesus Christ, his only Son, our Lord, who was born of the Virgin Mary, was crucified, died, and was buried, rose from the dead, and is now seated at the right hand of the Father? Do you believe in the Holy Spirit, the holy Catholic Church, the communion of saints, the forgiveness of sins, the resurrection of the body, and life everlasting?

Since God is an infinite agent who brings about justification, he does not depend on the normal preparation of the human will. In all natural changes, there is a gradual change from one condition to another. This may or may not be the case with justification. The Apostles had three years of instruction by Christ; St. Augustine had about thirty. But God does not have to bring about such a change successively. He can instantaneously prepare a free will for conversion as was the case in the most famous conversion in the history of the Church, the conversion of St. Paul. Conversion is a moral change and God is not limited by the lack of malleability of the free will of the subject. He can dispose it to choose for him in an instant.

From the point of view of the manner of working, the greatest work of God is creation in which God brings something into existence from nothing. But creation is completed in time. Justification consists in God raising a created soul to the experience of eternity. Justification finishes in the nature of God, himself. For this reason, one justified soul from the point of view of the work itself is greater than the whole created universe put together. "The good of grace in one is greater than the good of the nature of the whole universe."[413]

Justification is miraculous if one looks at it from the point of view of human power. No human power can bring grace to the soul. The Pelagians taught that man could merit justification by his own power. All grace did was allow man to do what he could do by his own power. Grace makes it easier. Nothing could be further from the truth. There is no active power in man by which he can attain grace. Every work, which can be done by God alone, is miraculous in this sense. Sometimes the manner in which justification is carried out is beyond the usual way in which the will is formed in freedom and in that sense is miraculous. An analogy would be when a sick man recovers his health instantaneously, completely beyond the skill of art or nature. St. Paul's justification was like this. But for something to be completely miraculous there can be no passive potential in the nature of the thing for the particular action. For example, there is no power in asses to prophesy or in the wind and the sea to be calmed by the word of a man or a body to rise from the dead by the work of a man. Yet, Balaam's ass prophesied and Jesus raised the dead and calmed the wind and sea by his word. The potential for this kind of action is called obediential potency. This is merely the potential present in every created thing to be at the disposal of whatever action the Creator chooses to do. This is not the case with grace. There is a natural capacity in man for God and therefore for grace because of the natural desire in the intellect for God. "The justification of the impious is not miraculous because the soul is naturally capable of grace."[414] This is not the capacity to get grace, but to receive it by preparation. One opens himself to conversion by free choices. Here is the proof of St. Augustine's statement: "You have made us for yourself and our hearts are restless until they rest in you."[415]

One point must be crystal clear: no one merits justification by works. Man can prepare himself to receive the justification of grace by allowing God to move his free will, but this is not a human motion in origin. It is only a human motion in effect. The primary cause is God.

THE EFFECT OF GRACE: MERIT OR REWARD

Perhaps no idea in the whole tract on grace has caused more difficulty than that of merit and yet it is the capstone of the whole discussion of fundamental moral theology. For many, the term suggests that man can claim something in justice before God. A recent document of agreement between Catholic and Lutheran theologians states that if the term "merit" were only changed to "reward" or "wages" that this would go a long way to resolving the difficulty. After all, Matthew 25: 31-46 clearly teaches that one receives one's reward by doing things for the least of the brethren. Christ separates the just from the wicked in the Last Judgment on this basis.

The term "merit" has been used by Catholic theology to express the second great effect of grace, which is cooperating grace. All this term seeks to express is that when God gives a participation in his supernatural life, he gives it so that it will bear fruit. In conversion God moves the prepared free will. The person so prepared in turn moves all of the powers of his soul and body in the formation of the virtues which are necessary for spontaneous acts by which he can love God by a relationship of union. In this way, man also freely participates in his own salvation.

The term for this free participation, "merit" is used in an analogous way. Merit expresses the receipt of a reward and normally it means something given in strict equivalence to someone for something he has done according to the virtue of justice. A contractor builds a house and merits receipt of a certain payment based on the contract and the work performed. If the one who contracted the work does not pay, then he is guilty of injustice. This is called condign merit, which is merit in strict equality. This is the normal experience of human reward in human affairs.

There can be no such merit in divine affairs. God is infinitely distant from all his creatures so there can be no strict equality of any kind between God and man. No one merits the first grace from God. No one can merit justification. Yet, in light of justification, God who acts according to his wisdom in all his creation never acts against the nature that he himself has created. In the case of man, this means that any effect of God's in which man must morally participate demands man's action according to his free will if that is possible. God inspires the good work in us both by his gift of sanctifying grace and by actual grace. Man so inspired acts according to the lights God has given him. In every Christian work, whether it is taking care of a crying baby, cleaning the kitchen, writing a book or suffering an insult with a hidden act of patience, if done from charity or from the motive of the love of God, both God and the Christian work. Each works according to his own mode of action. By God's will, God has determined that the salvation of the human being will be given according to both God's part in the action, and also *proportionately* correspond to man's part. Each person receives the reward of heaven according to a proportionate equality. Man's portion is small but essential. It is the amount of truth and freedom with which he allows his actions to be motivated by God's supernatural life. This is called *congruent merit*. By God's wisdom and will, each man is rewarded proportionately according to his own participation in the work.

So, the foundation and initiation of all human merit is justification and the first grace given by God alone. No one merits grace or justification; in light of the grace of justification received one merits the reward for a life lived in freedom practicing divine love: heaven.

In every meritorious work, there are two factors which must be considered. The first is the act of the free will of man. From this point of view there is no condign merit possible before God, but only congruent merit. But the Holy Spirit is also present working in each of these acts. From the Holy Spirit's action, God rewards the work condignly, namely his own part in the action. He rewards his own gifts. "I will make in him a fountain of living water welling up to eternal life." (John 4:14) So there are two participants in every meritorious act: God and the Christian. God rewards his own part condignly and he rewards the proportionate participation of the individual Christian congruently.

One's enjoyment of God in heaven is determined by congruent merit which is different for each person. Since merit is a loving cooperation between God and the soul, each person's place in the hierarchy of heaven is determined by love. One knows God more in heaven depending on how much one has loved him on earth. This love begins in practical works of charity according to the duties of one's ordinary state. "You are glorified in the assembly of your Holy Ones, for in crowning their merits you are crowning your own gifts." (*Preface I for Holy Men and Women*, quoted in *CCC* n. 2006)

As to perseverance in grace, one must also make a distinction. Since the reward of heaven is a result of the prior grace given to man, one can merit the continual perseverance in grace when one is in heaven by congruent merit. One cannot merit the grace of final perseverance here on earth, though. This is why one must continue the pray for final perseverance every day and watch unceasingly for the final coming of Christ, first in one's own death and then in glory at the end of time. Everyone receives the ability to persevere in baptism, but that one actually perseveres is not a matter of merit. God has not left us adrift here though. Each day in the formation of moral freedom, Christians must pray for the grace to persevere. For example, the prayer of the fathers of the desert for perseverance was: O God, come to my assistance. Lord, make haste to help me." This is a prayer for actual grace, as is: "Lead us not into temptation, but deliver us from evil." St. Thomas ends his treatment of fundamental morals which includes all the wonderful principles of truth and freedom which contribute to the formation of man with the request for prayer: "What cannot be earned, can always be prayed for."[416]

CHAPTER THIRTEEN

"What eye has not seen, nor ear heard, neither has it entered into the heart of man, what things God has prepared for those that love him."
(1 Cor. 2:9)

I WANT TO SEE GOD

At the age of seven, Teresa of Avila ran away from home. When she was found and asked why she ran away she replied: "I want to see God and I must die before I can see him." In her search she reflects the response of humanity responding to the original intention of God when, out of love, he created the world to share his goodness.

This short introduction to the basic principles of the Catholic Church has as its purpose analyzing the various principles by which man can arrive at what God has prepared for those who love him. Man loves God because God has first loved man.

The whole inertia of creation is a result of divine truth and love. The world came forth from God, has God as its model and everything in its own way seeks to return to the unity from which it springs. "Come, Holy Ghost, Creator blest." God's being is the origin of all being, his Word is the primary source of the distinction of one thing from another thing and his Spirit is the force of love which moves "heaven and all the other stars" as Dante sings in the *Divine Comedy*.[417]

God created the world to share his goodness. Everything that exists comes forth from God and results from his goodness. Everything comes forth from the absolute unity of God and seeks to return to this unity. Rocks do this by their attraction to other material bodies. Once organic life occurs, then this diversity seeking unity takes a new turn. "To be" does not mean "to be in competition" but in cooperation. In *The Screwtape Letters*, C.S. Lewis has a senior tempter in hell lament about this dynamism toward union in goodness and the love as the very thing which distinguished nature from evil.

> The whole philosophy of Hell rests on recognition of the axiom that one thing is not another thing, and,

> specially, that one self is not another self. My good is my good, and your good is yours. What one gains, another loses. Even an inanimate object is what it is by excluding all other objects from the space it occupies; if it expands, it does so by thrusting other objects aside or by absorbing them. A self does the same. With beasts the absorption takes the form of eating; for us, it means the sucking of will and freedom out of a weaker self into a stronger. 'To be' means 'to be in competition.' Now, the Enemy's (i.e. Christ's) philosophy is nothing more nor less than one continued attempt to evade this very obvious truth. He aims as a contradiction. Things are to be many, yet somehow also one. This impossibility He calls *Love*[418], and this same monotonous panacea can be detected under all He does and even all He is—or claims to be.[419]

God created to the world from love, not because he needs something from the world, but because he wants to share his goodness. God's love is different from man's in that God creates the good in the thing he loves, whereas man merely finds the good and affirms it. The primary effect of divine affirmation of everything is that it exists.

> So if God loves a creature, some goodness will result at some time in that creature, though not co-eternally with the love itself. And because of differences in such goodness, we distinguish different love of God for creatures. One is the general love with which he loves everything there is, and which gives natural existence to all created being.[420]

In addition to the primary movement of divine love which God gives to every created thing which is expressed in its existence, God also loves man with a special love. He invites us to a relationship with him. "Nature loves God above everything else as the source and goal of all natural good; charity loves him as the object of all happiness with whom we enjoy a kind of spiritual communion."[421]

> Another is the special love with which he draws reasoning creatures above their natural condition to

share in his own good; and this is the way God loves creatures in an unqualified sense, willing them an eternal good which is nothing other than himself.[422]

This special love truly allows the diverse created order to become like God through man by a union of relationship in which man can know as God knows and love as God loves. This is the result of God's grace which "implies some supernatural gift flowing out from God into a man."[423]

Since this love of God is the most basic motivation of the entire world both of nature and of morals, all the history of the world is founded on union and love with God. Man's response to the love of God's grace can only be one of recognition of the gift received and a free response of cooperation in such a divine favor. The moral principles described in this study are the basic foundation for this cooperation.

This cooperation is rooted in the very nature of man himself. Because man is a spirit and a body, no human being can be brought to birth merely from the material forces of their parents. Animals can be. Their souls are material and die with them. Man cannot be. Though human parents generate the material principle, only God creates the soul by a direct act of his power, truth and love. Since man has a spirit, his whole inner self is characterized by the ability to choose well and since God is his immediate origin, choosing well in the ultimate analysis means choosing God as one's final purpose.

This ability to choose God must extend even to his vision, the desire for which is entirely beyond the capacity of human nature since God is infinite. Because man has an intellect, choosing this vision must be his destiny. Man can only realize the full measure of his intelligence when his very intellect is filled with the direct perception of the infinite light of God.

The powers of the human soul which must unite in combination for such a pursuit are those powers directly connected to human choice: intellect, will, and the passions. Actions of the body must also participate if this is possible and desirable. The combination of the these powers in one human choice are central to interior character formation, but no human choice can freely pursue the infinite light of God without a gift, a quality added to human nature. This gift cannot be in just one or other power, but must be in the very central core of the soul. This gift is sanctifying grace. God always acts and gives the initiative in human choice. Man cooperates. Even ordinary human choices could not exist without the original impetus of the Holy Spirit. "To sum up then: to know *any*[424] truth we need God's help to activate our minds; but we need new light supplementing the light we have by nature only to know truths beyond our natural ability to know."[425]

All of the truths about the formation of the moral determinants guiding the will and humanizing the passions have as their final purpose that "(t)his animal, this thing begotten in a bed, could look on him."[426] Man was originally created in grace which was the perfect formation of his freedom. God gave him special gifts to allow him to live in freedom and spontaneity a union of love with God. This grace was lost in Adam and Eve's sin when they abused their freedom and chose self instead of God.

Though God allowed this choice precisely because of human freedom, his loving design for the world was not frustrated by it. As God tolerates all evil for the sake of good, he brought from this evil an even greater mercy. In this case, that mercy was the Incarnation, the promise of the Redeemer made as soon as the punishments for the sins are enumerated. God says to the serpent: "I will put enmity between you and the woman, and between your seed and her seed; he shall bruise your head and you shall bruise his heal." (Gen. 3:15) In the wonder of the Word taking flesh, the power of God's love reaches new heights. God's love united man to him in nature by sanctifying grace. Now God's love unites man to him in person in Christ. This is a sheer grace. This is, as the Scholastic theologians used to say in the Middle Ages, the *miraculum miraculorum* (the miracle of miracles).

The law of God was given to the world originally in Genesis to explain the limitations of man who enjoyed this wondrous grace. He received this grace as a gift of love and living the truth must be the manner in which to maintain it. The command given is symbolic and general not to eat the fruit of the tree. Man did not cooperate in freedom in this law. But this was not from weakness or ignorance.

After the sin, all of the history of the world until the coming of Christ is progressive preparation of a people living in "darkness and the shadow of death" (Lk. 1:79) to receive the light of the Messiah and to be able to live grace again in freedom and spontaneity. This was accomplished through both the natural law and the Old Law as St. Paul explains at the beginning of the Epistle to the Romans. These laws have many more commandments because of the ignorance of the human race following the sin. In Israel's' case, the great number of precepts was due to the God choosing them as his special people. Every aspect of their lives had to be permeated with the Trinity which, until the coming of Christ, they only experienced in seed.

The motivation for Christ redeeming us is thus also divine love, a desire on the part of God to bring us back to grace despite the reality of human sin. "For God so loved the world that he gave his only Son, that whoever believes in him should not perish but have eternal life." (Jn. 3:16)

Christ gives man back grace through the sacraments and teaches us the New Law through the presence of the Holy Spirit. Each man is now called to live again a life in which his freedom and spontaneity are internally formed by divine grace. Man's conduct in ethics must reflect this. No one can say he loves God and disobey his commandments, for obedience and love go together. No one can say he loves God who mistreats his neighbor.

Word and sacrament are essential for human fulfillment. So is the moral life. Acts of will are the means by which we carry out a salvation we did not cause in ourselves. Nevertheless, God never acts in something against its nature. Since man's nature is characterized by freedom, the depth of his humanity and his life of grace is determined by how spontaneously and lovingly he desires God in everyday choices.

This is why virtuous formation is so necessary and why morals cannot be reduced to playing it safe within the constraints of the external expression of laws. Though much of theological instruction after the Council of Trent has rightly emphasized confessional practice, the emphasis on interpretation of moral conduct in terms of the law sometimes had the effect of obscuring the equally important role in moral theology of accentuating both human happiness and the perfection brought by the formation of virtue, especially virtues which have their origin in grace. For the purposes of study, ascetical and mystical theology were often treated as different courses from moral theology. This led to the idea that the life of virtues lived through union with the Trinity had nothing to do with daily life and ethics.

The *aggiornamento* (updating) and *resourcement* (return to the sources) requested by Vatican II must be applied to morals. As John Paul II requested in *Veritatis Splendor*, this is the only basis on which to develop a renewal of moral theology. This renewal must take account of all the principles recounted in this study. It must clearly show how the fundamental principles of moral conduct, intellect, will and passions are formed or deformed internally by virtues and sins and aided externally by law and grace so that the judgments of conscience may truly be right. Only such judgments can really lead to acts of the will which either prepare man for grace or by which he perseveres in grace. If there is a flaw in the presentation of any of these principles, freedom suffers and man is not only enslaved to himself, but left unhappy.

The development of the spiritual life demands some understanding of all these principles. This may not be an academic understanding such as presented in this book, but whatever practical application one makes of the awareness of grace to self knowledge cannot deny or belittle any of these principles. To grasp this, one must consider in oneself the potential present in a freedom based on the truth and objective order and the slavery to passion and egotism caused by a freedom deformed with false and subjective ideas. The former makes man sublime. The latter should make him humble.

When one examines the disconnect between the freedom which realizing the image of God offers to him and the self-imposed limitations he places on this freedom by his failure to live according to the truth, this is the first great understanding of progress in the spiritual life and the man's first great cross. One becomes a martyr to his own conscience when he understands the vast horizon of potentials offered to him and his own refusals to freely embrace these.

The daily awareness and involvement in a person where he tries to develop his freedom based on virtue leads to his actions for good being "peaceful, dispassionate and firm."[427] The second great cross occurs when God elevates human freedom beyond anything man can understand or do to be like his own freedom. This is caused by the maturity of the mystical life and truly entails man looking at the world through God colored glasses. In our age, this point of view is much eclipsed and man has attempted to form his own freedom based merely on human values he can develop and understand himself. He is free but not a servant. Many authors have maintained that the failure of man to become God by his own power causes such great anguish that this is the origin of the drug culture, among other things. Drugs destroy the pain of realizing we are not God.

In fact, man can only be free when he is a servant. Love must be formed by truth and the divine truth form divine love. When this truth motivates freedom, then one not only perceives but loves the material world which is limited and time bound from an unlimited perspective which is God's and is eternal. Cardinal Newman put it well:

> Be in earnest, and you will speak of religion where, and when, and how you should; aim at things, and your words will be right without aiming. There are ten thousand ways of looking at this world, but only one right way. The man of pleasure has his, the man of gain his, and the man of intellect his. Poor men and rich men, governors and governed, prosperous and discontented, learned and unlearned, each has his own way of looking at the things which come before him, and each has a wrong way. There is but one right way; it is the way in which God looks at the world. Aim at looking at it in God's way. Aim at seeing things as God sees them. Aim at forming judgments about persons, events, ranks, fortunes, changes, objects, as God forms. Aim at looking at this life as God looks at it. Aim at looking at the life to come, and the world unseen as God does. Aim at 'seeing the King in his beauty'.[428]

When one experiences a freedom which is born of serving God, one experiences a peace within which must be shared with all one meets. This is beautifully expressed in an image of St. Teresa of Avila who was fascinated by the way silk was thought to be produced in her time. The little silkworm remains in darkness and the narrow confines of the cocoon until grace forms and hatches it into a moth. In the meantime, the worm just quietly produces the silk of the cocoon. When the moth is transformed and leaves the cocoon, it leaves the beautiful silk behind. "Who can guess what nature does for a silkworm …? All it needs is leaves, that is all. Nature does the rest. … But after several transformations the consummated soul receives wings with which to fly to heaven, leaving on earth a fertile seed to perpetuate its state in other souls." The moral life of everyday ordinary virtues lived with extraordinary love caused and supported always by grace truly forms a kind of divine freedom within. A life lived in such freedom allows the servant not only to serve God but to serve others and aid in the formation of such freedom and peace in the world.

Christians often look on the moral law as an imposition on their freedom when it is anything but this. Since the moral law expresses how man made in the image of God realizes his powers by his choices, it is actually the formation of freedom. One who is so formed by grace must not just do actions which conform to the moral law, but must love the goods which the actions command. In preparing for the vision of God, because the Trinity lives in his soul by grace, he can exist as God exists, know as God knows and love as God loves within the Trinity. He can get to intimately know and love as the Father, the Son and the Holy Spirit know and love each other. This is the sublimity of man. In the face of a humility caused respectively by our littleness and our awareness of our weakness, interior moral formation should help us to see ourselves as God sees us. Despite our weaknesses, human beings should see themselves as interiorly invited to return the love with which God created the world and them by sharing in his redemption and his spirit. Here is where freedom and servant-hood truly meet. In this meeting, where freedom is completely formed by the truth of God, the free servant must truly love interiorly what he practices exteriorly. Where serving truth and living freedom meet in joyous combination, one can finally personally fulfill in practice the saying of St. Gregory Nazianzen: "To be, rather than to seem to be, a friend of God."[429]

Endnotes

1. Pope John Paul II, *Veritatis Splendor*, n. 87. Cf. St. Augustine, *Ennaratio in Psalmum* XCIX, 7: CCL, 39, 1397.
2. Karl Rahner, *Foundations of Christian Faith* (New York: The Seabury Press, 1978), 449-450.
3. Bernhard Häring, "A Distrust that Wounds," *The Tablet* (23 October, 1993), 1378.
4. Richard McCormick, "Killing the Patient", *The Tablet*, (30 October, 1993), 1410.
5. Pope John Paul II, *Veritatis Splendor*, n. 44.
6. "[...] est. in horizonte, aeternitatis inferius et supra tempus." Thomas Aquinas, *Liber de Causis*, II, 2, n. 61.
7. Substance is a being which exists in its own right. A dog or cat is a substance. This term is used here to designate substance in the philosophical sense.
8. Vatican II, *Gaudium et Spes*, n. 14, 1; quoted in *Catechism of the Catholic Church* [henceforth: *CCC*], n. 364.
9. *CCC*, n. 365.
10. An accident is a being which cannot exist by itself, but must exist in a substance. White is an accident. One cannot simply have the color white without a white object.
11. Robert E. Brennan, O.P., *In the Image of His Maker*, (Bruce Publishing Company, Milwaukee: 1948) 128, note 26.
12. Brennan, *Image*, 132, note 28.
13. *Ibid*.
14. Thomas Aquinas, *In Comm. De Anima*, III, 3, n.794.
15. Anna A. Terruwe and Conrad W. Baars, *Psychic Wholeness and Healing*, (Alba House, New York: 1981) 9-10.
16. Thomas Aquinas, *Summa Theologiae* (henceforth *ST*), I, 78, 4, *ad corp*. Quoted in Brennan, *Image*, 156.
17. Robert E. Brennan, O.P., *Thomistic Psychology*, (The Macmillan Company, New York: 1941) 143.
18. Terruwe and Baars, *Psychic*, 10.
19. Brennan, *Image*, 165.
20. C.S. Lewis, *The Screwtape Letters, Letter IX*, (The Macmillan Publishing Company, New York: 1982) 41-42.
21. Aquinas, *Summa Theologiae*, I, 81, 1, *ad corp*.
22. Brennan, *Image*, 169.
23. I am indebted for these more contemporary terms and the general examples used in this section to Conrad Baars, *Psychic Wholeness and Healing*, 10-20.
24. *CCC*, 1767. Cf. Thomas Aquinas, *Summa Theologiae*, I-II, 24, 3, *ad corp*.
25. Aquinas, *ST.*, I-II, 26, *ad corp*.
26. *CCC*, 1765.
27. Terruwe and Baars, *Psychic*, 13.
28. *CCC*, 1765.
29. *CCC*, 1767.

30 "Est ergo tam in nobis quam in Deo circulatio quaedam in operibus intellectus et voluntatis; nam voluntas redit in id a quo fuit principium intelligendi: sed in nobis concluditur circulus ad id quod est extra, dum bonum exterius movet voluntatem , et voluntas tendit per appetitum et amorem in exterius bonum." Thomas Aquinas, *De Potentia Dei*, 9, 9, *ad corp*.

31 "Perciò esiste da semper uno stretto legame tra l'ethica e l'antropologia." (All translations of this work in the book are done by Fr. Brian Mullady, O.P.) Karol Wojtyla, *I Fondamenti dell'Ordine Etico*", (Vatican City: Libreria Editrice Vaticana: 1980) 32. Most of the ideas in this section come directly from these notes.

32 Wojtyla, *Fondamenti*, 32.

33 Metaphysics is the science beyond Physics and has as its subject being as being. Modern positivistic science tends to deny the existence of this science. Without it, all science would be reduced to only material description.

34 Epistemology is the science of how one knows truth, on the relationship of our experience in the senses to universal truths. It is the principal modern philosophical problem after Descartes.

35 "A suo parere, si può ridurre la moralità dell'uomo ad un particolare senso che ci permette di distinguere la virtù del peccato a partire dal particolare piacere che accompagna la prima e dal dolore che troviamo nel secondo." *Ibid.*

36 Wojtyla, *Fondamenti*, 33.

37 Wojtyla, *Fondamenti*, 43.

38 Wojtyla, *Fondamenti*, 34.

39 Wojtyla, *Fondamenti*, 44.

40 "Tuttavia, un'accurata analisi del sistema di Scheler dimostra che le associazioni perfezioristiche non sono pienamente guistificate. Questo perchè la persona, nella concezione di Scheler, non è affatto un'ente, ma è solamente un'unità di esperienze." Wojtyla, *Fondamenti*, 45.

41 Brennan, *Image*, 223.

42 Benedict XVI, General Audience, July 7, 2010.

43 For those who wish to examine the history of this rather complicated question there is no contemporary work as good as this. Cf. Servais Pinckaers, O.P., *The Sources of Christian Ethics*, (Washington, D.C: CUA Press, 1995) 103.

44 Thomas Aquinas, I-II, *prologue*.

45 I am indebted for this succinct presentation to the notes of Msgr. William Smith in his course for the International Catholic University called *The Moral Magisterium of John Paul II*.

46 John Paul II, *Veritatis Splendor*, n. 29.

47 Vatican II, *Dei Verbum*, 9; quoted in *CCC* 80.

48 Vatican II, *Dei Verbum*, 10, 2; quoted in *CCC*, 85.

49 *CCC*, 85

50 *Evangelium Vitae*, 62. Cf. also 57 and 65 where almost the same expression is used.

51 Josef Cardinal Ratzinger, *Doctrinal Commentary of the Concluding Formula of the Professio Fidei*, Congregation for the Doctrine of the Faith, June 29, 1998, 6.

52 Ratzinger, *Professio*, 11.

53 Vatican II, *Dei Verbum*, 10, #2; quoted in *CCC*, 86.

54 John T. Noonan, Jr., "Development in Moral Doctrine". *Theological Studies* 54 (1993), 662-677.

55 Noonan, *Development*, 673 cites Louis Vereecke, *Storia della teologia morale moderna*, (Rome: Lateran, 1979), 1, 4-5).
56 Noonan, *Development*, 675.
57 Noonan, *Development*, 676.
58 *Ibid.*
59 Noonan, *Development*, 677.
60 John Paul II, *Veritatis Splendor (henceforth, VS)*, 82.
61 *CCC*, 2267.
62 *CCC*, 2267 quoting, John Paul II, *Evangelium Vitae*, 56
63 Ratzinger, *Professio*, 5.
64 Ratzinger, *Professio*, 11.
65 Joseph Cardinal Ratzinger and Christoph Schönborn, *Introduction to the Catechism of the Catholic Church*, (San Francisco: Ignatius Press, 1994), 87.
66 Actionum quod ab homine aguntur, illae solae proprie dicuntur *humanae*, quae sunt propriae hominis inquantum est homo. Differt autem homo ab aliis irrationalibus creatures in hoc, quod est suorum actuum dominus. Unde, illae solae actions vocantur proprie humanae, quarum est dominus suorum actuum, per rationem et voluntatem: unde et liberum arbitrium esse dicitur: facultas voluntatis et rationis." Aquinas, *ST*, I-II, 1, *ad corp.*
67 John Paul II, *Theology of the Body*, (Boston: Pauline Books and Media, 1997) 38.
68 "Nam tota irrationalis natura comparatur ad Deum sicut instrumentum ad agens principale. [...] Et ideo proprium est naturae raionalis ut tendat ad finem quasi se agens vel ducens as finem." Aquinas, *ST*, I-II, 1, 2, *ad corp.*, translated by Timothy McDermott, (Westminster, Maryland: Christian Classics, 1992). This translation is a very good modern rendering which does not suffer from the more unfortunate difficulties of rendering Scholastic Latin into English. Where possible this translation will be used.
69 *CCC 2261*
70 "Quantum igitur ad rationem ultimi finis, omnes convenient in appetite finis ultimi: quia appetunt suam perfectionem adimpleri, quae est ratio ultimi finis [...] Sed ad id in quo ista ratio invenitur, non omnes homines convenient in ultimo fine [...] Sicut et omni gustui delectabile est dulce: sed quidbusdam dulcedo mellis, auth alicuius talium." Aquinas, *Summa*, I-II, 1, 6, *ad corp.*
71 "[...] illi qui peccant, avertuntur ab eo in quo vere invenitur ratio ultimi finis, non autem ab ipsa ultima finis intentione, quam quaerunt falso in aliis rebus." *Ibid.*
72 Fulton J. Sheen, *God and Intelligence in Modern Philosophy*, (Garden City, New York: Image Books, 1958), 231.
73 "Nam homo et aliae rationales creaturae consequuntur ultimum finem cognoscendo et amando Deum, quod non competit aliis creatures, quae adipiscuntur ultimum finem inquauntum participant aliquam similitudinem Dei, secundum quod sunt, vel vivunt, vel etiam cognoscunt. Nam beatitude nominat adeptionem ultimi finis." Aquinas, *Summa*, I-II, 1, 8, *ad corp.*
74 Cf., for example, Aristotle, *Nicomachean Ethics* and Boethius, *The Consolation of the Philosophy*.
75 Dicendum quod omnia corporalia obedient pecuniae, quantum ad multitudinem stultorum, qui sola corporalia bona cognoscunt, quae pecunia acquire possunt." Aquinas, *ST, I-II, 2, 1* ad 1.

76 John Paul II, *Theology*, 76.
77 John Paul II, *Theology*, 163-164.
78 Aristotle, *Metaphysics*, Book 1, 982b11-15; 983a24-25.
79 "Amplius. Naturaliter inest omnibus hominibus desiderium cognoscendi causas eorum quae videntur; unde propter admirationem eorum quae videbantur, quorum causae latebant, homines primo philosophari coeperunt, invenientes autem causam quiescebant. Nec sistit inquisition quousque perveniatur ad primam causam: et tunc perfecte nos scire arbitramur quando primam causam cognoscimus. Desiderat igitur homo naturaliter cognoscere primam causam quasi ultimum fienm. Prima autem omnium causa Deus est. Est igitur ultimus finis hominis cognoscere Deum." Thomas Aquinas, *Summa Contra Gentiles* (henceforth: SCG), III, c. 25, [2065].
80 Thomas de Vio Cajetan was a Dominican philosopher and theologian who was a contemporary of Martin Luther and actually met with him. He is said to have sympathized with Luther's criticism of the Church but stated that what Luther wanted was a different Church. He wrote a famous commentary on the *Summa Theologiae* of Thomas Aquinas. He is considered to be the founder of the school of NeoThomism.
81 Etienne Gilson, (1884-1978) French Thomistic philosophy and historian of philosophy was one of the leaders of the Thomistic revival of the 20th century.
82 Henri de Lubac, S. J. (1896-1991) was a French Jesuit who became a Cardinal. He is considered to be one of the most influential theologians of the 20th century. His research and writings were an important influence on Vatican II. He wrote an influential book called *Surnaturel* which led to his silencing from writing on nature and grace by the Congregation for the Holy Office. He was later exonerated.
83 Dominic Soto (1494-1560) was a Dominican theologian was a major figure in the philosophical movement known as the School of Salamanca. He was the emperor's representative at the Council of Trent and is considered the founder of modern mechanics.
84 "Haec glossa destruit textum, est tortuosa." Quoted in the *Letters of Etienne Gilson to Henri de Lubac*, (San Francisco: Ignatius Press, 1988), 101, note 3.
85 Germain Grisez (born 1929) is a prominent moral theologian who has tried to introduce a new natural law theory into Catholic moral theology. He is best known for his massive and controversial three volume work, *The Way of the Lord Jesus*, in which he attempts to redefine Catholic moral theology. Though lauded for his support of the *Humanae Vitae* at a time when it was almost universally rejected, his more recent theories have caused much discussion.
86 Germain Grisez, *The Restless –Heart Blunder,* Unpublished 2005 Aquinas Lecture, Center for Thomistic Studeis, University of St. Thomas, Houston, TX, 11.
87 "Item. Voluntas cum consecuta fuerit ultimum finem, quietatur eius desiderium. Ultimus autem finis omnis cognitionis humanae est felicitas. Illa igitur cognitio Dei essentialiter est ipsa felicitas, qua habita non restabit alicuius scibilis desideranda cognitio. Talis autem non est cognitio quam philosophi per demonstationes de Deo habere potuerunt: quia adhuc, illa cognitione habita, alia desideramus scire, quae per hanc cogntionem nondum sciuntur. Non est igitur in tali cognitione Dei felicitas." Aquinas, SCG, III, 39, 2172.
88 "Amplius. Per felicitationem, cum sit ultimus finis, naturale desiderium quietatur. Cognitio autem fidei non quietat desiderium, sed magis ipsum accendit: quia unusquisque desiderat videre quod credit. Non est igitur in cognitione fidei ultima hominis felicitas." Aquinas, *SGC*, III, 40, 2178.

ENDNOTES

89 Quamvis autem speculum quod est mens humana, de propinquiori Dei similitudinem repraesentet quam inferiores creaturae, tamen cognitio Dei quae ex mente humana accipi potest, non excedit illud genus congitionis quod ex sensibilibus sumitur: cum et ipsa anima de seipsa cognoscat quid est per ho cquod naturas intelligit sensibilium [...] Unde nec per hanc viam cognosci Deus altiori modo potest quam sicut causa cognoscitur per effectum." Aquinas, *SCG*, III, 48, 2245.

90 Aquinas, *SGC*, III, 48, 2260.

91 "In quo satis apparet quantam angustiam patiebantur hinc eorum praeclara ingenia. Aquibus angustiis liberabimur si ponamus, secundum probationes praemissas, hominem ad veram felicitatem post hand vitam pervenire posse, anima hominis immortali existente in quo statu anima intelligent per modum quo intelligent substantiae separatae." Aquinas, *SCG*, IIII, 48, 2261.

92 "In quo etiam satis apparet quod in nullo alio quaerenda est ultima felicitas quam in operatione intellectus: cum nullum desiderium tam in sublime ferat sicut desiderium intelligendae Veritatis. Omnia namque nostra desideria vel delectionis, vel cuiusque alterius quod ab homine desideratur, in aliis rebus quiescere possunt: desiderium autem praedictum non quiescit nisi ad summum rerum cardinem et factorem Deum pervenerit. [...] Erubescant igitur qui felicitatem hominis, tam altissimae, sitam, in infimis rebus quaerunt." Aquinas, *SCG*, III, 50, 2283.

93 "Ultima et perfecta beatitudo non potest esse nisi in visio divinae essentiae. [...] Ad perfectum igitur beatitudinem requritur quod intellectus pertingat ad ipsam essentiam primae causae. Et sic perfectionem suam habebit per unionem ad Deum sicut ad obiectum, in quo solo beatitudo hominis consistit." Aquinas, *ST*, I-II, 3, 8, ad corp. (McD)

94 "Unde, cum beatitudo nihil aliud sit quam adeptio summi boni, non potest esse beatitudo sine delectatione concomitante. [...] ex necessitate oportet quod operatio intellectus, quae est visio, sit potior delectatione." Aquinas, *ST*, I-II, 4, 1 and 2.

95 "Rectitudo voluntatis requiritur ad beatitudinem et antecedenter et concomitanter. Antecedenter quidem, quia rectitude voluntatis est per ordinem ad finem ultimum. [...] Et ideo nullus potest ad beatitudienm pervenire, nisi habeat rectitudinem voluntatis." Aquinas, *ST*, I-II, 4, a, ad corp. (McD)

96 "Desiderium animae separatae totaliter quiescit ex parte appetibilis, quia scilicet habet id quod suo appetitui sufficit. Sed non totaliter requiescit ex parte appetentis, quia illud bonum non possidet secundum omnem modum quo possidere vellet. Et ideo, corpore resumpto, beatitudo crescit non intensive, sed extensive." Aquinas, *ST*, I-II, 4, 5, ad 5.

97 "Felix indiget amicis, non quidem propter utilitatem, cum sit sibi sufficiens; nec propter delectationem, quia habet in seipso delectationem perfectam in operatione virtutis; sed propter bonam operationem, ut scilicet eis benefaciat, et ut eos inspiciens benefacere delectetur, et ut etiam ab eis in benefaciendo adiuvetur." Aquinas, *ST*, I-II, 4, 8.

98 "Cum enim ultima hominis beatitudo in altissima eius operatione consistat, quae est operatio intellectus, si nunquam essentiam Dei videre potest intellectus creatus, vel nunquam beatitudinem obtinebit, vel in alio eius beatitudo consistet quam in Deo. Quod est alienum a fide. [...]Similiter etiam est praeter rationem." Aquinas, I, 12, 1, *ad corp.*

99 "Quamvis enim homo naturaliter inclinetur in finem ultimum, non tamen potest naturaliter illum consequi, sed solum per gratiam [...]." Thomas Aquinas, *In Boeth. De Trinitate*, 6, 4, ad 5.

100 "Infelix homo qui scit omnia illa (scilicet creaturas), *te autem nescit, beatus autem qui te scit, etiam si illa nesciat. Qui vero te et illa novit, non propter illa beatior est, sed propter te solum beatus.*" Aquinas, ST, I, 12, 8, *ad 4*, quoting Augustine, *Confessions*, Book 5.

101 "Sicut natura non deficit homini in necessaries, quamvis non dederit sibi arma et tegumenta sicut aliis animalibus, quia dedit ei rationem et manus, quibus posit haec sibi conquirere; its nec deficit homini in necessaries, quamvis non daret sibi aliquod principium quo posset beatitudinem consequi; hoc enim erat impossibile. Sed dedit ei liberum arbitrium, quo possit converti ad Deum, qui eum faceret beatum. *Quae enim per amicos possumus, per non aliqualiter possumus*, ut dicitur in III Ethic." Aquinas, ST, I-II, 5, ad 1.

102 "Cum enim lapis movetur seipsum, principium huius motionis est extra lapidem: sed cum movetur deorsum, principium huius motionis est in ipso lapide." Aquinas, ST, I-II, 6, 1, ad corp.

103 "Perfecta quidem finis cognitio est quando non solum apprehenditur res quae est finis sed etiam cognoscitur ratio finis, et proportio eius quod ordinatur in finem ad ipsum. Et talis cognitio finis competit soli rationali naturae." Aquinas, ST, I-II, 6, 2, *ad corp.*

104 "Homo est dominus sui actus." Aquinas, ST, 6, 2, *ad 2*.

105 Karol Wojtyla, *The Acting Person*, trans. Andrzej Potocki. (Boston: D. Reidel Publishing Company, 1969), 171.

106 "Alii vero dixerunt, quod peccatum omissionis non habet aliquem actum, sed ipsum desistere ab actu est omissionis peccatum [...]", Thomas Aquinas, *De Malo*, II, 1, *ad corp.*

107 "Sed per se loquendo peccatum omissionis in ipsa cessatione ab actu consistit", Thomas Aquinas, *Ibid*. In all future quotations from *De Malo* I will make use of the translation of John Oesterle, University of Notre Dame Press, 1995.

108 "Sic ergo, per se loquendo, potest esse aliquod peccatum ad quod non requiritur aliquis actus, qui sit de essentia peccati", Aquinas, *De Malo*, II, 1, *ad corp.*

109 "Aliquid dicitur esse voluntarium, non solum quia cadit sub voluntatis actu, sed quia cadit sub potestate voluntatis", Thomas Aquinas, *De Malo*, II, 1, *ad 2*.

110 *CCC*, n. 1736.

111 "Non quaelibet potestas maior homine, potest movere voluntatem hominis, sed solus Deus," Thomas Aquinas, ST, I-II, 80, 3, *ad 1*.

112 "Quorum utrumque commovendo, potest inducere ad peccatum, potest enim operari ad hoc quod imaginationi aliquae formae imaginariae praesententur," ST, I, 80, 2, ad corp.

113 "Occasionaliter quidem et indirecte Diabolus est causa omnium peccatorum nostrorum, " ST, I-II, 80, 4, ad corp.

114 Joannes O. Gury, S.J. Compendium Theologiae Moralis (Lugduni, 1880; Ratisbonne, 1874) t. 1. "De Actibus Humanis", c. 2, n. 6-9.

115 F.J. Connell, New Catholic Encyclopedia, "The Principle of Double Effect", Volume 4, 1967.

116 Ibid.

117 CCC, 1737.

118 CCC, 1736.

119 "Voluntarium potest aliquid dici dupliciter, uno modo, secundum actionem, puta cum aliquis vult aliquid agere; alio modo, secundum passionem, scilicet cum aliquis vult pati ab alio", Aquinas, ST, I-II, 6, 5, ad 5.

120 Hoc autem quod per metum agitur, secundum hoc est in actu, secundum quod fit, cum enim actus in singularibus sint, singulare autem, inquantum huiusmodi, est hic et nunc; secundum hoc id quod fit est in actu, secundum quod est hic et nunc et sub aliis conditionibus individualibus. Sic autem hoc quod fit per metum, est voluntarium, inquantum scilicet est hic et nunc." Aquinas, ST, 6, 6, ad corp.

121 CCC,. 1451-3.

122 John Paul II, *Man and Woman He Created Them*, (Boston: Pauline Books and Media, 2006), 241.

123 "Bestiae carent ratione. Unde secundum hoc homo in coitu bestiali efficitur, quod delectationem coitus et fervorem concupiscentiae ratione moderari non potest. Sed in statu innocentiae nihil huiusmodi fuisset quod ratione non moderaretur, non quia esset minor delectatio secundum sensum, ut quidam dicunt (fuisset enim tanto maior delectatio sensibilis, quanto esset purior natura, et corpus magis sensibile); sed quia vis concupiscibilis non ita inordinate se effudisset super huiusmodi delectatione, regulata per rationem, ad quam non pertinet ut sit minor delectatio in sensu, sed ut vis concupiscibilis non immoderate delectationi inhaereat; et dico immoderate, praeter mensuram rationis." Thomas Aquinas, ST, I, 98, 2, ad 3.

124 "Virtus passiones [...] moderatas autem producit." ST, I-II, 59, 5.

125 John Paul II, *Male and Female*, 292 [TOB 41].

126 Aelred Squire, *Asking the Fathers*, (Westminster, Maryland, 1993: Christian Classics), 241.

127 "Et hoc ideo contingit, quia omnes potentiae radicantur in una anima, cuius intentio applicat unamquamque potentiam ad suum actum: et ita cum aliquis fuerit fortiter intentus circa actum unius potentiae, minuitur eius intentio circa actum alterius." Thomas Aquinas, *De Malo*, 9, 3, ad corp. (Henceforth DM), translated by John Oesterle, (Notre Dame, Indiana, 1993: Notre Dame Press)

128 "Per passiones autem fit aliqua immutatio circa corpus, ita quod interdum aliqui propter iram et concupiscentiam vel aliquam huiusmodi passionem in insaniam inciderunt. Et ideo quando huiusmodi passiones sunt fortes, per ipsam transmutationem corporalem ligant quodammodo rationem, ut liberum iudicium de particularibus agendis non habeat." Ibid.

129 Aquinas, *ST*, I-II, 24, 1, ad corp. cited in the *Catechism of the Catholic Church*, 1767.

130 CCC 2352

131 "Nescientia enim simplicem negationem scientiae importat." Aquinas, *DM*, 3, 7, ad corp.

132 "Ignorantia nihil est aliud quam carere scientia quam qui natus est habere: hoc enim est de ratione privationis cuiuslibet." *Ibid.*

133 "Ignorantia perversae dispositionis; puta, cum quis habet habitum falsorum principiorum et falsarum opinionum, ex quibus impeditur a scientia veritatis." *Ibid.*

134 "Error autem est approbare falsa pro veris." *Ibid.*

135 "Unde omnis homo tenetur scire ea quae fidei sunt, quia fides intentionem dirigit; et tenetur scire praecepta Decalogi, per quae potest peccata vitare, et bonum facere." *Ibid.*

136 "[...]propter laborem addiscendi, vel ne impediatur a peccato quod diligit, scientiam recusant." Aquinas, *DM*, 3, 7, ad 8.
137 "[...]per hoc quod voluntas contrariatur ei quod fit. Aquinas, *DM*, 3, 8, ad corp.
138 "[...] per solam remotionem actus voluntatis." *Ibid.*
139 "Cum ergo aliquis directe vult ignorare ut a peccato per scientiam non retrahatur, talis ignorantia non excusat peccatum nec in toto nec in parte, sed magis auget; ex magno enim amore peccandi videtur contingere quod aliquis detrimentum scientiae pati velit ad hoc quod libere peccato inhaereat." *Ibid.*
140 Conrad Baars was a psychiatrist who developed a theory of neurosis based on Thomistic rational psychology which contradicted Freud in that it placed the origin of neurosis not in a conflict between reason and the passions but among the passions themselves. What makes his work so helpful to Catholic moralists is that he believes that traditional Catholic moral formation is not only objectively true but leads to emotional health.
141 Conrad W. Baars, M.D. *Psychic Wholeness and Healing*, (New York, 1981: Alba House), 111 ff.
142 Pius XII, "Allocution to the Fifth International Congress of Psychotherapy and Clinical Psychology", *L'Osservatore Romano* April 16, 1953. Quoted in Baars, *Psychic Wholeness*, 125
143 "Actus autem humanus iudicatur voluntarius vel involuntarius, secundum cognitionem vel ignorantiam circumstantiarum." Aquinas, *ST,*, I-II, 7, 2, ad corp.
144 "[...] invenitur vel praetermittitur medium virtutis in humanis actibus et passionibus." Aquinas, *ST*, I-II, 7, 2, ad 3.
145 "quis, quid, ubi, quibus auxiliis, cur, quomodo, quando [...] circa quid", Aquinas, *ST*, I-II, 7, 3, ad corp.
146 "[...] non requiritur quod sit bonum in rei veritate, sed quod apprehendatur in ratione boni." Aquinas, *ST*, I-II, 8, 1, ad corp.
147 "Id autem quod est propter se bonum et volitum, est finis." Aquinas, *ST*, I-II, 8, 2, ad corp.
148 "Unde intellectus aliquando intelligit medium, et ex eo non procedit ad conclusionem. Et similiter voluntas aliquando vult finem, et tamen non procedit ad volendum id quod est ad finem." Aquinas, *ST*, I-II, 8, 3, ad 3. (Note: The author is aware that the translation in the text is very free for this passage, but it seems to capture the flavor and so I have left it intact.)
149 "Motio autem ipsius subiecti est ex agente aliquo. Et cum omne agens agat propter finem, ut supra ostensum est, principium huius motionis est ex fine." Aquinas, *ST*, I-II, 9, 1, ad corp.
150 "Primum autem principium formale est ens et verum universale, quod est obiectum intellectus. Et ideo isto modo motionis intellectus movet voluntatem, sicut praesentans ei obiectum suum." Aquinas, *Ibid.*
151 *CCC* 1731.
152 "Voluntas movet intellectum quantum ad exercitium actus, quia et ipsum verum, quod est perfectio intellectus, continetur sub universali bono ut quoddam bonum particulare. Sed quantum ad determinationem actus, quae est ex parte obiecti, intellectus movet voluntatem, quia et ipsum bonum apprehenditur secundum quandam specialem rationem comprehensam sub universali ratione veri." Aquinas, *ST*, I-II, 9, 1, ad 3.
153 John Paul II, *Veritatis Splendor* (Henceforth: *VS*), 31.

154 John Paul II, *VS*, 32.
155 *Ibid.*
156 Karl Rahner, "Concerning the Relationship of Nature and Grace", *Theological Investigations*, v. 1 (Baltimore: Helicon Press, 1963), 313-4.
157 Patrick J. Burke, "Conceptual Thought in Karl Rahner", *Gregorianum*, v. 75, 1 (1994), 92.
158 John Paul II, *VS*, 32.
159 John Paul II, *VS*, 40.
160 "Unde secundum quod homo est in passione aliqua, videtur sibi aliquid conveniens, quod non videtur extra passionem existenti [...] Et per hunc modum, ex parte obiecti, appetitus sensitivus movet voluntatem." Aquinas, *ST*, I-II, 9, 2, ad corp.
161 "Qualis unusquisque est, talis finis videtur ei." *Ibid.* Cf. Aristotle, *Nicomachean Ethics*, 5, 17 (1114 a 32)
162 "Est autem alius modus causandi proprius voluntati, quae est domina sui actus, praeter modum qui convenit naturae, quae est determinata ad unum." Aquinas, *ST*, I-II, 10, 1, ad 1.
163 John Paul II, *VS*, 33.
164 Robert Edward Brennan, *The Image of His Maker*, (Milwaukee: Bruce Publishing Company, 1948), 221.
165 "Etsi voluntas non possit facere quin motus concupiscentiae insurgat, de quo apostolus dicit Rom. VII, quod odi malum, illud facio, idest concupisco; tamen potest voluntas non velle concupiscere, aut concupiscentiae non consentire." Aquinas, *ST*, I-II, 10, 3, ad 1.
166 "Unde omnia movet secundum eorum conditionem, [...] Quia igitur voluntas est activum principium non determinatum ad unum, sed indifferenter se habens ad multa, sic Deus ipsam movet, quod non ex necessitate ad unum determinat." Aquinas, *ST*, I-II, 10, 4, ad corp.
167 "Et secundum hoc, Deus est causa actus peccati, non tamen est causa peccati, quia non est causa huius, quod actus sit cum defectu." Aquinas, *ST*, I-II, 79, 2, ad corp.
168 "Unde quod liberum arbitrium diversa eligere possit servato ordine finis, hoc pertinet ad perfectionem libertatis eius, sed quod eligat aliquid divertendo ab ordine finis, quod est peccare, hoc pertinet ad defectum libertatis.", Aquinas, *ST*, I, 62, 8, ad 3.
169 John Paul II, *VS*, 41.
170 The responsibility present in the commanded act is especially *ad rem* for the issue of both fundamental option and consequentialism.
171 "Propinquius autem ordinatur ad vitam hominis semen humanum, in quo est homo in potentia, quam quaecumque res exteriores; unde et philosophus in sua politica dicit in semine hominis esse quiddam divinum, in quantum scilicet est homo in potentia. Et ideo inordinatio circa emissionem seminis est circa vitam hominis in potentia propinqua." Aquinas, *DM*, 15, 2, ad corp.
172 Aquinas, *VS*, 49 and 50.
173 "Radix libertatis est voluntas sicut subiectum, sed sicut causa, est ratio." Aquinas, *ST*, I-II, 17, 1, ad corp.
174 Conrad W. Baars, *I Will Give Them a New Heart*, (New York: Alba House, 2008), 139.
175 Baars, *New Heart*, 134.

176 "Sicut autem in genere rerum naturalium, aliquod totum componitur ex materia et forma, ut homo ex anima et corpore, qui est unum ens naturale, licet habeat multitudinem partium; ita etiam in actibus humanis, actus inferioris potentiae materialiter se habet ad actum superioris, inquantum inferior potentia agit in virtute superioris moventis ipsam, sic enim et actus moventis primi formaliter se habet ad actum instrumenti. Unde patet quod imperium et actus imperatus sunt unus actus humanus." Aquinas, *ST*, I-II, 17, 4, ad corp.

177 "Unde philosophus dicit, in I Polit., quod ratio praeest irascibili et concupiscibili non principatu despotico, qui est domini ad servum; sed principatu politico aut regali, qui est ad liberos, qui non totaliter subduntur imperio." Aquinas, *ST*, I-II, 17, 7, ad corp.

178 A.A.A., Terruwe, *The Priest and the Sick in Mind*, (London: Burns and Oates, 1958), 4)

179 "Haec autem est ratio, unde bonum et malum in actibus humanis consideratur secundum quod actus concordat rationi informatae lege divina, vel naturaliter, vel per doctrinam, vel per infusionem, unde Dionysius ait IV cap. de Divin. Nomin., quod animae malum est praeter rationem esse, corpori praeter naturam." Thomas Aquinas, *DM*, 2, 4, ad corp.

180 John Paul II, *VS*, 48.

181 "Bonum autem quamdam perfectionem designat. Perfectio autem est duplex: scilicet prima, quae est forma vel habitus; et secunda, quae est operatio. Ad perfectionem autem primam, cuius usus est operatio, potest reduci omne illud quo utimur operando. Unde et e converso duplex malum invenitur. Unum quidem in ipso agente, secundum quod privatur vel forma, vel habitu, vel quocumque quod necessarium sit ad operandum: sicut caecitas vel curvitas tibiae quoddam malum est. Aliud vero malum est in ipso actu deficiente, sicut si dicamus claudicationem esse aliquod malum." Aquinas, *DM*, 1, 4, ad corp.

182 Sed haec duo mala aliter ordinantur in naturalibus et voluntariis; nam in naturalibus ex malo agentis sequitur malum actionis, sicut ex tibia curva sequitur claudicatio; in voluntariis autem e converso, ex malo actionis, quod est culpa, sequitur malum agentis, quod est poena, divina providentia culpam per poenam ordinante." *Ibid.*

183 *VS*, 34.

184 Epistemology is the study of the nature and characteristics of human knowledge.

185 *VS*, 34.

186 John Mahoney, *The Making of Moral Theology*, (Oxford: Clarendon Press, 1987), 203.

187 Karl Rahner, "On the Question of a Formal Existential Ethics", *Theological Investigations, vol. II*, translated by Karl H. Kruger (Baltimore: Helicon Press, 1963), 217-234.

188 Rahner, *Ethics*, 225.

189 *Ibid.*

190 Rahner, *Ethics*, 227-228.

191 Rahner, *Ethics*, 228.

192 Rahner, *Ethics*, 228, note 3.

193 *Ibid.*

194 Rahner, *Ethics*, 229.

195 Rahner, *Ethics*, 230.

196 Richard McCormick. "A Commentary on the Commentaries," in *Doing Evil to Achieve Good*, (Chicago: Loyola University Press, 1978), 238.
197 Richard McCormick. "Reflections on the Literature." In *Readings in Moral Theology: No. 1*, Edited by Chrales E.Curran and Richard A. McCormick, S.J., (New York: Paulist Press, 1979), 332.
198 Charles E.Curran. "Utilitarianism and Moral Theology", in *Readings, No. 1*, 335.
199 McCormick, "Commentary", 245.
200 Ibid., See also Richard A. McCormick, S.J. "Reflections", 318.
201 John Paul II, *VS*, August 6, 1993.
202 *VS*, 82.
203 Richard McCormick. "Killing the Patient" in *The London Tablet*, October 30, 1993, 9.
204 McCormick, "Killing", 10.
205 Ladislas Orsy. "The Sins of the Little One", *America* 129, December 8, 1973, 438-441.
206 Ladislas Boros. *The Mystery of Death*, (New York: Herder and Herder, 1965), 8.
207 Msgr. William Smith was one of the foremost moral theologians who defended the traditional moral teaching of the Church against proportionalism and consequentialism. He was a priest of the Archdiocese of New York and a professor at St. Joseph's Seminary, Dunwoddie, NY.
208 Msgr. William Smith. *Moral Magisterium of John Paul II*, International Catholic University, published notes, Lesson Twelve, 2. I am indebted to this article for a succinct description and critique of this school of thought.
209 Orsy, *Sins*, 438.
210 Orsy, *Sins*, 440.
211 Orsy, *Sins*, 440.
212 Smith, *Moral Magisterium*, Lesson Twelve, 2.
213 John Paul II, *Reconciliatio et Paenitentia*, 17. Cf. VS, 70 and CCC 1857-59.
214 Mark S. Latkovic, "Natural Law in the Moral Thought of Benedict Ashley, O.P.", published on the Internet, 2.
215 Christopher Tollefsen, "The New Natural Law Theory", 2, *Lyceum*, Fall, 2008.
216 "Propinquius autem ordinatur ad vitam hominis semen humanum, in quo est homo in potentia, quam quaecumque res exteriores; unde et philosophus in sua politica dicit in semine hominis esse quiddam divinum, in quantum scilicet est homo in potentia. Et ideo inordinatio circa emissionem seminis est circa vitam hominis in potentia propinqua. Unde manifestum est quod omnis talis actus luxuriae est peccatum mortale ex suo genere. Et quia appetitus interior accipit bonitatem vel malitiam ex eo quod appetitur, inde est quod etiam appetitus huiusmodi actus inordinati est peccatum mortale, si sit completus, scilicet cum ratione deliberata; alioquin est peccatum veniale." Thomas Aquinas, *DM*, 15, 2, ad corp.
217 John Paul II, *VS*, 47-49.
218 "Sicut autem res naturalis habet speciem ex sua forma, ita actio habet speciem ex obiecto; sicut et motus ex termino." Thomas Aquinas, *ST*, I-II, 18, 2, ad corp.
219 "Ita primum malum in actionibus moralibus est quod est ex obiecto, sicut accipere aliena." *Ibid*.
220 C. S. Lewis, *The Screwtape Letters*, (New York: Macmillan Publishing Company, 1961), 83.

221 "Actio mala potest habere aliquem effectum per se, secundum id quod habet de bonitate et entitate. Sicut adulterium est causa generationis humanae, inquantum habet commixtionem maris et feminae, non autem inquantum caret ordine rationis." Aquinas, *ST*, I-II, 18, 1, ad 3.

222 John Paul II, *VS*, 78.

223 "Loquimur autem nunc de actibus hominis: unde bonum et malum in actibus, secundum quod nunc loquimur, est accipiendum secundum id quod est proprium hominis in quantum est homo. Haec autem est ratio, unde bonum et malum in actibus humanis consideratur secundum quod actus concordat rationi informatae lege divina, vel naturaliter, vel per doctrinam, vel per infusionem, unde Dionysius ait IV cap. de Divin. Nomin., quod animae malum est praeter rationem esse, corpori praeter naturam." Thomas Aquinas, *DM*, 2, 4, ad corp.

224 *CCC*, 1751.

225 John Paul II, *VS*, 78.

226 *Ibid*.

227 *CCC*, 2258.

228 *CCC*, 2261.

229 In this last phrase, the Pope is not speaking about executing the mentally unstable, but about resisting even to the point of the killing of the aggressor in the heat of battle.

230 John Paul II, *Evangelium Vitae*, March 25, 1995, 55.

231 John Paul II, *EV*, 56.

232 Josef Cardinal Ratzinger. Letter to Theodore Cardinal McCarrick and Bishop Wilton Gregory, June, 2004. Reprinted in *L'Espresso*, July 2004.

233 John Paul II, *Familiaris Consortio*, November 22, 1981, 32.

234 *Ibid*.

235 John Paul II, *Man*, 153.

236 CCC 2402-3.

237 *Ibid*.

238 CCC 2406.

239 CCC 2408.

240 *Ibid*.

241 Richard McCormick. "*Killing*", 10 (1411).

242 "Actus generationis ordinatur ad bonum speciei, quod est bonum commune. Bonum autem commune est ordinabile lege; sed bonum privatum subiacet ordinationi uniuscuiusque. Et ideo quamvis in actu nutritivae virtutis, quae ordinatur ad conservationem individui, unusquisque possit sibi determinare cibum convenientem sibi; tamen determinare qualis debeat esse generationis actus non pertinet ad unumquemque, sed ad legislatorem, cuius est ordinare de propagatione filiorum, ut etiam philosophus dicit in II Polit." Aquinas, *DM*, 15, 2 *ad 12*.

243 "Gravitas ergo peccati quam habet ex specie sua, attenditur ex parte obiecti, sive materiae; et secundum hanc considerationem gravius peccatum dicitur ex suo genere quod maiori bono virtutis opponitur. Unde cum bonum virtutis consistat in ordinatione amoris, ut Augustinus dicit, Deum autem super omnia diligere debeamus; peccata quae sunt in Deum, sicut idololatria, blasphemia et huiusmodi, secundum suum genus sunt reputanda gravissima. Inter peccata autem quae sunt in proximum, tanto aliqua sunt aliis graviora, quanto maiori bono proximi opponuntur. Maximum autem bonum proximi est ipsa vita hominis, cui opponitur

ENDNOTES 253

peccatum homicidii, quod tollit actualem hominis vitam; et peccatum luxuriae, quod opponitur vitae hominis in potentia, quia est inordinatio quaedam circa actum generationis humanae. Unde inter omnia peccata quae sunt in proximum, gravius est homicidium secundum genus suum; et secundum locum tenet adulterium et fornicatio, et huiusmodi peccata carnalia; tertium autem locum tenet furtum et rapina et huiusmodi, per quae in exterioribus bonis laeditur proximus." Aquinas, *DM*, 2, 10, *ad corp.*

244 "Ideo dicitur communiter, quod actus quidam sunt boni vel mali ex genere; et quod actus bonus ex genere, est actus cadens supra debitam materiam, sicut pascere esurientem; actus autem malus ex genere est qui cadit supra indebitam materiam, sicut subtrahere aliena; materia enim actus, dicitur obiectum ipsius." Aquinas, *DM*, 2, 4, *ad 5.*

245 " Circumstantiae se habent ad actus morales sicut accidentia, quae sunt praeter rationem speciei, ad res naturales. Actus autem moralis, sicut dictum est, recipit speciem ab obiecto secundum quod comparatur ad rationem." *Ibid.*

246 "Sed supra hanc bonitatem vel malitiam potest supervenire alia bonitas vel malitia ex aliquo extrinseco, quod vocatur circumstantia, sicut ex loco vel tempore aut conditione agentis aut huiusmodi; puta, si subtrahat non sua ex loco sacro, vel propter indigentiam, aut aliquid huiusmodi." *Ibid.*

247 *CCC* 2267.

248 *CCC* 1754.

249 "Unde etiam aliquis antequam habeat virtutem, operatur actum virtuosum; aliter tamen postquam habet virtutem [...]Sic ergo patet quod triplex est gradus bonitatis et malitiae in actibus moralibus: primo quidem secundum suum genus et speciem, per comparationem ad obiectum sive materiam; secundo ex circumstantia; tertio vero ex habitu informante." Aquinas, *DM*, 2, 4, ad 11.

250 "Et oportet quod quilibet individualis actus habeat aliquam circumstantiam per quam trahatur ad bonum vel malum, ad minus ex parte intentionis finis." Aquinas, *ST*, I-II, 18, 9, *ad corp.*

251 In actu autem voluntario invenitur duplex actus, scilicet actus interior voluntatis, et actus exterior, et uterque horum actuum habet suum obiectum. [...]Et ideo actus humani species formaliter consideratur secundum finem, materialiter autem secundum obiectum exterioris actus." Aquinas, *ST*, I-II, 18, 6, *ad corp.*

252 "Et ideo actus humani species formaliter consideratur secundum finem, materialiter autem secundum obiectum exterioris actus." *Ibid.*

253 "Sic igitur quando obiectum non est per se ordinatum ad finem, differentia specifica quae est ex obiecto, non est per se determinativa eius quae est ex fine, nec e converso." Aquinas, *ST, I-II,* 18, 7, *ad corp.*

254 "Sic igitur in actione humana bonitas quadruplex considerari potest. Una quidem secundum genus, prout scilicet est actio, quia quantum habet de actione et entitate, tantum habet de bonitate, ut dictum est. Alia vero secundum speciem, quae accipitur secundum obiectum conveniens. Tertia secundum circumstantias, quasi secundum accidentia quaedam. Quarta autem secundum finem, quasi secundum habitudinem ad causam bonitatis. [...]Et secundum hoc, contingit actionem quae est bona secundum speciem suam vel secundum circumstantias, ordinari ad finem malum, et e converso. Non tamen est actio bona simpliciter, nisi omnes bonitates concurrant, quia *quilibet singularis defectus causat malum, bonum autem causatur ex integra causa*, ut Dionysius dicit, IV cap. de Div. Nom." Aquinas, *ST*, I-II, 18, 4, *ad corp., ad 3.*

255 *CCC*, 1755-1756.
256 Msgr. William Smith, *Moral Magisterium of John Paul II*, International Catholic University, published notes, "Reconcilication and Sin (Mortal and Venial), IV: 12.
257 John Paul II, *VS*, 67.
258 Cf, Post-Synodal Apostolic Exhortation *Reconciliatio et Paenitentia* (December 2, 1984), 17; AAS 77 (1985) 77 (1985), 218-223, quoted in John Paul II, *VS*, 70.
259 John Paul II, *VS*, 44.
260 An ancient school of philosophy which originated in Greece with Zeno of Citium. The Stoics believed that the will should accord with nature, but a nature which for them meant moral determinism. The passions interrupted this and generally were to be disregarded completely. The school was also very influential in Rome.
261 Karol Wojtyla, *Love and Responsibility*, (San Francisco: Ignatius Press, 1993), 58-59.
262 Anna A. Terruwe and Conrad W. Baars, *Psychic Wholeness and Healing*, (New York: Alba House, 1981), 123.
263 Wojtyla, *Love and Responsibility*, 62.
264 Catholic Theological Society of America, *Human Sexuality*, ed. Anthony Kosnick, Doubleday, 1979.
265 Msgr. John F. McCarthy, J.C.D., S.T.D., president of the Roman Theological Forum, Rome, Italy, delivered at the 1978 Annual Meeting of the National Federation of Catholic Physicians' Guilds in New Orleans, Louisiana. Quoted in the *Anti-Catholicism New Times*, Alphonse de Valk, April 2005.
266 *CCC*, 1767 quoting Thomas Aquinas, *ST, I-II, 24, 3*.
267 "Unde Aristoteles dicit in politica sua, quod anima dominatur corpori dispotico principatu, sicut dominus servo, qui non habet facultatem resistendi in aliquo imperio domini; ratio vero dominatur inferioribus animae partibus regali et politico principatu, id est sicut reges et principes civitatum dominantur liberis, qui habent ius et facultatem repugnandi quantum ad aliqua praecepta regis vel principis." Aquinas, *DVC*, 1, 4 ad corp.
268 "Non autem ad virtutem pertinet quod ea quae sunt subiecta rationi, a propriis actibus vacent, sed quod exequantur imperium rationis, proprios actus agendo." Aquinas, *ST*, I-II, 59, 5, *ad corp*.
269 "Virtus passiones inordinatas superat, moderatas autem producit." Aquinas, *ST*, I-II, 59, 5, *ad 1*.
270 "Et sic per redundantiam huiusmodi, quanto virtus fuerit perfectior, tanto magis passionem causat." Aquinas, *ST*, I-II, 59, 5, *ad corp*.
271 "Stoici enim dixerunt tristitiam in sapientem non cadere, Peripatetici vero dixerunt sapientem quidem tristari sed in tristitiis secundum rationem moderate se habere, et haec opinio veritati concordat. Ratio enim condicionem naturae auferre non potest; est autem naturale sensibili naturae ut et convenientibus delectetur et gaudeat et de nocivis doleat et tristetur: hoc igitur ratio auferre non potest sed sic moderatur ut per tristitiam ratio a sua rectitudine non divertat. Concordat etiam haec opinio sacrae Scripturae, quae tristitiam in Christo ponit, in quo est omnis virtutis et sapientiae plenitudo. Sic igitur Iob ex praenarratis adversitatibus tristitiam quidem sensit, alias patientiae virtus in eo locum non haberet, sed propter tristitiam ratio a rectitudine non declinavit quin potius tristitiae dominabatur. Ad hoc igitur ostendendum dicitur *post haec aperuit Iob os suum*. Dicit autem *post haec*, idest post septem taciturnitatis dies; ex quo manifestum fit quod verba quae

sequuntur sunt secundum rationem prolata per tristitiam non perturbatam; si enim ex perturbatione mentis dicta fuissent, prius ea protulisset quando vis tristitiae vehementior erat: tristitia enim quaelibet longitudine temporis mitigatur et in principio magis sentitur; unde propter hoc tandiu tacuisse videtur ne perturbata mente loqui iudicaretur. Quod etiam ostenditur per hoc quod dicitur *aperuit os suum*; cum enim aliquis loquitur ex impetu passionis, non ipse aperit os suum sed agitur passione ad loquendum: non enim per passionem nostri actus domini sumus sed per solam rationem." Aquinas, *In Comm. Super Job*, III, 1.

272 Baars, *Psychic*, 240-1.
273 John Paul II, *VS*, 4.
274 *Ibid*.
275 "Quod autem ratio humana sit regula voluntatis humanae, ex qua eius bonitas mensuretur, habet ex lege aeterna, quae est ratio divina." Thomas Aquinas, *ST*, I-II, 19, 4. *ad corp*.
276 John Paul II, *VS*, 32.
277 *Ibid*.
278 John Paul II, *VS*, 46.
279 *Ibid*.
280 John Paul II, *VS*, 43.
281 "Et secundum hoc, lex aeterna nihil aliud est quam ratio divinae sapientiae, secundum quod est directiva omnium actuum et motionum." Aquinas, *ST*, I-II, 93, *ad corp*.
282 "Quaedam rationis ordinatio ad bonum commune, ab eo qui curam communitatis habet, promulgate." Aquinas, *ST*, I-II, 90, 4, *ad corp*.
283 Conrad W. Baars, *I Will Give Them a New Heart*, (New York: Alba House, 2008), 136.
284 John Paul II, *The Acting Person*, (Boston: D. Reidel Publishing Company, 1979), 339-340.
285 *CCC*, 1907-09.
286 John Paul II, *VS*, 43.
287 John T. Noonan is a Senior Circuit Judge on the United States Court of Appeals for the Ninth District in San Francisco. He also is a very committed Catholic layman who writes much on the subject of the natural law.
288 John T. Noonan, "Development in Moral Doctrine", *Theological Studies* 54 (1993), 662.
289 Noonan, "Development", 669.
290 Bernard Häring, *My Witness for the Church*, trans. Leonard Swindler (New York: Paulist Press, 1992). 122, quoted in Noonan "Development", 672.
291 Noonan, "Development," 673 cites Louis Vereeke, *Storia della teologia morale moderna*, (Rome: Lateran, 1979), 1. 4-5.
292 Noonan, "Development", 675-6.
293 "always the same".
294 "The more things change, the more they remain the same."
295 *Ibid*, 676-7.
296 John Paul II, *VS*, 44.
297 Leo XIII, *Libertas Praestantissimum* (June 20, 1888), quoted in John Paul II, *VS*, 44.

298 Benedict XVI, Wednesday Audience Conference, December 16, 2009.
299 "Sed quantum ad proprias conclusiones rationis practicae, nec est eadem veritas seu rectitudo apud omnes; nec etiam apud quos est eadem, est aequaliter nota. Apud omnes enim hoc rectum est et verum, ut secundum rationem agatur. Ex hoc autem principio sequitur quasi conclusio propria, quod deposita sint reddenda. Et hoc quidem ut in pluribus verum est, sed potest in aliquo casu contingere quod sit damnosum, et per consequens irrationabile, si deposita reddantur; puta si aliquis petat ad impugnandam patriam." Aquinas, *ST*, I-II. 94, 4, *ad corp.*
300 "Sicut philosophus dicit, I Rhetor., *melius est omnia ordinari lege, quam dimittere iudicum arbitrio.* Et hoc propter tria. Primo quidem, quia facilius est invenire paucos sapientes, qui sufficiant ad rectas leges ponendas, quam multos, qui requirerentur ad recte iudicandum de singulis. Secundo, quia illi qui leges ponunt, ex multo tempore considerant quid lege ferendum sit, sed iudicia de singularibus factis fiunt ex casibus subito exortis. Facilius autem ex multis consideratis potest homo videre quid rectum sit, quam solum ex aliquo uno facto. Tertio, quia legislatores iudicant in universali, et de futuris, sed homines iudiciis praesidentes iudicant de praesentibus, ad quae afficiuntur amore vel odio, aut aliqua cupiditate; et sic eorum depravatur iudicium. Quia ergo iustitia animata iudicis non invenitur in multis; et quia flexibilis est; ideo necessarium fuit, in quibuscumque est possibile, legem determinare quid iudicandum sit, et paucissima arbitrio hominum committere." Aquinas, *ST*, I-II, 95, 1, *ad 2*.
301 Wojtyla, *Acting Person*, 326.
302 "Rationis autem prima regula est lex naturae, ut ex supradictis patet. Unde omnis lex humanitus posita intantum habet de ratione legis, inquantum a lege naturae derivatur" Aquinas, *ST*, I-II, 95, 2, *ad corp.*
303 "Si vero in aliquo, a lege naturali discordet, iam non erit lex sed legis corruptio." *Ibid.*
304 Leo XIII, *Diuturnum Illud*, 15.
305 Aquinas, *ST*, I-II, 100, 5, *ad corp.*
306 *CCC*, 1961.
307 *CCC*, 1962.
308 St. Augustine quoted by the Council of Trent in DS 1536 and DS 3718.
309 *CCC* 1963.
310 CCC, 1964
311 Thomas Aquinas, *ST*, I-II, 107, 1 ad 2; cf. Rom 5:5; quoted in *CCC*, n. 1964.
312 *CCC*, 1972.
313 Servais Pinkaers, O.P., *The Sources of Christian Ethics*, (Washington, D.C.: Catholic University Press, 1995), 271.
314 Pinkaers, *Sources*, 272.
315 *Ibid.*
316 *Ibid.*
317 *CCC*, 1780.
318 Vatican II, *Gaudium et Spes*, 16.
319 John Paul II, *VS*, 55.
320 *Ibid.*
321 John Paul II, *VS*, 56.

ENDNOTES

322 John Paul II, *VS*, 59 quoting the Supreme Sacred Congregation of the Holy Office, Instruction on 'Situation Ethics' *Contra Doctrinam* (February 2, 1956): *AAS*, 48 (1956), 144.
323 John Paul II, *VS*, 60.
324 John Paul II, *VS*, 62.
325 Cf. for example, Dominic Prümmer, OP; *Handbook of Moral Theology*, (Fort Collins, CO, Roman Catholic Books, 1957), 60
326 "Certitude", *Catholic Encylcopedia*, 1917, New Advent Website.
327 "Ratio primo quidem et principaliter est universalium, potest tamen universales rationes ad particularia applicare (unde syllogismorum conclusiones non solum sunt universales, sed etiam particulares); quia intellectus per quandam reflexionem se ad materiam extendit [...] Tamen per experientiam singularia infinita reducuntur ad aliqua finita quae ut in pluribus accidunt, quorum cognitio sufficit ad prudentiam humanam.: Aquinas, *ST*, II-II, 47, 3, ad 1 and 2.
328 "Non videtur autem possibile quod aliquis peccatum evadat, si conscientia, quantumcumque errans, dictet aliquid esse praeceptum Dei sive sit indifferens sive etiam per se malum; si contrarium, tali conscientia manente, agere disponat. Quantum enim in se est, ex hoc ipso habet voluntatem legem Dei non observandi; unde mortaliter peccat.", Aquinas, *De Veritate*, 14, 4, *ad corp.*
329 "[...] rectam ligare simpliciter, quia ligat absolute et in omnem eventum." Aquinas, *Ibid.*
330 "[...] non ligat nisi secundum quid quia sub conditione." *Ibid.*
331 "[...] per accidens, secundum quid." *Ibid.*
332 "Conscientia erronea errans in his quae sunt per se mala, dictat contraria legi Dei; sed tamen illa quae dictat, dicit esse legem Dei. Et ideo transgressor illius conscientiae efficitur quasi transgressor legis Dei; quamvis etiam conscientiam sequens, et eam opere implens, contra legem Dei faciens mortaliter peccet: quia in ipso errore peccatum erat, cum contingeret per ignorantiam eius quod scire debebat." Aquians, *DV*, 17, 4, *ad 3*.
333 "Unde per hoc non probatur quod conscientia erronea non liget dum manet, sed solum quod non ligat simpliciter et in omnem eventum." Aquinas, *DV*, 17, 4, ad 4.
334 "Concludit autem verum, quando ipse error non est peccatum: utpote cum contingit ex ignorantia facti. Si autem ex ignorantia iuris, sic non concludit, quia ipsa ignorantia peccatum est." Aquinas, *DV*, 17, 4, ad 5.
335 *CCC*, 1792, quoting *Vatican II, Gaudium et Spes*, 16.
336 "Quod ille qui habet conscientiam faciendi fornicationem, non est simpliciter perplexus, quia potest aliquid facere quo facto non incidet in peccatum, scilicet conscientiam erroneam deponere; sed est perplexus secundum quid, scilicet conscientia erronea manente" Aquinas, *DV*, 17, 4, ad 8.
337 *CCC*, 1794.
338 *CCC*, 1791.
339 John Mahoney, S.J., *Making*, (Oxford: Oxford University Press, 1987), 113-114.
340 Professor of Moral Theological Ethics at Marquette University.
341 Daniel G. Maguire, "Morality and Magisterium," in *Readings in Moral Theology: No. 3*, eds. Charles E. Curran and Richard A. McCormick, S.J. (New York: Paulist Press, 1982), 45.
342 *Ibid.*, 46.

343 This term refers to the union of throne and altar in a state. The confessional state is one in which there is a state religion.
344 Leo XIII, *Libertas Praestissimum*, 30.
345 *Dignitatis Humanae*, 2.
346 "[…] quod infidelium quidam sunt qui nunquam susceperunt fidem, sicut gentiles et Iudaei. Et tales nullo modo sunt ad fidem compellendi, ut ipsi credant, quia credere voluntatis est. Sunt tamen compellendi a fidelibus, si facultas adsit, ut fidem non impediant vel blasphemiis, vel malis persuasionibus, vel etiam apertis persecutionibus." Thomas Aquinas, *ST, II-II, 10, 8 ad corp.*
347 *Dignitatis Humanae*, 1.
348 *CCC*, 2108.
349 Pinkaers, *Sources*, 232.
350 Pope Benedict XVI, Wednesday Audience Discourse, July 10, 2010.
351 Brennan, *Image*, 232.
352 **Peter Lombard** or **Petrus Lombardus**; (c. 1100 — July 20, 1160 in Paris) was a scholastic theologian and bishop and author of *Four Books of Sentences*, which became the standard textbook of theology, for which he is also known as **Magister Sententiarum**.
353 "Virtus est bona qualitas mentis, qua recte vivitur, qua nullus male utitur, quam Deus in nobis sine nobis operatur." Aquinas, *ST*, I-II, 55, 4, obj. 1.
354 "Quod quidem fit per habitum; qui cum sit per modum cuiusdam naturae, operationem sibi propriam quasi naturalem reddit, et per consequens delectabilem. Nam convenientia est delectationis causa; unde philosophus, in II Ethic., ponit signum habitus, delectationem in opere existentem." Thomas Aquinas, *De Virtutibus in Communi* (Henceforth: DVC), translated by Ralphy McInerny, (South Bend, IN: St. Augustine's Press, 2009) 1, 1, ad corp.
355 "Qua quidem scientia existente, in particulari actu contingit iudicium rationis intercipi, ut non recte diiudicet; et propter hoc dicitur parum valere ad virtutem, quia ea existente contingit hominem contra virtutem peccare. Sed ad prudentiam pertinet recte iudicare de singulis agibilibus, prout sint nunc agenda: quod quidem iudicium corrumpitur per quodlibet peccatum. Aquinas, *DVC*, 1, 6, ad 1.
356 "Unde voluntas non indiget aliquo habitu virtutis inclinante ipsam ad bonum quod est sibi proportionatum, quia in hoc ex ipsa ratione potentiae tendit; sed ad bonum quod transcendit proportionem potentiae, indiget habitu virtutis. […]Sic ergo duae virtutes sunt in voluntate sicut in subiecto; scilicet caritas et iustitia." Aquinas, *DVC*, 1, 5, ad corp.
357 John Paul II, *Man*, 187.
358 "Homo inquantum propria voluntate facit illud quod debet, meretur. Alioquin actus iustitiae quo quis reddit debitum, non esset meritorius." Aquinas, *ST, I-II*, 114, ad 1.
359 1 Cor. 13:1-4 quoted in *CCC* 1826.
360 *CCC*, 1827.
361 Francis de Sales, *Introduction to the Devout Life*, III, 1.
362 Karol Wojtyla, *The Acting Person*, (London: D. Reidel Publishing Company, 1979), 253.
363 Wojtyla, *Acting*, note 72, 313.
364 Pinkaers, *Sources*, 466.

365 Ibid.
366 Karl Menninger, *Whatever Became of Sin?*, (New York: Hawthron Books, 1973).
367 Pope Pius XII, Radio Message to the U.S. National Catechetical Congress in Boston (October 26,1946): Discorsi e Radiomessaggi VIII (1946) 288.
368 John Paul II, *Reconciliatio et Paenitentia*, 18.
369 "Secundum hoc igitur tria inveniuntur opponi virtuti. Quorum unum est peccatum, quod opponitur sibi ex parte eius ad quod virtus ordinatur, nam peccatum proprie nominat actum inordinatum, sicut actus virtutis est actus ordinatus et debitus." Aquinas, *ST*, I-II, 71, ad corp.
370 *Dictum vel factum vel concupitum contra legem aeternam.*" *CCC*, 1871, quoting St. Augustine, *Contra Faustum* 22: *PL* 42, 418 and Thomas Aquinas, *ST, I-II*, 71, 6, arg. 1.
371 *CCC*, 2408.
372 "Et ideo peccata specie distinguuntur ex parte actuum voluntariorum, magis quam ex parte inordinationis in peccato existentis. Actus autem voluntarii distinguuntur specie secundum obiecta, ut in superioribus ostensum est. Unde sequitur quod peccata proprie distinguantur specie secundum obiecta." Aquinas, *ST*, I-II, 72, ad corp.
373 Terruwe and Baars, *Psychic*, 26.
374 Terruwe and Baars, *Psychic*, note 26, 32.
375 *CCC*, 1859.
376 *CCC*, 1860.
377 "Ratio ligatur ex hoc quod intentio animae applicatur vehementer ad actum appetitus sensitivi; unde avertitur a considerando in particulari id quod habitualiter in universali cognoscit." Aquinas, *DM*, 3, 10, ad corp.
378 "Applicare autem intentionem ad aliquid vel non applicare, in potestate voluntatis existit. Unde in potestate voluntatis est quod ligamen rationis excludat. Actus ergo commissus, qui ex tali ligamine procedit est voluntarius, unde non excusatur a culpa etiam mortali. Sed si ligatio rationis per passionem in tantum procederet, quod non esset in potestate voluntatis huiusmodi ligamen removere, puta si per aliquam animae passionem aliquis in insaniam verteretur, quidquid committeret, non imputaretur ei ad culpam, sicut nec alii insano. Nisi forte quantum ad principium talis passionis quod fuit voluntarium." Aquinas, *Ibid*.
379 "Et ideo quanto motus voluntatis fuerit fortior ad peccandum, tanto peccatum est maius; sed quanto passio fuerit fortior impellens ad peccandum, tanto fit minus." Aquinas, *DM*, 3, 11, *ad 3*.
380 *CCC*, 1860.
381 *CCC*, 2352.
382 "[...]sed potius pati ex electione boni vel mali." Aquinas, *DM*, 3, 11, *ad corp*.
383 John Paul II, *Man*, 264, 309.
384 *CCC*, 1859. The changes in the verbs are the author's
385 *CCC*, 1860
386 *Ibid*. The changes in the verbs are the author's.
387 *CCC*, 1860
388 "Si ergo contingat quod aliquis in tantum velit aliqua delectatione frui, puta adulterio vel quocumque huiusmodi appetibili, ut non refugiat incurrere deformitatem peccati, quam percipit esse coniunctam ei quod vult [...]unde adulter

et delectationem vult quidem principaliter, et secundario vult deformitatem," Aquinas, *DM*, 3, 12, *ad corp.*

389 "Sed in eo qui peccat ex malitia, voluntas inclinatur in actum peccati manente habitu, qui non transit, sed perseverat, ut forma quaedam iam immanens et connaturalis facta." Aquinas, *DM*, 3, 13, *ad corp.*

390 "habet enim firmatum propositum ad peccandum." *Ibid.*

391 "Sic ergo gravissime et periculose peccat qui peccat ex malitia, et non potest de facili revocari, sicut revocatur ille qui peccat ex infirmitate, in quo ad minus manet bonum propositum." *Ibid.*

392 "Uno modo, ipsum obiectum propositum, sicut dicimus quod cibus excitat desiderium hominis ad comedendum. Alio modo, ille qui proponit vel offert huiusmodi obiectum. Tertio modo, ille qui persuadet obiectum propositum habere rationem boni, quia et hic aliqualiter proponit proprium obiectum voluntati, quod est rationis bonum verum vel apparens." Aquinas, *ST*, I-II, 80, *ad corp.*

393 "Daemones autem ad hominis malum; vel quantum ad effectum peccati, prout scilicet homo ex his quae apprehendit, movetur ad superbiam, vel ad aliquod aliud peccatum; vel ad impediendum ipsam intelligentiam veritatis, secundum quod per aliqua apprehensa ducitur homo in dubitationem quam solvere nescit, et sic trahitur in errorem." Aquinas, *DM*, 16, 12, *ad corp.*

394 "Daemon quibusdam nebulis implet omnes meatus intelligentiae, per quos pandere lumen rationis radius mentis solet." *Ibid.*

395 "Deus est universale principium omnis interioris motus humani, sed quod determinetur ad malum consilium voluntas humana, hoc directe quidem est ex voluntate humana; et a Diabolo per modum persuadentis, vel appetibilia proponentis." Aquinas, *ST*, I-II, 80, ad corp.

396 "Sic ergo privatio originalis iustitiae, per quam voluntas subdebatur Deo, est formale in peccato originali, omnis autem alia inordinatio virium animae se habet in peccato originali sicut quiddam materiale." Aquinas, *ST*, I-II, 82, 3, *ad corp.*

397 "Manifestum est autem quod peccatum actuale primo invenitur in aliquo principio, scilicet in voluntate, quae primo est susceptiva peccati, ut supra dictum est, et ab ea derivatur in alias potentias animae, et etiam in membra corporis, secundum quod moventur a voluntate." Aquinas, *DM*, 4, 6, *ad corp.*

398 John Paul II, *Reconciliatio et Paenitentia*, Post-synodal exhortation, December 2, 1984, 17.

399 *CCC*, 1855.

400 John Paul II, *RP*, 31, 1.

401 "Veniale autem non convertitur ad bonum commutabile ut ad finem; et ideo non convertitur ad ipsum ut ad alium terminum a Deo, ut propter hoc sit necessarium a Deo averti." Aquinas, *DM.* 7, 1, *ad 3.*

402 *CCC*, 1457.

403 Pinkaers, *Sources*, 264.

404 "Alio modo dicitur iustitia prout importat rectitudinem quandam ordinis in ipsa interiori dispositione hominis, prout scilicet supremum hominis subditur Deo, et inferiores vires animae subduntur supremae, scilicet rationi. Et hanc etiam dispositionem vocat philosophus, in V Ethic., iustitiam metaphorice dictam." Aquinas, *ST*, I-II, 113, *ad corp.*

405 Quoting the Council of Trent (1547): DS 1528)

406 "Alia autem est dilectio specialis, secundum quam trahit creaturam rationalem

ENDNOTES

supra conditionem naturae, ad participationem divini boni." Aquinas, *ST*, I-II, 110, *ad corp.*

407   *CCC*, 1997.

408   "Et sic mensura et regula virtutis theologicae est ipse Deus [...]Et sic mensura et regula virtutis theologicae est ipse Deus." Aquinas, *ST,* I-ii, 64, 4, *ad corp.*

409   *CCC*, 2000.

410   "[...] inquantum scilicet percipit se delectari in Deo, et contemnere res mundanas; et inquantum homo non est conscius sibi alicuius peccati mortalis." Aquinas, *ST*, I-II, 112, 5, *ad corp.*

411   Cf, *CCC*, 2005.

412   *CCC*, 1988.

413   "Sed bonum gratiae unius maius est quam bonum naturae totius universi." Aquinas, *ST*, I-II, 113, 9, *ad* 2.

414   "Iustificatio impii non est miraculosa, quia naturaliter anima est gratiae capax." Aquinas, *ST*, I-II, 113, 10, *ad corp.*

415   Augustine, *Confessions*, 1, 1.

416   "Etiam ea quae non meremur, orando impetramus." Aquinas, ST, I-II, 114, 9, ad 1.

417   Dante Alighieri, *The Divine Comedy: Paradiso*, canto XXXIII.

418   Italics original.

419   C.S.Lewis, *Screwtape*, 81.

420   "Patet igitur quod quamlibet Dei dilectionem sequitur aliquod bonum in creatura causatum quandoque, non tamen dilectioni aeternae coaeternum. Et secundum huiusmodi boni differentiam, differens consideratur dilectio Dei ad creaturam. Una quidem communis, secundum quam diligit omnia quae sunt, ut dicitur Sap. XI; secundum quam esse naturale rebus creatis largitur." Aquinas, *ST*, I-II, 110, 1, *ad corp.*

421   "Natura enim diligit Deum super omnia, prout est principium et finis naturalis boni, caritas autem secundum quod est obiectum beatitudinis, et secundum quod homo habet quandam societatem spiritualem cum Deo." Aquinas, *ST*, I-II, 109, 3, *ad 1.*

422   "Alia autem est dilectio specialis, secundum quam trahit creaturam rationalem supra conditionem naturae, ad participationem divini boni. Et secundum hanc dilectionem dicitur aliquem diligere simpliciter, quia secundum hanc dilectionem vult Deus simpliciter creaturae bonum aeternum, quod est ipse." Aquinas, *ST*, 110. 1, *ad corp.*

423   "Significatur quiddam supernaturale in homine a Deo proveniens." *Ibid.*

424   Italics original.

425   "Sic igitur dicendum est quod ad cognitionem cuiuscumque veri, homo indiget auxilio divino ut intellectus a Deo moveatur ad suum actum. Non autem indiget ad cognoscendam veritatem in omnibus, nova illustratione superaddita naturali illustrationi; sed in quibusdam, quae excedunt naturalem cognitionem." Aquinas, *ST*, I-II, 109, 1, *ad corp.*

426   Lewis, *Screwtape*, 148.

427   Francis de Sales, *Introduction to the Devout Life*, III, 10.

428   John Henry Cardinal Newman, *Parochial and Plain Sermons*, (San Francisco: Ignatius Press, 1987), 978.

429   St. Gregory Nazianzen, *Carmen de Vita Sua*, 324.